People & organisations.

Ownership and Value Creation

Strategic Corporate Governance in the New Economy

Rolf H. Carlsson

JOHN WILEY & SONS, LTD
Chichester · New York · Weinheim · Brisbane · Singapore · Toronto

Copyright © 2001 by John Wiley & Sons Ltd,
Baffins Lane, Chichester,
West Sussex PO19 1UD, England

National   01243 779777
International (+44) 1243 779777
e-mail (for orders and customer service enquiries): cs-books@wiley.co.uk
Visit our Home Page on http://www.wiley.co.uk
or http://www.wiley.com

Other Wiley Editorial Offices

John Wiley & Sons, Inc., 605 Third Avenue,
New York, NY 10158-0012, USA

WILEY-VCH Verlag GmbH, Pappelallee 3,
D-69469 Weinheim, Germany

Jacaranda Wiley Ltd, 33 Park Road, Milton,
Queensland 4064, Australia

John Wiley & Sons (Asia) Pte Ltd, 2 Clementi Loop #02-01,
Jin Xing Distripark, Singapore 129809

John Wiley & Sons (Canada) Ltd, 22 Worcester Road,
Rexdale, Ontario M9W 1L1, Canada

British Library Cataloguing in Publication Data

A catalogue record for this book is available from the British Library

ISBN 0-471-63219-8

Typeset in 10/12 Palatino by Deerpark Publishing Services Ltd
Printed and bound in Great Britain by Biddles Ltd, Guildford and King's Lynn
This book is printed on acid-free paper responsibly manufactured from sustainable forestation, for which at least two trees are planted for each one used for paper production.

For Eric Rhenman
My late mentor

Contents

Part III. CONCEPTUALISATION AND PROFESSIONALISATION

'Corporate governance and active ownership have received increased attention in recent years. The Anglo-Saxon model is being vitalised by active American institutions and is spreading also to Continental Europe and Japan where bank- or cross-ownership networks have previously dominated. Rolf H. Carlsson gives a valuable historical review and illustrates with cases how active ownership has played an important role in company development. Finally, the book gives some interesting views on where corporate governance is heading and some advice on how to make it work well.'

Percy Barnevik, Chairman, ABB, Astra Zeneca

'Who owns the modern company? And how should owners behave? For European companies, moving towards the Anglo-Saxon model of company finance, these are becoming the central questions of corporate governance. Rolf H. Carlsson brings a fresh eye and historical depth to the issues of ownership, management and value creation that every firm *and* its owners must consider.'

Frances Cairncross, Management Editor, The Economist

'Institutional investors are faced with the huge challenge of transcending from reactive shareholders to *shareowners*, competent enough to play a proactive role in the process of value creation. There are lessons to be learnt from his insightful analysis of the active ownership of the Wallenbergs, now in their fifth generation of sustained success having fostered many leading multinational corporations of Swedish origin. Carlsson also outlines a powerful frame of reference and analytical tools to address issues of value creation and the role of active owners. This book is a significant contribution to the all-important issues of corporate governance. I was intrigued and pleased to read it.'

Richard H. Koppes, Jones Day and Stanford Law School;
former General Counsel, CalPERS

'This innovative book puts the spotlight on those who have the ultimate responsibility for corporate governance, the owners. It provides a useful insight into the ways of effective ownership.'

Professor Jay W. Lorsch, Harvard Business School

'It is not only pertinent to the point as regards key corporate governance issues. It adds new perspectives by highlighting the demanding challenges of globalisation. A remarkable new book on the crucial issues of ownership and corporate governance.'

Dr. R. Marsch-Barner, Senior Counsel, Deutsche Bank AG

'Rolf H. Carlsson's book on ownership (has been) eagerly awaited by the governance community. Carlsson is uniquely able to illumine those areas in which Swedish corporate structuring has been ahead of the world. The focus on ownership is particularly important when evaluating the frequent involvement of government. So also is the pattern of family control in a society celebrated for egalitarian consciousness. Carlsson will bring much new material to the discussion. It is a book that we all look forward to reading.'
Robert A.G. Monks, Principal, Lens Investment Management

'...Rolf H. Carlsson's book addresses an often neglected issue: what does it take to be an owner? What constitutes good ownership, and why do we need it? The nuanced and rich analysis of ownership competence which can be found in Rolf H. Carlsson's book goes far beyond the traditional debate and provides truly interesting and valuable insights for investors, industrialists, entrepreneurs, and owners both in the private and the public sectors.'
Richard Normann, Professor, Chairman, SMG

'For almost 150 years now the idea has been to build, support and develop businesses to create long-term shareholder value. We are involved with a wide range of companies, from small early-stage businesses to large multinational corporations. Rolf H. Carlsson has analysed this process, in which our model for corporate governance is the key, and provides valuable insights into our approach to business.'
Marcus Wallenberg, CEO, Investor AB

Preface

We need passion for ownership since true ownership itself has a strong element of passion. Owner/entrepreneurs who have changed the world – the Henry Fords (Ford), the Bill Gates (Microsoft), the Ted Turners (CNN), and the Ingvar Kamprads (IKEA) to name but a few – have all been passionate about their ideas and visions as well as for the sustainable prosperity of their companies. However, direct ownership of this type, or involving less spectacular individuals, is exceptional today. In terms of market capitalisation, the lion's share is owned by institutions of various kinds – mutual trusts, pension funds, insurance companies. Corporate ownership has become anonymous, predominantly faceless in many developed economies.

What is worse, this has happened in parallel with – or maybe because of – neglecting the importance of ownership for business as well as overall prosperity.

This book has come about because of a concern for, and I dare say, a passion for ownership. Ownership makes a difference. Ownership has an indispensable role to play in creating sustainable value in companies, for overall prosperity.

Since ownership has been neglected, it is crucial to spread the *gospel* of the blessings of ownership. I hope this book will support that cause by making its own distinctive contribution concerning the themes of ownership and value creation as outlined in the Introduction.

This book is based on one I published in Swedish (1997). However, this English version is largely rewritten to address an international audience as well as updated to reflect the current situation and new challenges of ownership, e.g. those generated by the *new economy*. The work on this version has also made it possible to deepen and expand my case study of the Wallenberg sphere. Hopefully, I have learnt a few lessons in the meantime as well.

Acknowledgements

I am indebted to a large number of individuals as well as several institutions for the realisation of this book.

In the process of updating and adapting the original book to an international audience, ambitions grew during the course of the project resulting in the present version, which is about 80 percent new. These ambitions were enhanced, not least because of a series of interviews and discussions with an extensive number of knowledgeable – many being the best qualified you can find as regards issues of corporate governance, ownership, and value creation – and most stimulating persons. I would like to express my sincere gratitude to all the persons included in the interview list (Appendix 1). They all willingly and enthusiastically shared their ideas and experiences with me. Of course, I am solely responsible for what became the final result of these interviews and deliberations in the book.

However, I am even more indebted to several of the individuals on the interview list who gave me additional assistance in a variety of ways, e.g. by granting me several extensive interviews, helping me with contacts to additional interviewees, allowing me to quote them in the book, reading my drafts and giving valuable feedback, supplying me with data and input material. I am much obliged to Jean-Pierre Auzimour, Percy Barnevik, Bo Berggren, Erik Berglöf, Clas Bergström, Bob Boldt, Ramsay Brufer, Sir Dominic Cadbury, Frances Cairncross, William D. Crist, Stephen Cruz, Michelle Edkins, Donald Gogel, Lennart Grabe, Finn Johnsson, Richard H. Koppes, Håkan Lindgren, Jay W. Lorsch, Olof Lund, Reinhard Marsch-Barner, Lars Millberg, Ira Millstein, Robert A.G. Monks, Richard Normann, Daniel Nyberg, Anders Perlinge, Henrik Rhenman, Björn Savén, Per Spångberg, Bengt Stymne, Marcus Wallenberg, Dennis Weatherstone, and Christer Zetterberg.

I would like to thank Diane Taylor, publishing editor at John Wiley & Sons Ltd, for believing in the idea and prospects of this book as well as for her patience in accepting repeatedly postponed deadlines. Her feedback on progress drafts of the book during the course of this project has been most constructive and encouraging.

I am much obliged to Bertil Ekerlid who facilitated the publication of this book by yielding the rights of Ekerlids Förlag to the Swedish version.

Financially this project has been made possible by research grants from the SIAR Foundation and Industri Kapital AB. I would like to convey my sincere thanks for these grants to the Board of the SIAR Foundation and to Björn Savén, the CEO of Industri Kapital, respectively. I am indebted to Gemini Consulting for granting me leave of absence to pursue this project as well as for allowing me to draw upon its infrastructure.

My warmest thanks to Karl-Magnus Westerberg, who helped me with the initial research as well as the final editing. Anna Björkdahl provided excellent assistance by retrieving a lot of information for me, not to mention all the teaching she bestowed on me so that I could manage on my own out in cyberspace.

All readers should be grateful to Izabella Hallberg who scrutinised and improved my English significantly. If you still find strange expressions and grammatical errors, I am to blame for the last minute changes and additions in the manuscript. I am deeply indebted for her persistent efforts, and, hopefully, some of the many language lessons she has taught me will stick.

Last, but not least, I owe a lot to Gun Johannesson who typed my extensive interview dictations and scribbling, put what I typed myself in order and did all what I cannot do on the computer, e.g. graphs and tables. Many thanks, Gun.

Stockholm, December 2000
Rolf H. Carlsson

Introduction

The title of this book – *Ownership and Value Creation – Strategic Corporate Governance in the New Economy* – conveys the following messages that form the book's main propositions:

- Ownership makes a difference! The *ownership function* fulfills an indispensable role in the market economy. Its quality makes all the difference for sustainable value-creation.
- Ownership will be a key aspect in this new millennium. Globalisation and the *new economy* – to mention two mega change forces – offer new challenges. All the fantastic new technologies coming out currently as well as a proliferating entrepreneurial spirit are fabulous assets. However, *competent and diligent ownership* has to be added if we are going to succeed in transforming such assets into sustainable value-creation, business prosperity.
- Owners of corporations, of business entities have to take on the crucial challenges of being owners and prepare for them.
- Corporate governance activists must be more concerned about business prosperity aspects in the governance of corporations and business entities. To mark this aspect, *Strategic* has been added to the generic term *corporate governance*.
- Competence, adequate *owner competence* will be required to perform a value-creating ownership role, a critical development challenge that still remains to be accepted by many *shareholders* if they should become *shareowners*.

FOCUS AND PURPOSE

The focus of this book is the role of ownership and sustainable value-creation as well as the competence and other prerequisites required to performing such a role. In addition to an analysis to prove the relevance of the above propositions, the purpose is to offer assistance to owners who wants to enhance their capabilities for value-creation, e.g. regarding:

- a frame of reference for value-creation and the role of the owner;
- development of the ownership function as a whole and differentiation between owners;

- lessons to be learnt from successful owner specialists;
- analytical tools for active owners to manage key issues of the value-creation process;
- differentiation between the roles of owners, boards and executive management;
- enhancement of the governance process.

SOME OBSERVATIONS TRIGGERING THE NEED AND FOCUS OF THIS BOOK

The title of this book – *Ownership and Value Creation: Strategic Corporate Governance in the New Economy* – should be seen against the spectacular development of stock markets and market capitalisation in recent years. Rapidly expanding flows of funds invested in stock markets and mounting expectations of future value returns – mutually reinforcing – are powerful driving forces behind this amazing development. However, will these, often hyped, future expectations automatically entail fundamental value-creation in the future? Most sensible people realise that this will not be the case. Still, the question remains: to what extent will there be a convergence between future expectations as reflected in current stock market prices and fundamental value-creation in the end?

The stock market – a wonderful innovation

The stock market is a wonderful innovation. It facilitates the mobilisation of risk capital from thousands and millions of savers/investors and then channels that to the many companies needing risk capital to grow and prosper. It accommodates the small and the big. The small saver, with a few dollars to spare, can participate in financing a billion-dollar equity company. The stock market sets a price on the shares so that you, the investor, know the value of your fortune every day. Each listed company is valued so that it has continuously updated knowledge of what asset value the company represents, on what value, i.e. market capitalisation, it has to yield a return.

So, what is the problem? Having this wonderful market mechanism of risk capital exchange and pricing – why can't we live happily ever after?

Unfortunately, it can be argued, the stock market is always wrong!

Most people would argue the opposite, of course. The market is always right – and they are right, in the sense that the market decides at what price you can trade your share, on what terms the company can get new risk capital etc. At the same time, the market is fundamentally wrong since nobody can predict the future and the price of a stock is supposed to be a reflection of future earnings.

However, the correctness of the heading is particularly relevant in the context of this book. Although the trading and pricing of a company on the stock exchange is related to the fundamental, value creation processes within the company, the logic at work on the stock market and in the company, respectively, are different. One small example should be sufficient argument: a stockholder can sell his/her shares whenever and immediately he/she changes his/her assessment of future prospects; the company is stuck – for a varying length of time and with the ensuing 'boom or bust' – once it has committed its resources to something. Thus, the stock market and the individual company are worlds apart – still, these two worlds have to be accommodated, the gulf between them has to be bridged.

The ownership function – accommodating the different logic

One of the main theses of this book is that the actual outcome and answer to the initial question (to what extent will there be a convergence between future expectations as reflected in current stock market prices and fundamental value creation in the end?) will depend on the quality of – what in this book will be called – the *ownership function*. This is based on the view that the role of the ownership function is to link the sources of risk capital in stock markets to the fundamental processes in corporations and individual businesses so as to achieve sustainable value-creation. It will be argued in this book that owners – provided they are active, competent, and well positioned – have a crucial role to play in the processes of creating value, for business prosperity.

In the complex markets of today, the ownership function is constituted by a variety of actors, playing different roles, fulfilling part-functions of the ownership function as a whole: institutional investors, e.g. pension funds, mutual trusts, insurance companies – as well as, what will be called owner specialists, e.g. venture capitalists, LBO/MBO and private equity companies, investment companies, multi-business corporations – and many more, in addition to private individuals.

The corporate governance movement – enhancing the ownership function

The most important, if not spectacular, thing that has happened concerning the ownership function is the corporate governance movement that started in the mid-1980s. It has aimed to enhance the ownership function by reinstating owners in the governance role of corporations, thus making boards and executive management accountable to their owners. Corporate governance is more than demands for *shareholder value,* which has emerged as some kind of *mantra* during the same period of time. A pioneer of the corporate governance movement, the state of California pension fund, CalPERS (see Chapter 2 for a thorough review of CalPERS achievements!) is a strong advocate for the word *shareowner*instead of *shareholder* to mark the significance as well as the rights and obligations of owners. Being particular with this term, signals an ambition to establish a new order regarding the governance of corporations.

The impact of the corporate governance movement on the ownership function

Thus, an obvious topic of this book includes an assessment of the corporate governance movement. What has been done to enhance the ownership function and to safeguard fundamental value-creation, now and for the future? Without pre-empting the conclusions of that analysis in ensuing chapters, let us already at this point highlight one observation made by the most recent corporate governance committee of the UK, the much respected Hampel Committee (Chapter 4 will elaborate on this). The corporate governance movement has been more concerned with one of two important aspects of corporate governance: *Accountability* has predominantly been in focus while the other key aspect, the enhancement of *business prosperity*, has got much less attention. There are probably several factors explaining this, but it would be fair to suggest that key reasons are the difficulties involved and the *competence* it takes to have an impact on value-creation as an owner. This book shares the Hampel Committee's concern for sustainable value-creation. There is also a subsequent concern regarding what needs to be done to make the owner competent and potent as value-creator. Therefore, a key focus of this book is *ownership competence* and what is required to achieve sustainable value creation.

APPROACH AND STRUCTURE OF THIS BOOK

To prove the relevance of the propositions initially stated, and to fulfil the purposes set out in this book, three main topics and issues have to be covered, namely:

1. **Corporate governance and the ownership function.** Have the initiatives and activities of the corporate governance movement led to a more competent and potent *ownership function* and how well positioned is it to take on the challenges ahead?
2. **Lessons of successful ownership.** What are the competence elements and other key success factors explaining *sustainable value-creating ownership*? What are the experience lessons to be learnt from proven success in real life?

3. **Conceptualisation and its implications.** How to conceptualise owner-ship and value-creation as well as other aspects of corporate governance to provide useful tools to enhance the competence of owners as well as the ownership function as a whole? What are the conclusions and implications of this for further action?

Assessing the corporate governance development and positioning the ownership function

Where does corporate governance stand today? Before the 1990s very few were aware of this term and phenomenon. Today, corporate governance is known everywhere in the global business and financial community. But what has been achieved concretely so far in terms of – to use the two key aspects of corporate governance emphasised by the Hampel Report (see chapters 1 and 4!) – *accountability* and *business prosperity*. Are boards and executive management of corporations accountable to their owners to a larger extent today than before the whole corporate governance movement started? Are owners doing their job of demanding accountability, and are those in charge of running the corporations responding? To what extent has corporate governance contributed to enhancing business prosperity? These and many other questions become obvious when attempting an assessment of concrete achievements of corporate governance so far. As obvious as the following: Where is the corporate governance movement heading? Are corporate governance standards and practices being globalised? What challenges, of accountability and business prosperity, will be on the corporate governance agenda of the future?

To make these general questions operational we need to define what is meant by *accountability* and decide how it can be assessed. Some criteria for a review of business prosperity achievements have to be added. Finally, we need to limit the study to make it manageable within the scope of this book.

Accountability and business prosperity

Although useful to separate for analytical as well as action purposes, it is important to emphasise that *accountability* and *business prosperity* are inte-grated aspects of corporate governance. In the first place, accountability has to do with delivering business prosperity, sustainable value-creation.

Accountability applies to the chain of command of owners, the board of directors and executive management. The board is accountable to the owners and executive management to the board (complications in this straight model caused by the so-called stakeholder model and blurred borderlines between the board and executive management will be discussed in the book as well).

Since delivering business prosperity requires considerable freedom of action on the part of the board of directors and executive management as well, there is always a risk that such power is misused and abused. The incumbent board and executive management can promote their own interests in various ways. They can entrench themselves in their position even if business performance is faltering. By favouring certain groups of shareholders they can protect their own power position. Granting themselves over-generous remuneration packages is another example. They can promote their own personal business interests, employ their own, often unqualified, *buddies*, and such like. Accountability aspects of corporate governance are much concerned with issues of this type.

To ensure accountability in all these respects – value-creation demands as well as abuse of shareholder rights in other respects – corporate governance standards and practices can be grouped into three main categories, namely.[1]

Quality and accessibility of information

Information is the key to preventing abuse of power as well as to keeping a check on performance – involving the financial community at large and the media in that monitoring work. A fundamental requirement is that all shareholders are treated equal, have the same access to information. Key features of this aspect of corporate governance include:

- general transparency making it possible to analyse performance, discover irregularities etc;
- accountability standards to make sure definitions of terms are consistent and allow comparison – benchmarking with other companies and so forth;
- disclosure of remuneration principles, practices and figures as well as if the company is involved in litigation cases or is exposed to other risks, not yet visible in the accounts.

Formal control aspects

In this category one can include arrangements to safeguard the formal rights of shareholders, the owners of the company, as well as the rights of a third party. Two important institutions in this area include:

- The AGM, the Annual General Meeting where all shareholders can exercise their voting rights to discharge the board, elect a new board etc. All prerequisites to make this work properly are of key concern for the corporate governance agenda.

• Auditing is an important control instrument for shareholders as well as for other stakeholders. The professional quality, integrity, and independence of auditors as well as how the auditing process is implemented can make a big difference in the control of the corporation, its board and executive management.

Balance of power and content of corporate governance

Is the balance of power between owners on the one hand and the incumbent board/executive management on the other well balanced or distorted? Is executive management challenged as well as supported when it comes to the content of business decision making? These questions highlight the most crucial aspects of corporate governance, namely whether *the bosses* are accountable and whether sustainable value is created. The focus here is on the board of directors – the key instrument of the owners through which to exercise ownership of the corporation – the key aspects of which include:

• The independence and competence of the board.
• The recruitment and election of board members.
• The composition of the board.
• The renewal of the board.
• Organisation of the work of the board.
• Information access, resource support etc.

Assessing corporate governance and positioning the ownership function with respect to accountability involves an analysis of the status and progress of the aspects exemplified above. It should be obvious that such an assessment must be done primarily in the institutional context that is specific to each country.

Assessment of business prosperity achievements

This is a tricky aspect to assess, particularly since our aim is to understand the sustainability of value-creation. Improved financial performance can be a result of short-term measures, which might even have counterproductive effects on long term performance. In addition, it is not always easy to distinguish what improvements are attributable to the ownership function and what is due to external factors. Furthermore, a thorough analysis of sustainable value-creation could easily become a Herculean task, completely outside the scope of this book. So, the assessment that will be done in this context will be based on finding indicators of renewal in corporations and business at large in the countries included. Such renewal indicators include LBO/MBO (Leveraged Buy-Out/Management Buy-Out) deals highlighting the pace of restructuring in the *old economy* corporations. In addition, it is important to review venture capital activities and IPO (Initial Public Offering = the first listing of a company on a stock exchange) intensity indicating the creation of new companies, e.g. reflecting the *new economy*.

Limiting the geographical scope of the corporate governance review

Since our purpose is to assess the impact of the corporate governance movement on the ownership function and positioning the latter as regards current and future challenges, limiting our study to a handful of the leading countries, as regards corporate governance, and the largest economies in the world should be enough. Two of the countries, the USA and the UK, are included for two significant reasons. The corporate governance movement started in the USA and hooked on quite early in the UK. The development in both countries has had a major international impact, setting examples for other countries to follow. This impact is also a consequence of the dominating role particularly the US financial institutions but also the British have on global capital markets. Three countries have been added to the study sample: France, Germany, and Japan. Thus, the sample includes the five largest economies in the world. However, the three latter countries represent very different corporate governance traditions and institutional frameworks – compared to each other as well as to the USA and the UK.

In addition to the country reviews and their comparison, a handful of large cross-border mergers are also studied as a potential vanguard of international convergence of corporate governance practices.

Lessons of successful ownership

If ownership makes a difference, it would be interesting to analyse the factors explaining success. Thus, the first thing to do is to identify examples of sustainable success of active ownership. The lessons to be learnt have to be derived in two steps: the first step explaining the success factors in the particular case or cases identified for study; the second step seeing whether such success factors can be interpreted in a more generalised framework.

The general character of business and ownership success

Developing a successful business takes time. Success stories such as IKEA and Tetra Pak needed some twenty years to achieve the stage of business breakthrough that opened opportunities for international expansion and eventual global leadership. Some success stories may have shorter lead times but business success does not occur as some kind of instant magic trick. Developing a business is a demanding and often arduous learning process. Furthermore, as we will discuss thoroughly in this book, sustainable success is subject to incessant renewal demands.

Thus, to prove the success of a successful owner specialist, and to identify the key factors explaining that success necessitates an analysis of the performance and achievements of such a specialist during a long period of time. Sustainable success as an owner specialist must be based on repeated success at developing new and successful businesses as well as on repeated ability to renew and sustain the success of already established businesses.

The Wallenberg sphere – a case study of ownership success

The selection of the Wallenberg sphere as the case to be studied in this context was based on its proven success during a long period of time. As a leading active owner it has managed to develop, renew and sustain a considerable number of multinational corporations, e.g. ASEA (now ABB), Astra (now Astra Zeneca), Atlas Copco, Ericsson, Scania, SKF, and Stora (now Stora Enso) – many of which hold leading positions in their global markets.

Identifying and analysing key elements of owner competence

To identify and understand the core competence elements explaining the success of the Wallenberg sphere, four dimensions or basic questions are analysed:

- Are there certain types of business where the sphere has been more successful? Has a pattern of specialisation emerged? In that case – what patterns can we distinguish, what historical driving forces explain them, and what characterises these businesses?
- How has the sphere organised and managed its relations with the individual companies? What characterises the interventions of the sphere representatives? In other words, what constitutes its corporate governance system and what experience explains it?
- What has been the external relations policy of the sphere? How has it legitimised itself in the business community in Sweden as well as internationally – and in society at large? How has it managed its various stakeholders?
- What is the philosophy behind the formation of the sphere? What are the values that have been guiding the actions taken? Could one distinguish a basic owner idea that has propelled and directed all the sphere's energetic efforts?

Additional analyses and synthesis – the success formula

Specialist competence, and contact networks are reviewed, in addition to the analysis of competence elements, career patterns of leading chief executives and directors of the boards of the sphere as well as the concrete structure of supporting resources.

The study also includes a presentation of how the various competence elements and supporting structure are integrated into one *success formula* as well as how that formula has been renewed and adapted to changing external business and institutional environments.

The findings are then tested and lessons to be learnt explained in a generalised, conceptual framework where examples from other owner specialists are used as well.

Conceptualisation and its implications

Issues of sustainable value-creation, the role of owners and the ownership function, organisational issues of role differentiation, and other issues addressed in this book offer many conceptualisation challenges. A primary mission of this book is to present a frame of reference for the importance of the ownership function and the indispensable role of the owner in the process of sustainable value creation. The propositions listed in the beginning of the Introduction require a logically consistent reasoning to make sense.

The conceptual framework presented in this book includes ideas developed by others as well as concepts taken from the SIAR School,[2] and concepts developed by this author.

The conceptual analysis addresses three fundamental sets of questions:

- **Why is** ownership and the role of the owner crucial?
- **What** is ownership all about, and what distinguishes ownership from other roles in the process of value-creation? What competence and other prerequisites are required?
- **How** are value-creation contributions made, and how should ownership be exercised to be successful?

The conceptual analysis of these questions takes it points of departure from three fundamental propositions concerning:

- The overall nature of the market economy – the concept of the *process of creative destruction* and demands for *incessant renewal*.
- The fundamental rationale of the individual firm – the concept of *the firm as a learning centre*.
- Ownership and risk – the two parameters of risk.

The implications of these propositions are analysed. Concepts and analytical tools for the active owner to address key issues of value-creation, management of demands for renewal and various kinds of risk are developed. Alternative views and misconceptions of fundamental concepts are also examined. Conclusions and recommendations are presented for the enhancement of ownership competence, the ownership function as a whole as well as for the organisation and exercise of corporate governance.

WHAT ARE THE KEY CONTRIBUTIONS OF THIS BOOK AND WHAT MAKES IT DIFFERENT FROM OTHER BOOKS ON THE TOPICS COVERED?

This book is written for people of action – chairmen and chief executives, directors of boards and people in various management positions as well as for their advisors, i.e. lawyers, consultants and analysts – in the investment, financial and business communities of the world. Many of the issues discussed are also addressed to politicians and public administrators. Hopefully they will find the book easy to read as well as full of *action content*. However, giving the book this action profile has been combined with an ambition to apply a certain methodological rigour to make the book useful for researchers and students as well. The most visible expressions of this include an extensive number of footnotes, a list of reference literature, and an appendix with comments on this author's frame of reference and methodological principles.

As regards the subject matter of the book, one main theme and two supporting subjects are included.

Main theme: ownership and value creation

This book puts the active owner at centre stage by combining an analysis of value-creation with that of the role of the owner and the ownership function. The logic of value-creation is analysed at the macro level as well as at the micro level of a corporation. The value-creation hierarchy of a corporation (single business, multi-business, and owner levels, respectively) is distinguished. A role differentiation model for these levels is presented based on the value-creation contribution appropriate at each level. The value-creation contribution at the owner level is further elaborated, and concepts and analytical tools to be used by the active owner are outlined. In addition, the organisation and role differentiation of the chain of command between owners, boards of directors and executive management are discussed and normative ideas provided. Suggestions for the enhancement of the process of governance are also included.

Other books rarely combine the topic of ownership with that of the logic of value creation. Comparable books usually belong to one of two categories:

- One category discusses ownership issues, not least books on corporate governance. These books focus on accountability aspects, balance of power issues and the cost of separating ownership and the control of corporations. Generally, they have very little to say about the logic of value-creation and how the owner can contribute in the process of value-creation, what competence is required and so forth.
- Another category is focused on value-creation issues but as a matter of concern solely for executive management. In most books on value-creation and strategic issues, at least concerning large corporations, the owners are not supposed to be involved.

Supporting subject 1: corporate governance

The review of the corporate governance development, included in this book, aims at positioning the ownership function in its institutional context and stage of progress. Thus, it provides input for the conceptual analysis of ownership and value-creation. However, this requires a very concrete study of the corporate governance situation and dynamics in the five largest economies of the world. It has been necessary to apply a historical perspective to understand the particular institutional setting in each country under review as well as to identify the driving forces behind the emergence of the corporate governance movement. To position the ownership function in front of current and future issues it has been important to identify and analyse the dynamics of globalisation and other driving forces, e.g. new technologies and changing demographics. As a consequence the corporate governance review should not only be seen as background information for conceptualisation of the value-creating role of ownership. It offers the reader a current update of the agenda of key issues and controversies of corporate governance in several leading countries as well as in the global context.

A distinguishing contribution of this book as regards the corporate governance review is its application of an action perspective. Key issues are identified and conclusions are generated on how to enhance the ownership function and sustainable value-creation. The views presented in this book will not be shared by all readers and actors addressed. Some readers may even find some of the views provocative. Hopefully, if the advice given will not be followed, at least, further discussion will be stimulated.

Supporting subject 2: the case study of a successful owner specialist

The identification and analysis of the key elements of owner competence of the Wallenberg sphere, as well as the *success formula* explaining these achievements, must be based on actions and performance during a long period of time. Although studies made by several economic historians have provided important input, the case study in this book is not a summary presentation of the history of the Wallenberg sphere. The historical facts have been used to explain the success of the sphere as an owner specialist. In addition, this provides crucial input for extracting lessons to be learnt concerning ownership and sustainable value-creation in other contexts.

Thus, the case study of the Wallenberg sphere distinguishes this book from studies made by economic historians. Furthermore, the in-depth analysis presented here goes beyond frequent studies made by investment analysts and economic journalists of Investor, the investment company and key owner instrument of the sphere, and the Wallenberg dynasty, respectively. In addition to the analysis of past performance in order to identify the owner competence and success formula, the case study includes a review of current and future challenges of the sphere as well as a discussion of its strategic options.

There are also some additional benefits to be gained from this study for various categories of readers, e.g.:

- The study provides facts and analysis of several of the large multi-national corporations of the sphere for those interested in ABB, Ericsson, Saab, and Scania, for instance.
- Some of the background explanations of the factors driving the emergence of Sweden as a global hotbed of Internet technologies and applications, not least those related to mobile communications, are given in this study. The Wallenberg sphere as well as Ericsson have played crucial roles in this development in the past – and still do.
- For readers interested in the historical development of the Swedish economy at large as well as those interested in why the Swedish Stock Exchange had the best performance of all during the 20th century, an understanding of the Wallenberg sphere in the perspective of this study may prove useful.

OUTLINE AND MAIN CONTENT OF THIS BOOK

This book is structured in three parts. The purpose and the main content of each part are summarised below.

Part I. Activating and renewing ownership

The multiple purpose of this part include the following main aspects:

- The emergence of corporate governance as we understand it today.
- A critical review of the corporate governance situation in the five largest economies of the world including how it has emerged as well as an identification of current issues.
- Observations concerning the position of the ownership function in each country with regard to accountability and business prosperity aspects.
- A comparative analysis and assessment of the process of international convergence of corporate governance standards and practices in each country as well as cross-border mergers of large multi-national corporations.
- Future prospects and challenges facing the ownership function and the corporate governance movement.

After a brief introduction (Chapter 1) of what is meant by corporate governance, the presentation continues with an analysis of why and how the corporate governance movement emerged. Thus, the historical roots, driving forces and emergence of corporate governance in the USA are reviewed. This includes a case study of CalPERS as the early instigator and pioneer of corporate governance (Chapter 2). A review and critical analysis of the current corporate governance situation in the USA follows after that (Chapter 3). The development and implementation of the *Combined Code* in the UK is another landmark achievement with great international impact, which is covered. Analyses of current corporate governance issues in the UK and the position of the ownership function are also included (Chapter 4). The current corporate governance situation in the remaining three countries of the five largest economies of the world – Germany, France, and Japan – are analysed in a historical as well as an international perspective (Chapters 5–7, respectively). A comparative analysis of the five countries is presented, including a review of different board concepts – unitary and two-tier boards, respectively, as regards formal status as well as actual implications concerning balance of power and differentiation of roles between independent and executive directors. Cross-border mergers and other driving forces for international convergence of corporate governance practices are discussed as well (Chapter 8).

This part of the book ends (Chapter 9) by applying a dynamic perspective of corporate governance, including a future outlook of ownership and corporate governance challenges. Implications of the business logic of the emerging *new economy* are discussed. An overall conclusion is that corporate governance and the role of ownership will be even more indispensable, and more important for sustainable value creation in the future than it has been, or has been allowed to be in the past.

Part II. Ownership makes a difference. a case study of the Wallenberg sphere

The purpose of this part is threefold:

1. To present a concrete case of successful ownership. To show what actual ownership, as exercised by a successful owner specialist, is all about. To understand the competence elements and the "success formula" at work in the Wallenberg sphere.
2. To provide input for conclusions about lessons to be learnt and possibly applied in other contexts.
3. To provide concrete observations and examples for the conceptual analysis of various issues of value-creation, the role of ownership, and more in Part III.

The case study of the Wallenberg sphere is presented in two chapters (chapters 10 and 11). Additional background information is provided in a separate appendix (Appendix 3).

Throughout its history, the Wallenberg sphere has experienced repeated cycles of renewal as well as earlier *new economies*. The first Chapter of Part II (Chapter 10) analyses and presents the key elements of the owner competence of the Wallenberg sphere as well as its comprehensive *success formula* based on how historical challenges have been managed.

After an initial summary of the core competence elements, the Wallenberg sphere is briefly introduced and its proven success illustrated. This is followed by an analysis of the key aspects of its ownership competence, including:

- *Competence* to manage certain types of business, *risk logic* and *dynamics*.
- The *meta-management* skills of the Wallenberg sphere.
- The *legitimisation* policy and the key factors explaining the *institutionalisation* achievements of the sphere.
- The *ownership idea* in the Wallenberg sphere and its supporting *system of values*.

After a review of supporting resources and networks of key associates as well as external contact networks, a synthesis – *the distinctive ownership competence* of the sphere – is presented.

This chapter ends with a discussion of the *real learning* and the dynamic elements of the lasting success of the sphere.

In the second chapter (Chapter 11), recent performance as well as the current situation and future challenges of the sphere are reviewed.

Initially the performance of the fourth generation, which handed over the executive responsibilities of the sphere to the fifth generation in recent years, is summed up. Impressive achievements as well as shortcomings are identified and reviewed.

This is followed by a review of the programmes for active ownership presented by the new leadership, particularly involving Percy Barnevik, the new chairman of Investor, and the representative of the fifth generation, Marcus Wallenberg as new CEO of Investor. Performance to date is assessed.

Key challenges for the renewal of the sphere are identified and the new strategy – called *The Bridge*, marking the ambition of the sphere to integrate investments in the *new economy* with active renewal initiatives in the core holdings of the *old economy* – launched by Marcus Wallenberg is discussed.

Open issues of future challenges are identified and some strategic options are put forward. Thus, the case study of the Wallenberg sphere ends as a good case should – leaving the conclusions about future prospects and renewal options for the reader to consider.

The appendix to Part II (Appendix 3) provides the reader with additional facts about the current structure of the sphere as well as a review of some critical events in the past, which have had a formative impact on the sphere. A couple of mini-cases of how active ownership has been exercised in ASEA/ABB and the Saab/Scania groups are also included.

Part III. Conceptualisation and professionalisation

Based on our review of corporate governance development and its future challenges in Part I of the book, and the analysis of a successful owner in Part II, the purpose of Part III is twofold:

1. 1 To develop a conceptual framework of ownership and sustainable value creation, and related issues. This is done in Chapter 12 and includes a variety of aspects.

   - The logic of value creation.
   - The fundamental value creating contributions by an owner.
   - Different risk management strategies.
   - Different types of risk as well as differentiated risk logic and dynamics.
   - How the role and contributions of the owner differ from that of other key actors.
   - What type of owner competence is required and why.
   - Differentiation of competence to fit the situation of a company depending on risk logic, development stage, business and institutional environment etc.
   - A comprehensive theory of ownership and its prerequisites.
   - Alternative views and misconceptions – Marxist-inspired views and the stakeholder model.
   - The concept and importance of capital.

2. To outline some normative ideas of how to improve and enhance the ownership function. This is done in Chapter 13 by applying four different perspectives.

- *Value creation perspective* – how can basic ownership competence be developed to support the value creation role of ownership?
- *Industry development perspective* – how can ownership, seen as an industry of many different actors, be developed in order to increase the overall efficiency of the ownership function in the economy?
- *Organisational perspective* – how should the chain (of command) of owner- board of directors-executive management be organised so that a rational and constructive differentiation of tasks, roles and responsibilities can be achieved?
- *Governance perspective* – how should ownership be exercised so that renewal, sustainable value creation and accountability be guaranteed?

This chapter and the book ends with a brief concluding summary of what the corporate governance movement has achieved to date regarding the enhancement of the ownership function as well as pinpointing the huge challenge that still remains to be tackled.

PART I

Activating and Renewing Ownership

Emergence, Driving Forces, Current Agendas,
and Future of Corporate Governance

An Introduction to Corporate Governance

1

CORPORATE GOVERNANCE – A GLOBAL PHENOMENON

During the 1990s the term *corporate governance* became a household name, not only in the business and financial communities, but also with the public at large. Like so many other new ideas, trends and fads, corporate governance originated in California. An account of this really quite exciting story is given later (Chapter 2). Starting in California it has become more than just an American phenomenon. It has spread all over the world – especially since the mid-nineties. A recent review of corporate governance guidelines and codes of *best practice*[1] identifies some sixty entries in 22 countries around the world including a handful issued by international organisations. Some fifty of these entries have come about or have been updated since 1995.

It should be obvious that such a list with so many relatively fresh documents reflects a wide variety of situations when it comes to corporate governance realities. These situations span from long experience of sophisticated Corporate Governance Programmes, e.g. as pioneered and practised by CalPERS, the State of California pension fund (See Chapter 2!), and The *Combined Code* as part of the listing rules of the London Stock Exchange at one end to mere *paper tigers*, wishful recommendations to improve practices without any response to date in many countries at the other end of the scale. The pace and dedication by which new corporate governance practices are being introduced also vary a lot. 'Just now (1999) things seem to be moving faster in many European countries' remarked Bob L. Boldt, Senior Investment Officer at the Global Public Markets Investments department of CalPERS[2].

Before reviewing the current corporate governance situation in somewhat more detail in a handful of important countries, it would be useful to discuss briefly the concept of *corporate governance* and explore its meaning by narrating how it all started, developed and came to be practised in the USA by CalPERS. For an understanding of the international development of corporate governance, the development in the UK that started with the Cadbury Report, what initiated it and what it lead to is also important and will be included in a following review of the corporate governance situation in the UK.

WHAT IS MEANT BY CORPORATE GOVERNANCE?

Since corporate governance was initially developed and implemented in the USA and then passed to the United Kingdom, the English term of what from the beginning was an Anglo-American phenomenon has also been accepted in its international proliferation.

In order to understand the meaning of corporate governance let us begin with the purpose of it. The so-called *Hampel Report*[3] offers some help in this respect – already in its first sentence: 'The importance of corporate governance lies in its contribution both to *business prosperity* and to *accountability*' (author's italics). Thus, in one sentence, that British committee has captured the very essence of corporate governance. More about this later (Chapter 4).

Another important aspect of corporate governance is how it is organised. As the term indicates it is about governance of corporations but it does not explicitly say anything about who should govern. A method of conceptualising corporate governance has been suggested by Dr. Bo Berggren, retired chairman of Stora (now StoraEnso, the world's largest producer of pulp and paper products) and Astra (the Swedish pharmaceutical company, now AstraZeneca), with long experience from the Wallenberg sphere (see Part II). In an address to an OECD seminar in 1995, where he made a comparative analysis of the institutional differences between Sweden and some other countries as regards corporate governance, he stated: 'There are actually only two externally defined levels – the owners and the concrete operations of a business. How we choose to organise the relations between these two levels, how corporate governance is organised, how accountability is demanded varies between countries and is reflected in different institutional arrangements'. Berggren illustrated his point by means of Figure 1.1.

In his information-rich illustration, Berggren has positioned the various institutions as how far they are from the owners and from operations, respectively. The role of the chairman in the three corporate governance systems is also highlighted.

Later in Part I, the differences between corporate governance in some of the leading countries are further explored as a starting point for a discussion of indications and forces driving international convergence of corporate governance principles and practices.

It should also be recognised that there are deviating opinions from the basic owner-related concept of corporate governance. The prerogative of owners is questioned by advocates of the so-called *stakeholder* model. They argue that other stakeholders, primarily employees, are also legitimate co-governors of corporations. We come back to the stakeholder model several times since it is unavoidable in discussing, e.g. the situation in Germany (Chapter 5) and the historical driving forces of today's corporate governance. In discussing the fundamental role of ownership it is also important to

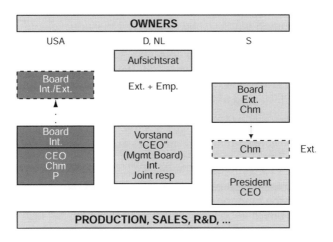

Figure 1.1 ''...only two externally defined levels ...'' the concept of corporate governance. Source: reproduced by permission of Dr. Bo Berggren.

critically review the underlying assumptions of the stakeholder model (Chapter 12).

The concept and practice of corporate governance today cannot be well understood without an awareness of how it emerged and was developed by the pioneering efforts of CalPERS (abbreviation of **Ca**lifornia **P**ublic **E**mployees **R**etirement **S**ystem), one of the pension funds of the state of California. A brief account of this exciting story as a decisive part of the development of corporate governance in America as well as a driving force of international initiatives in this arena follows in Chapter 2.

However, it should be said that corporate governance in the USA today is not the same thing as practiced by CalPERS. In an immensely pluralistic USA far from all share CalPERS' views on corporate governance. There are many deviating ideas. Furthermore, many other actors have been involved in the shaping of corporate governance in the USA. So, before coming to the CalPERS' story, let us end this introduction to corporate governance by providing a bird's eye view of how corporate governance was established in its first arena, *Corporate America*.

MAKING CORPORATE AMERICA ACCOUNTABLE

The calendar of critical events in Table 1.1 summarises the development of corporate governance in the US since the mid-1980s. Some of the most important actors making it happen are mentioned in the list: CalPERS, of course, but also individuals, e.g. Bob Monks and Dale Hanson. Bob Monks has been

Table 1.1   Important dates in the corporate governance revolution[a]

1985	Founding of CII
1985	Bob Monks founds ISS
1986	Boone Pickens founds USA
1987	CalPERS files first Shareholder Proposals
1988	U.S. DOL issues 'Avon' letter re Value of Proxy Voting
1989	CalPERS asks SEC for Proxy Reforms
1991	Dale Hanson letter to GM Board
1991	New Compact for Owners & Directors in HBR
1992	Bob Monks Ad in WSJ on Sears Board
1992	GM Board fires CEO Stempel
1992	SEC's Proxy Reforms Enacted
1993	CEO heads roll (AMX, IBM, Whse, Kodak, etc.)
	Fortune Magazine: 'The King is Dead'
1994	GM Board issues corporate governance guidelines
	CalPERS asks top 300 companies to compare
1995	Securities Litigation Reform Act passed over Clinton Veto
1996	Teamsters issue Least Valuable Directors list
1996 & 1997	Business Week cover stories on Best & Worst Boards
1996	NACD Report on Director Professionalism
1997	CalPERS (draft) on 'Ideal' corporate governance standards
1997	BRT Report on corporate governance standards
1998	TIAA-CREF files shareholder proposal on Independent Board at Disney
1998	CalPERS Final Draft of Corporate Governance Guidelines
1998	Texaco Poison Pill put to Shareholder Vote/Passes
1998	TIAA-CREF Kicks Out Entire Corporate Board (Furr's)
1999	OECD and World Bank adopt Corporate Gov Principles

[a] *Richard H. Koppes, Jones, Day, Reavis & Pogue, Stanford Law School, September 1998.* Published by courtesy of Mr. Koppes.

called the 'grandfather of American corporate governance'[4]. He founded Institutional Shareholder Services (ISS) in 1985. ISS is a consulting organisation providing various services, e.g. as a voting agent, to institutional investors. It was instrumental in the emergence of the corporate governance movement. Dale Hanson was the chief executive of CalPERS' from 1987 until 1995 and the daring leader in designing and executing its corporate governance programme. Some of the events listed as well as some of the institutions and names mentioned are discussed later. However, before continuing with the CalPERS story it should be said that in the list of events there is at least one important name missing, Richard H. Koppes. Koppes was the chief counsel of CalPERS from 1986 until 1996 who in tandem with Hanson pioneered many features of what we see today as modern corporate governance in America. The following will explain this further.

The CalPERS Story: Pioneering and Establishing Corporate Governance in the USA

2

'LIKE HELL!'

That indignant outburst came from Jesse Unruh, a seasoned Kennedy politician in California and a powerful trustee of the state pension fund CalPERS in California. The indignant reaction was provoked by Texaco's management and board, which at that time was entirely dominated by members who were also in the executive management, who had seen off a hostile bid for Texaco by means of a so-called *greenmail operation*[1] in 1984. Bass Brothers, who were the ones considering a take-over, had acquired a significant minority holding in Texaco as the starting point for a bid for the whole company. The Texaco management saw this as a threat to its own position. By exploiting the American Companies Act whereby a company can buy back its own shares from existing owners, and in addition making their offer only to Bass Brothers, they were able to stave off the threat. Nor was there anything to prevent the management from using *greenmail* (referring to the colour of the dollar bill); in other words offering an exorbitant price – in this case US\$55 per share compared with the market price which was around US\$35 at that time (1984). What annoyed Jesse Unruh was not just that they were robbing the other shareholders, including CalPERS (the excess being paid in this case corresponded to a total of US\$137 million, thus reducing the net value of the company by the same amount and hence the value of the remaining shareholders' stakes to a similar degree), but also that such goings on were possible at all.[2]

Jesse Unruh was unable to do anything about this particular affair, but one could claim that this incident was the trigger for the whole American Corporate Governance movement.

An important resolution

The CalPERS' board immediately adopted a resolution which stated that as long-term investors they would not accept behaviour similar to that of

Texaco from companies they had invested in and that they expect these companies to follow practices that are not prejudicial to the shareholders. CalPERS decided to use its power as a shareholder at the general meetings to see through its resolution and also to work in other ways to get to grips with the unsatisfactory state of affairs on the American stock market and in American corporations. Apart from the greenmail abuse, which was one of the worst offences, there were a lot of other issues to tackle, for example the boards' dependence on the management, the competence and appointment of the boards, the boards'/managers' salaries, emoluments and incentive system, so-called *poison pills*(various arrangements to prevent or obstruct hostile take-overs).

The mission and investment policy of CalPERS

Before getting on to what happened next, more background information is needed to understand the underlying motives and driving forces behind the actions.

CalPERS, which was among the inner circle of the largest public pension funds even in 1984, is now the largest in the USA, with total assets of more than US$160 billion.

Towards the end of the 1960s legal restrictions on pension funds' possibilities of investing in shares were lifted. Increased requirements for growth in

Table 2.1 CalPERS current asset allocation mix by market value and policy target percentages as of January 31, 2000[a]

Asset class	Market value ($ Billion)	Current allocation (%)	Target (%)
Cash equivalents	1.6	1.0	1.0
Fixed income			
Domestic	35.3	21.2	24.0
International	5.8	3.5	4.0
Total fixed income	42.7	25.7	29.0
Equities			
Domestics	74.9	45.1	41.0
International	34.5	20.8	20.0
Alt. Inv./Private Eq.	5.6	3.4	4.0
Total equities	115.0	69.3	65.0
Real estate	8.3	5.0	6.0
Total fund	166.0	100.0	100.0

[a] Source: http://www.calpers.ca.gov/invest/asset/asset.htm. Published by permission of CalPERS.

these pension funds, in order to guarantee civil servants' pensions, have meant that the proportion in shares has been increasing all the time. Table 2.1 shows CalPERS' total assets as of January 31, 2000 of which the dominant portion consists of shares.

The pension commitments are of the *defined benefit* type, in other words a certain pension is guaranteed to the beneficiary. With the increasingly tight finances in the state of California, there was increasing pressure on CalPERS to raise the return on its existing funds so the current budget was debited with the lowest possible charges so as to ensure the consolidation of the pension liability. In recent years, CalPERS' investments have generated a surplus return far above pension liabilities to the extent that it has been possible to raise pension benefits (compare that with the cumbersome state of affairs in most European countries where pension funds covering present and future pension benefits are minimal, if they exist at all).

Since the early 1970s, CalPERS investments in shares have predominantly been made on the basis of an index tracking strategy. This means that the total share portfolio reflects the whole stock market and that the yield is thus expected to follow the development of the general index. There are several reasons why this strategy was chosen. First of all, a pension fund is a long-term investor. It is the long-term yield, which is the decisive factor. It is not exposed to the competition, which unit trusts and personal pension insurance companies are, where the current yield is often an important factor in competition. By simply making changes in its own portfolio when the whole composition of the stock market changes, CalPERS avoids any effects its own reinvestments may have on the share prices. The number of reinvestments is also limited to a minimum and they are in principle carried out on an automatic signal from the data program, which monitors the composition of the portfolio. The transaction costs for the purchase and sale of shares are thus minimised, not just in the form of charges saved but also in personnel and analysis costs, which would be incurred in operating an active *stock picking* and transaction strategy. Being part of the state administration in California meant that CalPERS also had difficulty in attracting sufficiently qualified personnel for an active transaction strategy, owing to the wage restrictions imposed within that administration.

The index strategy and long term approach mean that people are not as interested in the relative yield for CalPERS as it is in the absolute. Only if the latter increases do CalPERS' chances of keeping its pension promises and reducing the need for contributions from the principal improve. Against that background it is easy to understand Jesse Unruh's indignation and the decision and actions which followed when people tried to do something about the fundamental deficiencies in the governance of *Corporate America*.

Initiating CII

One of the first actions, which Jesse Unruh initiated was, together with two other pension funds for public employees (New York City and New Jersey State), the formation of the CII (the Council of Institutional Investors) in 1985. The purpose of CII was to take care of the shareholders' interests, especially the institutional owners, such as the pension funds of state employees.

The CII came to play an important part as a lobbying body for changes in the legislation to better safeguard the interests of shareholders and obtain more shareholder-friendly management among the American corporations. It should be noted that the American legislation and legal system have a series of features, which have made it difficult for shareholders, not least institutional investors, to assert their rights vis-à-vis the companies[3]. This is connected with the fact that anti-trust legislation had, and still has, a strong position in the regulation of American economic life. Furthermore, since the 1930s capital market legislation has been designed to promote liquidity and flexibility on the stock market. Among other things this meant that share-holders were forbidden to collaborate before a general meeting. A share-holder was not allowed to contact another shareholder direct to propose a common mode of action, ask for a proxy etc., unless he sent the same proposal to all shareholders (compare this with the Texaco management's possibility of buying out a shareholder by *greenmail!*) Cooperation in the CII thus had to be of a general nature and it could not become a forum for cooperation in specific individual situations. One of the changes which the CII has contributed to is that the proxy ban – on canvassing for proxies – and restrictions on communication between shareholders before an AGM have been lifted. This only occurred in 1992 after CalPERS had filed an application to SEC asking for Proxy Reforms (see Mr. Koppes list of events!).

Building up its own resources

An even more important initiative of Mr. Unruh, following the appalling Texaco greenmail offense, was to develop the internal organisation and competence of CalPERS to exercise its rights as share owner (CalPERS makes a point of using the term *share owner* instead of shareholder to empha-sise the importance, rights and obligations are that of an owner of shares in a corporation.). The first step was to recruit a chief counsel, Mr. Koppes to reinforce CalPERS' formal competence in the exercise of voting rights at annual general meetings. A new chief executive, Mr. Dale Hanson, was also recruited, who proved very dynamic, persistent and fearless in the confrontations which became a recurring feature of CalPERS shareowner activism – particularly during the first few years. But it was to take a long

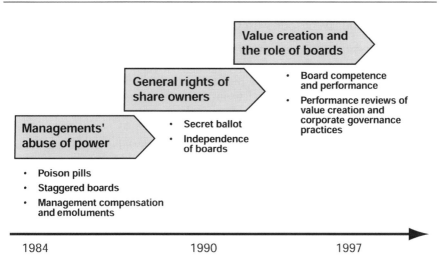

Figure 2.1 CalPERS Corporate Governance programme – a development in three (overlapping) phases.

learning process, with a lot of trial and error, before they had carved out their procedures for the exercise of ownership and until it was possible to record ultimate progress. The focus of CalPERS corporate governance programme varied from the mid-1980s onwards. At least three different phases can be distinguished as Figure 2.1 shows.

There is no room here to report on CalPERS' learning process in detail during these phases but a couple of aspects need to be emphasised in brief.

The first major lesson: focus on performance

Initially CalPERS chose to act at AGMs in companies where it had noted abuses of good Corporate Governance standards, e.g. *poison pills* to hinder hostile take-over attempts, staggered boards (preventing the AGM to elect an entire new board), lacking competence and independence of the board etc. For example CalPERS tried to introduce an *anti-poison pill* in McDonalds backed by proxies representing 30 percent of the votes. However, at the AGM CalPERS received no support whatsoever for this from shareholders present at the meeting – for the simple reason that McDonalds was producing brilliant results and proposing shareholder-friendly offers, among other things a share split. That experience was one of the reasons why it primarily came to focus on companies having poor and unsatisfactory results – an important step on the road to the success, which they eventually achieved.

Lesson number two: focus on the board

Another important milestone was reached when CalPERS realised it made sense to direct their action at board level, in particular its independent members, rather than trying to achieve changes directly in material matters. Changes to the board, intended to enhance its competence and independence in relation to the executive management, thus became a key instrument. An important milestone happened in 1992 when the chairman/CEO of General Motors, Robert Stempel, was ousted because of incompetence. Although there are different opinions about who should be credited for this – if anybody but the GM board itself that got their act together – the persistent pressure that CalPERS exercised against the board was most probably a contributing factor. About a year later CalPERS' owner activism set a veritable avalanche of CEO/Chairman heads rolling which was talked about as *the boardroom revolution*. This happened in several major corporations, e.g. in American Express, IBM, Westinghouse, and Kodak, as indicated in Mr. Koppes' list above.

It was obvious by then that CalPERS corporate governance activism had started to make a difference among institutional investors and to have significant impact in *Corporate America*. A more detailed analysis will follow later in this section but some observations about the factors behind this success are appropriate to highlight already at this point. In summary, the success factors are to be found in the way CalPERS corporate governance programme was carried out as well as in the quality and style of its leadership.

Achieving leverage – what really mattered

By focusing on poor performance CalPERS gained legitimacy for its viewpoints and actions. Making it clear that the board, solely, is accountable for the performance and corporate governance practices of the company, as well as for any changes needed – or be changed itself – further added to the legitimacy of CalPERS activism. Another key lever was to use media to get attention and raise pressure on incumbent boards and management to take notice of CalPERS demands. Important leverage was also achieved by mobilising other activists.

However, the success of CalPERS is most of all attributable to the key people involved and the leadership that was exercised. Three aspects of this are particularly important:

1. CalPERS managed to recruit two individuals who turned out to be extremely well qualified for the task of developing and implementing the CalPERS way of exercising corporate governance. One was the new CEO, Dale Hanson, who came on board in 1987, and the other key indi-

vidual was Richard H. Koppes, the chief counsel, who was recruited the year before.

2. Mr. Hanson and Mr. Koppes were not only well qualified individually. Together, they made an outstanding team. Their skills complemented each other and they seemed to have enjoyed working together. The audacity and drive of Mr Hanson made an effective combination with the cool, systematic style and proficiency in legal matters of Mr. Koppes. As a result, actions – usually spearheaded by Mr. Hanson – against poor performers and corporate governance abusers were well prepared, systematic and persistent. The latter point, not least, was crucial since it took repeated and varied efforts over a period of time – at least two years in most cases – to get the board of a company to initiate necessary changes.

3. The board of CalPERS provided consistent support to the actions taken. Governed by a policy of fiduciary duty, it managed to avoid that political special interests interfered with the corporate governance activities of CalPERS.

Confirmation of value-creation

CalPERS' progress was further acknowledged from outside and illustrated when an independent consultancy company, Wilshire Associates, in an analysis of CalPERS' 1994 Corporate Governance programme, was able to pinpoint remarkable improvements in the results of the companies which had been the subject of CalPERS' action. As the diagram in Figure 2.2 shows, the analysis even showed that the more intensive CalPERS' action had been, the greater was the improvement in the results. It was proven (several studies by other analysts have since confirmed these results and subsequent follow-ups have actually shown even greater improvements) that Corporate Governance, active ownership, could be profitable.

The diagram shows the accumulated development five years prior to and five years after CalPERS instigated Corporate Governance actions against selected companies. The scale on the left is negative, which thus means that there was a negative discrepancy of about 65 percent in the accumulated result as against the comparable sector average for the respective company before CalPERS' intervention. In the five years after CalPERS began its programmes, development in these companies correspondingly showed a positive discrepancy of slightly more than 40 percent.

In the diagrams of Figure 2.3, a distinction has been made between the early years of CalPERS shareholder activism and the later years of the study period. In the later years, CalPERS programme of action became better developed and comprised a total Corporate Governance programme. The

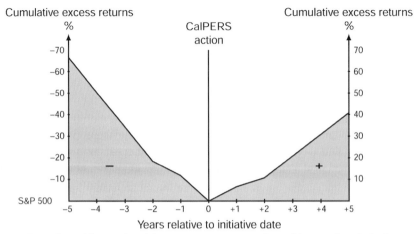

Note: Not adjusted for market risk, excess returns are also evident and statistically
significant at the 95 % level when adjusted for industry and market risk
Source: Wilshire Associates Incorporated

Figure 2.2   US owner activism – CalPERS shows the way. In 1994, the Wilshire
study showed that governance yielded substantial shareholder returns (42
companies, where CalPERS initiated actions 1987–92).

study thus showed that it was the latter, which brought about a radically
greater improvement in the results of the chosen companies.

A system of successful corporate governance

The main elements in the system for the successful exercise of Corporate
Governance that CalPERS developed included:

1. Focus on companies, which have systematically shown poorer results
   than comparable companies. Each year CalPERS selects about ten (maximum) companies for action. Today, this is called *The Focus List*, earlier the
   Target List. It attracted great attention, not least as a result of the fact that it
   was also given another, more vulgar name – *The Shit List*. Nobody wanted
   to be on it and companies and boards still don't want to be on it! This list
   has been a favourite item for publication by the business press and by
   other media. Today, everybody can download it from CalPERS website
   (*www.calpers.ca.gov*). The selection criteria used by CalPERS are threefold:

   - Sustainable shareowner value (dividends + stock price development).
   - Economic Value Added (EVA©).
   - Corporate Governance deficiencies.

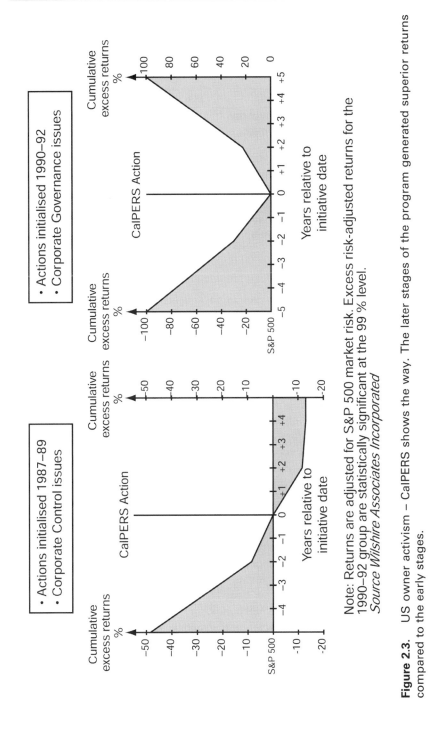

Figure 2.3. US owner activism – CalPERS shows the way. The later stages of the program generated superior returns compared to the early stages.

Note: Returns are adjusted for S&P 500 market risk. Excess risk-adjusted returns for the 1990–92 group are statistically significant at the 99 % level.
Source Wilshire Associates Incorporated

Table 2.2 CalPERS Focus List 1999

Top focus	Financial performance (5 years)	Change (%)	Corporate governance deficienceies
1. Tyson Foods Inc.	Stock performance	+59	Dual class of stocks (differentiated voting
	Benchmark	+156	rights)
2. Circus Circus Enterprises	Stock performance	−37	Board not independent
	Benchmark	+13	
3. Mallinkrodt	Stock performance	−31	Lack of independent directors on the audit
	Benchmark	+330	committee

Further monitoring
4. Cummins Engine
5. National Semiconductor
6. Pacific Century Financial
7. Pioneer Resources
8. Sierra Health
9. St. Jude Medical

The latest (when this book is written) list – published April 21, 1999 – includes nine companies sorted in two categories as shown in Table 2.2. Three companies, which have not responded to CalPERS' requests are listed in the first category containing top-priority companies for further actions. The additional six companies in the second category have started to take measures so they are just included for further monitoring.

2. When communicating with the company, CalPERS contacts the board through its chairman. CalPERS emphasises that it is the board, which is responsible for the company and that as owners CalPERS has no ambition *to micro-manage the corporation.*

3. CalPERS demands changes to correct the unsatisfactory results in the chosen companies. It turned out that without exception these companies revealed shortcomings in terms of Corporate Governance in some respects, e.g. as regards the board's independence and competence. This led to CalPERS successively making a more comprehensive assessment, including both financial performance and corporate governance practices criteria, to identify candidates for its focus list. A common phenomenon in the USA is that the CEO[4] and the chairman are one and the same person. In many cases, where CalPERS focused its activism, this meant that the person concerned has been forced to resign and that

the company board thereafter has been more independent through having a 'non-executive chairman' or by having an independent so-called *lead director*. As mentioned earlier, changes on this point became so manifest and affected so many companies at one time in the early 1990s (1993) that people talked about *the boardroom revolution* in the USA.

4. The basic approach at CalPERS when it started its programme of measures against a company has been to achieve the desirable changes through dialogue with the company's chairman and board. Only if that proved impracticable did it bring in the heavy artillery in the form of publicity, open action at general shareholders' meetings etc. In many cases this proved to be necessary, not least in the early years when CalPERS and other institutional shareholders were not acknowledged at all as legitimate claimants by many boards/managers.

SO WHAT HAS BEEN ACHIEVED AND CAN ALL OF IT BE ASCRIBED TO CALPERS?

Before moving on to American corporate governance today and what CalPERS and other activists are doing now, it could be useful to sum up what had been achieved around the mid-1990s and what were the driving forces behind it.

– '… a major, major change'

It should not be claimed that CalPERS alone changed the American Corporate Governance game plan. On the contrary, a forceful and important element in the success was CalPERS's ability to co-operate and collaborate with other players and interests. (Several key actors involved in this drama, or *The Corporate Governance Revolution* as Mr. Koppes refers to it, are mentioned in his list: CII, Mr. Monks, TIAA-CREF among others.) On the other hand, CalPERS did play a leading role by taking the decisive initiatives, being persistent and not being afraid of conflicts. In this way CalPERS became the activist shareholder who quickly learned what worked in exercising their rights and obtaining results. Against that background it has seemed appropriate to study CalPERS' development in order to understand what actually happened to *Corporate America*.

This assessment is supported by persons who have had the possibility of observing what happened over a long period, e.g.:

• David Batchelder – for a long time partner in T. Boone Pickens, renowned as a so-called *corporate raider*[5] and a founder of USA[6] – who now has his own investment company, has pointed out in conversations with the author that CalPERS, as a state pension fund, is more independent than many other types of institutional investors, for example insurance companies, in relation to the companies it invests in. As a result it is 'in a better position to battle *Corporate America*.'

• Another very knowledgeable person in this context is Dr. Ira Millstein, senior partner[7], the very experienced and respected lawyer and corporate governance advisor. He claims among other things that the pension funds previously believed that they did not have any possibility of influencing the companies, of making any impact with their demands etc. 'until CalPERS showed that they could.'

Ira Millstein also summed up what had been achieved in the following way:

> I think that the key governance development of the last ten years is the new found voice of institutional shareholders. The disempowered and fragmented shareholder component of the Berle and Means[8] model has been largely overcome. The united voice of shareholders – through powerful institutional shareholders – can now be heard, and they are demanding improved performance. That is a **major, major** change.

What Dr. Millstein is referring to is that the whole climate had changed and that it had become legitimate for institutional shareholders to make demands as well and that boards and management had realised and accepted that they were accountable to their owners.

Corporate America had changed

A clear indication of the fact that Corporate America had changed and that the climate of shareholding had palpably improved was the fact that the aforementioned United Shareholders Association (USA), which was founded by T. Boone Pickens in 1986, was dissolved in 1993. Its board recommended this on the grounds that 'the objectives of USA had been realised'. The purpose of USA had been to support small shareholders so that they 'could unite and attempt to influence the governance of large US corporations'.

This type of change in the shareholding climate was also manifestly observable at CalPERS. When it began to make initial contact with the companies where CalPERS wanted change, in many cases it received from the chairman the answer 'Mind your own business!' A few years later, when CalPERS organised an award ceremony to choose the company which had most thoroughly implemented the Corporate Governance demands, the 'whole of Corporate America' came to CalPERS and the winner was very proud to receive such an honour. After that, CalPERS does not have to ask for information from companies, or to ask for an audience with chairmen and top executives. These often come on their own initiative to Sacramento, the state capital of California, where CalPERS has its head office, to report on the development of their company, the work of the board etc.

But the actual changes and results were also very evident:

1. The Wilshire analysis showed that the effect on CalPERS' own shareholdings in the companies which had been the subject of action had been to increase the value of CalPERS' share portfolio by amounts in the billion dollar category during the period studied. The value had increased because these companies, after being the focus of CalPERS' activism, were fundamentally running better. But CalPERS' holding is a maximum of 5 percent in each company, often only 1–2 percent. The remaining shares have naturally increased just as much in value, to the benefit of the other shareholders.

2. The effect on results and value-creation was not however confined just to the companies, which had been the subject of action. The attention which CalPERS and other activists' actions attracted caused boards and management in many other companies to pull their socks up. Nobody wanted to land on *The Shit List*, no board member wanted to see his reputation destroyed because his competence had been questioned, or because of unjustifiable salaries, nor through attention from the press and the media. Results improved throughout a very wide circle of companies. There were even those who would ascribe the whole of the productivity improvement which took place in the early 1990s in American companies mainly to corporate governance.

   Such a claim is naturally impossible to verify. Many other forces had been at work. The focus on shareholder value was strongly supported by the corporate governance activists but it had other sources too. International competition forced corporate executives to act, regardless of shareholders' demands, and so on.

3. CalPERS itself instigated a survey of the 300 biggest companies in the USA in 1994. It emerged that over half of them were developing, or had developed, guidelines for corporate governance and had also carried out an evaluation of their actual implementation. In almost 90 of those companies, CalPERS was able to record that implementation went well beyond the normal requirements.

4. A new type of corporate raider had been created. Instead of acquiring total control, they content themselves with creating a minority holding which offers the possibility of demanding representation on the board and thus influencing the board's decisions and the demands placed on the company.

   In principle it was CalPERS' model, which this new type of *corporate raider* was inspired by: to identify companies having unexploited *shareholder value potential*, force through changes to improve the fundamental performance and thus have a positive effect on the price, with a knock-on effect on the holding they have themselves. In this change there may be great value potential for the shareholders affected but also for the economy as a whole. In traditional raiding there was often an element of capital destruction. Whoever took over the company with full control often made short-term reductions in the form of radical cost-cutting, for example in research and development work, to improve the short term profitability and thus make it easier to realise the capital gain and pay off the loans which had financed the take-over. In many cases, these short-term changes spelled damage to long term value creation. The new form of raiding requires an improvement in the target company's basic performance at the same time as it has to gain the trust of the stock market so that the price of the shares go up and produces a return on the stake invested.

Since this breakthrough there are also passive followers of CalPERS, investment funds who buy shares in the companies which CalPERS has just put on its focus list. They hope to benefit from the improved results and increased share price, which are the results of CalPERS' activities.

The corporate governance activities up to the mid 1990s focused directly on the very largest and well established corporations. They represented the big numbers on the stock market and accounted for a major part of the American economy. It was also there that the major need for change – and resistance to change – was to be found. The share owner activism which CalPERS and other institutional investors had brought to bear had achieved significant progress and had been of major importance. Indirectly this corporate governance activism also meant that the development of the whole risk capital and stock market had been stimulated, e g through the transformation of corporate raiders as indicated above.

5. Finally, CalPERS, CII and other funds had very actively contributed to institutional changes, which had reinforced shareholder power, for example, the abolition of the proxy ban, which prevented communication and consultation between shareholders.

6. To sum up, it can thus be said that the American market economy had been strengthened through a better functioning corporate governance (control of each corporation by its owners) and also through an improved and further developed *institutionalised market for corporate control*. It was not just competition that had become more effective, the whole stock market had increased its capacity and ability to create value added and growth.

HOW COME IT ALL GOT STARTED IN THE MID-1980S?

This review has shown what event back in 1984 triggered Jesse Unruh to initiate a series of decisions that snowballed into what could be called the *corporate governance movement* (alternatively *revolution* as Mr. Koppes calls it). But why did Mr. Unruh react at that time? That was not the first time a majority of owners had been conned by greenmail instigated by incumbent executives controlling a corporate board. Neither had anything happened that suddenly gave institutional investors such as CalPERS a possibility to exercise its rights as owners of shares. On the contrary, ERISA (Employee Retirement Income Security Act of 1974) had obligated pension funds to vote their shares a long time ago. However, the legislator had other considerations in mind at the time. 'The idea that pension funds should vote their shares was just 'a footnote of a footnote', says Dr. William D. Crist, President of the Board of Administration of CalPERS referring to his background as a labour economist.[9]

Owner activism on the part of pension funds and similar institutions had also been seen before but this had focused on social and moral issues, e.g. anti-apartheid boycotts against investments in South Africa. TIAA-CREF (Teachers' Insurance and Annuity Association – College Retirement Equities Fund), a non-profit organisation and the largest private pension fund (currently some US$260 billion under management) was one of the activists at that time.

Obviously, there were other driving forces behind CalPERS pioneering initiatives. In fact, the same driving forces that had triggered a set of corporate raiders to target a whole range of companies, where they could identify unutilised value creation potentials because of *poor financial performance* as well as an unwillingness or incompetence by incumbent management to take necessary improvement measures. Overall, financial performance among the largest US corporations had stagnated after the oil crises in the 1970s, deteriorated in the early 1980s and stayed at a low level during the rest of that decade. This unsatisfactory development was further aggravated by the management of these large corporations granting themselves huge salary increases and various emoluments. So, while profitability stagnated or decreased, management's compensation increased by some 250 percent during the same ten-year period from the late 1970s. Thus, one could argue that it was the raiders that showed the way, although CalPERS and some other institutional investors reacted to the same fundamental phenomena.

US Corporate Governance since the Mid-1990s and Current Agenda

3

Thus, after some milestone events in the first half of the 1990s, e.g. the ousting of Robert Stempel as chairman/CEO at GM in 1992, SEC's proxy reforms the same year, *the boardroom revolution* in 1993, *GM Board Guidelines On Significant Corporate Governance Issues* in 1994, to mention some of the most significant – the corporate governance movement had reached a breakthrough. The Wilshire assessment of CalPERS systematic owner activism in 1994 confirmed this breakthrough and legitimised the way institutional investors addressed corporate governance issues and their right to do so. CalPERS received a further boast from a survey among representatives of *Corporate America* the result of which was summarised in the following feedback: 'we need you to keep our bosses accountable'.

CALPERS – A REVISED STRATEGY AND A WIDER SCOPE

CalPERS decided – against this background – to continue its owner activism and outlined a revised strategy in 1995 to include:

- A wider sample of corporations in its holdings, in addition to the 200 largest companies who had been in focus until then.
- Increased allocation of funds to so-called relation investments in small and mid cap companies. This type of investment is outsourced to professional investors, e.g. to the company, Batchelder & Partners, owned by the interview person quoted earlier. Relation investments mean that the investor usually takes a larger stake in companies with value creation potential where the investor also involves himself in the value creation process, e.g. by becoming director of the board, having an active dialogue with executive management or replace the CEO if needs be.
- Introducing corporate governance programmes internationally as well, e.g. in Japan, France, Germany and the United Kingdom. In the UK, CalPERS has teamed up with the most progressive British institutional activist, Hermes.

A policy statement, dated August 1995 – *Why Corporate Governance Today?* – provided a basis for CalPERS revised strategy. In 1997 and 1998 this was followed by updated and new documents: *Corporate Governance Core Princi-*

ples& *Guidelines* for the United States and separate and locally adapted documents for the international markets in focus.[1]

Although CalPERS has continued to develop its role as an ardent owner activist there are some modifications in the way its initiatives are implemented. While creative ways of attracting media attention was an integrated and quite efficient instrument to start a dialogue with *mind-your-own-business-type*chairmen and boards in the earlier phase, the current approach is less conspicuous. There are several factors behind this change, e.g.:

- Currently, there are new people managing CalPERS corporate governance programme after first Dale Hanson, the CEO, and later also Richard Koppes, the general counsel, left the organisation. Some observers the author talked to recently (autumn 1999) even claim that CalPERS has lost some of its lead position as owner activist since '(it has)... shut its two cannons'. This view is by no means shared by everyone. There are also other factors that should be recognised.
- CalPERS is still publishing its focus list every year but this now attracts less media attention. It is not considered *news* in the same way as before and the focus lists now include smaller companies of less national interest. Furthermore the focus list is available on the Internet.
- Following the breakthrough CalPERS is well recognised by everybody in Corporate America and does not need media backing to start a dialogue with a focus list candidate.
- A handful of other public pension funds and institutional investors have become active, successful and well recognised for their achievements. They work somewhat differently from the earlier CalPERS way.

THE TEDDY ROOSEVELTS OF CORPORATE GOVERNANCE

This headlined an article by John A. Byrne in the May 31, 1999 issue of Business Week about the way TIAA-CREF (T-C)[2] is practising owner activism. In the article, a manager of shareholder affairs at Coca-Cola Co in commenting on T-C's corporate governance achievements was quoted saying: 'They are the Teddy Roosevelts of corporate governance. They speak softly but carry a big stick'. T-C has hired senior executives from large corporations to their corporate governance department. These people, e.g. B. Kenneth West, who is a former CEO of Harris Bankcorp Inc. in Chicago, and who was hired in 1995, have credibility, so when they contact corporate governance abusers they know the ropes and are able to establish a constructive dialogue and not to be taken for a ride. Behind such a diplomatic and *softly* approach is a *big stick* in several respects. T-C has gained institutional power status through a long track record of mobilising and voting proxies. It has joined forces with CalPERS and other activists in several cases, although, by tradition, T-C does not enter into membership of associations such as the CII (Council of Institutional Investors). In addition, T-C can muster quite a lot of financial clout, managing funds totalling some USD 270 billion. Its investment allocation strategy is made up of approximately 80 percent of total funds being index funds and 20 percent based on discrete stock selection. Its domestic portfolio comprises some 3000 US corporations of which 200 are actively held, i.e. each one being closely monitored by T-C's investment office. This does not mean that the *Wall Street walk* principle is applied. The investment horizon is some 30 years since, with the kind of pension schemes that dominate, liquidity requirements can be forecasted quite accurately. However, each company in the active portfolio has to defend its position by its future value creation prospects. The domestic equity portfolio accounts for some 2/3 and international for 1/3 of total share holdings. All international holdings are considered active but based on some distribution according to industries and countries. TIAA-CREF does not outsource any of its investment management which means that it has quite a sizeable investment staff and is not engaged in the type of relation investment that CalPERS is.

Another type of focus list

T-C also makes a focus list but it is not published like that of CalPERS. T-C has built up a database of some two thousand companies which are continuously monitored according to criteria that differ somewhat from those of CalPERS in that T-C puts less emphasis on current financial performance and more on corporate governance practices. The reason for this, in T-C's view, is that financial performance can only be assessed retrospectively while current corporate governance practices will be decisive for the future performance of a company.

As owner activist, T-C has gained fame in recent years by some spectacular achievements. On Mr Koppes' list there is a spectacular one mentioned concerning the Furr company where T-C, as the first institutional investor ever, managed to get an entire board unseated.

Recently, T-C has distinguished itself concerning a corporate governance issue called *the dead hand poison pill*. Kenneth A. Bertsch, Director, Corporate Governance of T-C explains in his memo: 'In the metaphor-crazed world of mergers and acquisitions, there can be few terms with more lethal connotations than "dead hand poison pill", an anti-takeover device.' What makes this dead hand poison pill special is not only that it is a deterrent mechanism against hostile take-overs, and that it 'would substantially dilute the would-be acquirer's holdings'. This type of poison pill is also connected to 'provisions providing that only directors on the board at the time the pill was adopted, or their chosen successors, can redeem the pill. This is frequently called a "continuing director" provision'. Mr. Bertsch, in his memo, could also report quite spectacular success:

> CREF, the equity arm of TIAA-CREF, submitted shareholder resolutions on this subject to 11 companies for 1999 annual meetings. Seven of these 11 companies voluntarily removed their dead hand provisions, leading to CREF's withdrawal of the resolutions. Shareholders at three companies where boards initially declined to take this action – Bergen Brunswig, Lubrizol and Mylan Laboratories – voted by large majorities (averaging 70 percent of shares voted) in favour of resolutions to redeem or put the dead hand pills to shareholder votes. This is an unprecedented level of voting support, particularly for what in essence is a new issue. (CREF is in discussions with the eleventh company.)

OTHER OWNER ACTIVISTS

CalPERS and TIAA-CREF have been presented here because of their pioneering corporate governance activities, spectacular achievements, and because of their size. There are several other institutional investors, which would also qualify for a presentation based on the merit that they are owner activists. Among public pension funds, Wisconsin is often mentioned for its creativity and investment strategy (larger stakes than other pension funds generally and focusing on mid-cap companies). Also, private funds are more frequently mentioned in corporate governance contexts, e.g. the pension fund of American Express, Franklin Mutual, and others. However, it would be outside the scope and purpose of this book to extend this presentation any further.

THE CURRENT AMERICAN CORPORATE GOVERNANCE AGENDA

The current corporate governance agenda cannot solely be defined from the progress made since this movement started. We also have to take into account the quite dramatic changes that have taken place in the overall macro economic environment.

- A fundamental driving force during the first phases of the corporate governance movement in the 1980s was poor financial performance and a stagnant stock market. Most of the 1990s have seen an unprecedented stock market bonanza, especially since the middle of the decade.
- When the owner activists started to get some response from the big corporations in the early 1990s a huge untapped potential of cost cutting was there for the taking. We learned a new set of buzzwords: *downsizing, delayering, core business* focusing, and – of course – *BPR, Business Process Re-engineering, benchmarking,* and *shareholder value.* The formidable purge

of cost squeezing, layoffs, and shedding of non-core business that established companies went through – not only in the United States but in Western Europe as well, with some time delay – was also driven by a general business downturn and mounting international competition. Quick results were achieved in many corporations and we saw new *heroes* made, often short-lived though, e.g. Ian *chainsaw* Dunlop, the CEO who led the purge of Scott Paper and sold the remains. But there were also more thoughtful people who wondered what would happen next. The author had the opportunity to interview some senior board members of both US mega corporations and leading European companies about this issue in 1994–95. While both sides of the Atlantic emphasised the urgency of starting to focus on the *top line*, i.e. how to achieve growth, it was also possible to record the following, typical statement: 'we have been so absorbed by issues of cutting costs and reducing capital employed for such a long time that – when it comes to creating new business and growth – we are at loss'. However, the stage changed quickly and dramatically. The US economy is now (early 2000) in its ninth year of business upturn and high annual growth figures, especially since the middle of the 1990s. The driving forces behind this growth wave, which most large corporations are riding high on, however, are more likely to be found outside these corporations than internally in the form of recently gained wisdom of how growth is generated from within. It is the new economy of new technologies, new companies and, not least, the stock exchange bonanza that creates great future expectations of prosperity among large strands of the population (more than fifty percent of American households hold listed equity/mutual funds).

- To a large extent an explanation of the current boom in the US economy has to be found rather far back, in the economic policy – *Reaganomics*– that was introduced in the early 1980s. This was made clear by a comparative study of the economic development of the state of Ohio and Sweden.[3] The rationale for the study was that Sweden and the state of Ohio are about the same size by population and the traditional industry structure was also quite similar – in particular raw materials based, and engineering industries. But why had, by the middle of the 1990s, Ohio had many years of high economic growth, and an unemployment rate that was lower than the comparatively low overall US rate, while the Swedish economy during the same period had minimal growth and – during the 1990s – an unemployment rate several times higher? Many interesting conclusions could be drawn from this comparative study but there are at least two deserving to be highlighted in this context, namely:

1. While *Reaganomics* forced US companies in mature industries to reconsider and even close down many of their traditional businesses after

the *oil shocks*of the 1970s, the Swedish Government introduced a series of devaluations that instantly restored international cost competitiveness but conserved the old industry structure (and fed a new vicious circle of inflation, cost efficiency problems and new rounds of devaluations/currency depreciations). In Ohio, a process of renewal started that to a large extent took place outside the existing companies in a creative, dynamically interactive process between academic research, new entrepreneurs and venture capitalists. This type of dynamics either did not exist at that time in the Swedish economy or was practically negligable(radical renewal rather took place within some of the large corporations, e.g. within Ericsson in mobile telephony; see also Part II!).

2. A second point worth mentioning is that such successful renewal processes take time. The initiatives in the early 1980s did not start to materialise until a decade later.

• What happened in Ohio was only a reflection of what happened in the US economy as a whole. Sweden is to some extent a special case but what was done or not done in Sweden was also typical for many other European countries, the UK under Thatcher was an exception, in coping with the economic crisis in a way that delayed structural reforms. Renewal processes – mainly outside many of the large established corporations, e.g. by channelling venture capital to new start-ups – were initiated already in the early 1980s in the USA. The first results were to a large extent seen in biotechnology and life sciences. Successively during the 1990s, IT-related businesses have taken over and since the middle of the decade internet-related business development is the name of the game.

Issues of executive pay

Against this background of recent formidable value growth in fundamentals but most of all in stock markets it is not surprising to find one particular issue at the top of the agenda – the multifaceted one of *executive pay*. There are at least four controversial aspects of this issue, namely:

• *The absolute level of compensation.* 'The American culture is extremely materialistic', says Dr. Crist, President of the Board of Administration of CalPERS, 'it is quite OK to argue in our culture that if an executive gets more pay he/she will become more productive. This is quite different to, e.g. the French culture where other values, such as honour, may be even more important.' Some cases of remuneration abuse have been targeted by TIAA-CREF and others, as a prelude to bringing up more fundamental issues of board independence and competence, e.g. concerning the Disney

Corporation. Reacting to a proposed new, exorbitant pay package to Mr. Eisner, the CEO of Disney, TIAA-CREF was able to change the board of Disney by getting two new and independent directors elected. In addition, procedures were improved as regards the re-election of the board. Instead of a *staggered* board there are now annual elections of all directors.

- *The formula for remuneration.* The basic idea in this respect is to pay for performance. However, in many cases performance formulas contain too many external factors rather than such elements of performance where management has made a difference. Performance aspects are also closely connected to the forms of payment as outlined below.
- *Alignment of share owners' and executive management's interests.* The popular stock option plans are now being questioned by institutional investors. 'They are not related to downside risk', says Kenneth A. Bertsch, Director, Corporate Governance at TIAA-CREF. 'An option has the same zero value whether the share price stay stagnant or if it goes down. If compensation is in the form of stock it may promote better decisions about appropriate risk-taking', explains Mr. Bertsch. However, T-C is not totally against stock options. Mr. Bertsch adds: '…we support stock options for executives if programs are reasonable in size and are well-designed.'
- *A fourth issue, finally, is how stock options should be accounted for.* They represent a cost to the company as well as to other shareholders. Negligence to account for stock options is often excused by arguments that the actual future cost is uncertain and difficult to calculate. Warren Buffet of Berkshire Hathaway seems to be leading the discussion concerning the accounting aspects of stock options. In one of his entertaining essays[4] he ridicules this type of argument by reminding the reader of 'how accounting abounds with imprecision'. Cases in point include the cost of heavy capital items, e.g. a 747 jumbo jet – just because it is difficult to know how long it will last is no acceptable argument for not entering annual depreciation of it into the books.

Still owner unfriendly

Another aspect of corporate governance that has been affected by the booming economy and bullish bourses is some increased resistance from incumbent boards of directors to comply with demands put forward by owner activists. Why should they change if performance is OK is a frequent counter reaction to such proposals.

One way of coping with this new situation, observes David Batchelder, owner/CEO of Batchelder & Partners, is that institutional owner activists apply *the short slate rule.* This means that, instead of trying to change the entire board, they try to get one or two new directors elected who can infuse new ideas and demands in the board.

Richard H. Koppes confirms this appreciation of the current situation and thinks that institutional corporate governance activists are planning to get their own candidates elected to corporate boards – either their own officers or people closely associated to the activist institution.

'American legislation and corporate environment are still "owner unfriendly", says Dr. Crist of CalPERS – thus indicating that, despite all achievements so far by the corporate governance movement, there are still lots of unfinished business for owner activists. One dominating theme then is the independence of boards, including the many aspects that that entails, and sub-issues still to be dealt with. At the same time it should be recognised that quite dramatic changes of corporate boards have taken place already. Dennis Weatherstone, retired chairman of J.P. Morgan, and a director of the boards of GM, Merck, and Air Liquide as well as of several non-profit organisations, marks the significant change that has taken place by referring to an earlier situation as *the rubber stamp era*. Mr. Weatherstone: 'During the rubber stamp era, boards only reacted to what management proposed. Now, boards have really become pro-active'.[5]

Performance and independence of boards

CalPERS is initiating corporate governance audits and TIAA-CREF is continuously monitoring the corporations contained in its 2000 + data base of holdings to control the independence and performance of boards and subsequently taking actions to correct shortcomings. They are supported and complemented by other activists and followers.

In most boards of listed corporations there is now a majority of non-executive directors. However, this is no guarantee for board independence. Institutional investors, such as CalPERS and TIAA-CREF are now trying to achieve and support board independence, e.g. by:

- Applying *the short slate rule* mentioned above: if it is not necessary or possible to change the entire board, at least try to get one or two candidates elected whom you know and trust as being independent and competent.
- If it is not possible to separate the Chairman and CEO positions, at least get a non-executive *Lead Director* appointed to lead the non-executive board members.

Still, in some 80 percent of US corporations, the chairman and CEO positions are held by the same person. For an outsider, such as this author, it is difficult to understand why change to separate the two positions and roles does not happen faster – at least a priori. How can a board's independence and ability to carry out its governance role be guaranteed if the chairman, the head of the board, is supposed to govern himself as CEO?

The combined Chairman/CEO issue

The chairman/CEO combination seems to have become an institution in Corporate America. A corporate career – if the ambition is to reach the top – is expected to end up in the combined chairman/CEO position. In the 20 percent of the cases where the positions are separated, most of them are explained by exceptional circumstances, e.g. it is a matter of a transition period. A case in point is General Motors where John Smale, retired Chairman/CEO of Procter & Gamble, took on the chairman role until the new CEO, John Smith, felt prepared to take on the combined position. A more recent example is the AOL/Time Warner merger where a separation of the two roles seems to be the *Solomonic solution* of what to do with one Chairman/CEO of each company. In the merged colossus, Steve Case, Chairman and CEO of America Online, will become Chairman of the Board and Gerald M. Levin, Chairman and CEO of Time Warner, will become Chief Executive Officer. Other cases that could be mentioned would refer to family controlled companies where the family would be in charge anyway. Being such a strong institution also means that it is quite difficult to change.

In BRT's (The Business Round Table – An association of Chief Executive Officers Committed to Improving Public Policy) Statement on Corporate Governance from September 1997 – which can be found on Mr. Koppes' list of significant advances in *The Corporate Governance Revolution* – there is no change on the issue of separation of the roles of Chairman and CEO: 'Most members of The Business Round Table believe their corporations are generally well served by a structure in which the CEO also serves as chairman of the board.' Ram Charan[6], a consultant to chief executives, argues in his book against a board structure with a non-executive chairman as well as *Lead director*, clearly indicates that an underlying assumption is that the CEO should be the most powerful institution of the whole corporation. A key worry seems to be that, a counter veiling power created by a non-executive chairman or *lead director*, would lead to confusion about accountability and the direction of the corporation. The BRT quotation cited above continues: 'They (most members) believe that the CEO should set the agenda and the priorities for the board and for management and should serve as the bridge between management and the board, ensuring that management and the board are acting with common purpose.' It could hardly be expressed more clearly: The CEO is and should be the boss! On the other hand – these views are not surprising coming from CEOs and other self-interested parties whom one might expect to have a biased view.

A variety of views

However, opinions do differ from those of the BRT. The author has talked to several persons with concrete experience, in connection with active ownership, of a separation of the two roles, who prefer such a structure in corporations. People with this view include Mr. Koppes, former general counsel of CalPERS and now a lawyer, senior advisor and lecturer (Stanford University) on corporate governance, David Batchelder of Batchelder & Partners, a relation investment firm and Donald J. Gogel, President and CEO of Clayton, Dubilier & Rice, Inc (CD&R), a very successful and much admired private equity firm. Mr. Gogel believes that firms like his have established a model of effective corporate governance.

> We work hard to create a structure of ownership and incentives to ensure that shareholders and managers have common interests. We believe in relatively flat organisations that allow for flexibility and speed of decision. We also believe that Boards should be led by a non-executive Chairman and should consist primarily of independent (non-executive) directors. This approach is essential not only during periods of transition when our companies are private, but also when they are listed public companies. In our view, these practices are applicable and beneficial to all companies.

According to Mr. Gogel, 'The single most important corporate governance issue is the independence of the Board, including the Chairman.'

Pragmatists

In between these *camps* for and against a separation of the chairman and CEO positions there is also a *midfield* of pragmatists. A statement, which the author has heard from a very experienced representative of Corporate America, and which probably is typical for this category of pragmatists, is: 'I believe in what works'. Principles aside, it is rather a matter of people involved and the pre-requisites of the concrete situation that should determine the governance structure, is their line of argument. In this camp of pragmatists there are good reasons to include one very enlightened persons with an open mind for new solutions, namely William G. Bowen who has written a book[7] in which he makes a distinguished and systematic review of arguments for and against a separation of chairman and CEO. His inventory of arguments include studies and books by distinguished scholars on the subject, e.g. by professor Lorsch[8], Harvard Business School. In addition, he refers to several situations where he has personal experience (he has been a board member of major corporations such as American Express, Merck, NCR among others, as well as of a multitude of non-profit organisations) of individuals who have skilfully mastered this dual role and responsibility. Mr. Bowen also reaches rather pragmatic conclusions in his analysis. While there are proven general arguments for the currently dominating structure, he proposes more experimentation with a separation of the two positions. However, at the time of writing he stated that the most important corporate governance imperative is to have a governance committee of non-executive directors, and chaired by a non-executive chairman, which would ensure that the board performs its corporate governance mission.

There is a strong mechanism to preserve the status quo in companies which are running well and where the board is satisfied with the existing CEO/chairman or with a CEO who wants to become chairman as well. There is hardly any board, which could put the performance of the corporation at risk by insisting on a corporate governance principle and which might induce the CEO to go to another corporation. Thus, it is not surprising to find that when a separation of chairman and CEO positions is done it is done in connection with tackling a serious crisis in that corporation.

Another possible reason why change does not happen might be that many people, including corporate key actors, are not aware of how different and how demanding each of the two roles are. A senior executive and chairman in Corporate America told the author that when he was appointed chairman – in addition to his role as CEO at the time – he had no idea about this difference. Hence, there is reason to believe that the demands on a combined Chairman/CEO are underestimated.

The leading institutional owner activists, e.g. CalPERS and TIAA-CREF are also members of the pragmatist camp in this respect. They do not have a general demand that Chairman and CEO should be separate. Their minimum demand is to have a lead director. This concept reportedly functions well if it has been introduced conscientiously enough. Cases in point that have been mentioned include General Motors and Campbell Soup.

The Chairman/CEO issue – conclusion

Thus, in conclusion, the driving forces to achieve a separation of the Chairman and CEO positions are too weak and the resistance too strong to currently expect much to happen in this matter in the near future.

Maybe a new crisis, involving many big corporations, is needed to succeed with an attack on the combined Chairman/CEO *fortress*. Mr. Boldt, Senior Investment Officer of CalPERS, had one hypothesis[9], which could be applicable in predicting such a milestone change, when he suggested that the real test of the quality of current corporate governance structures will come when the ongoing general growth wave is over.

The Combined Code and Corporate Governance Situation in the UK

4

INTRODUCTION

The Cadbury Committee in the UK and its report, *The Financial Aspects of Corporate Governance*, presented in December 1992, is a landmark in the development of corporate governance – not only in the UK but also internationally. This British pioneering effort – initiated by reasons explained below – became a trigger and inspiration for corporate governance initiatives in many other countries. In particular, three features contributed to this:

- The Cadbury Committee was appointed at an early stage in the development of corporate governance codes, compared to what happened in the USA. *General Motors Board Guidelines on Significant Corporate Governance Issues*, which is regarded as a breakthrough in corporate governance in Corporate America, was outlined and decided as late as 1994.
- Secondly, the content of the Cadbury report was rich, well structured and thought through. Furthermore, its content was subsequently supplemented and enhanced by study groups and committees producing reports on corporate governance issues, in particular the Greenbury (1995) and Hampel (1998) Reports.
- The implementation aspect was considered and present from the beginning since the London Stock Exchange (LSE) was one of the main sponsors of these committees and study groups. The final recommendations, *The Combined Code* have been integrated into the Listing Rules of the LSE.

In the USA we saw how the development of CalPERS' corporate governance activities and the instigation of the Council of Institutional Investors were triggered by abuse of shareholder rights by incumbent management in greenmail operations. In the UK, the Cadbury committee was the result – at least indirectly – of another kind of shareholder abuse and outright criminal offences. A number of scandals, or *affairs*, occurred in the late 1980s – The Guinness affair, The Polly Peck affair, BCCI – the bank scandal, and others – that made the Conservative Government at the time quite uncomfortable. The Government made it clear to the private sector that legislative measures had to be taken unless private industry put its own house in order.

The response to this challenge was that the Financial Reporting Council, the London Stock Exchange, and the accountancy profession set up the Committee on The Financial Aspects of Corporate Governance, chaired by Sir Adrian Cadbury, hence the name by which the committee and its report are known. The purpose of this endeavour was 'to review those aspects of corporate governance specifically related to financial reporting and account-ability'.[1] There was a lot of concern about the low level of confidence that was perceived among investors as well as the general public regarding financial reporting and auditors ability to safeguard against bad practise. The composition of the membership of the committee reflected this overall concern and purpose. In addition to leading representatives of the organisa-tions sponsoring the Committee, it included chartered accountants, account-ing experts as well as representatives of other organisations and societies who had an interest in these issues or could bring expertise to the table, e.g. the Law Society, and the Institute of Directors.

When the Cadbury Committee started its work, its expectations of public attention – although issues in focus were of great importance for the func-tioning of companies and the economy as a whole – was rather low. After all, these issues concerned quite technical aspects of accounting and reporting. However, after the committee had already begun its work one of the biggest cases of financial and accounting fraud was unveiled, the Maxwell case. This dramatic event and the magnitude of the fraud Mr. Maxwell had committed put the spotlight on the work and expected recommendations of the Cadbury Committee.

During the course of the committee's work it turned out that the issues in focus could not be analysed and acted upon within the rather narrow remit of the Committee. The issues of financial reporting and auditor responsibil-ities had to be seen in a wider context. Thus, the committee extended, on its own initiative, its mandate to include '... proposals ... to contribute posi-tively to the promotion of good corporate governance as a whole.'[2]

So, the final report is structured in three main sections:

1. A review of the structure and responsibilities of boards of directors which is summarised in a *Code of Best Practice*.
2. Deliberations on the role of auditors, and which are developed to address a number of recommendations to the accountancy profession.
3. A discussion of the rights and responsibilities of shareholders ending up in a set of normative ideas concerning accountability of boards to share-holders, shareholder communications etc.

One of the driving forces behind the Cadbury Committee was 'criticism of the lack of effective board accountability for such matters as directors' pay'.[3] The Cadbury Report includes a section on board remuneration, where, based on the principle of openness, a set of recommendations is outlined.

However, the Committee also recognised that the overall issue of directors' pay involves additional important aspects. In a sub-section of the summary recommendations, the Committee suggests that 'the rules for disclosure of directors' remuneration, and the role which shareholders could play', should be addressed by a successor body of the Committee.

In addition to this recommendation by the Cadbury Committee, a continued public interest soured by extensive press coverage, and pressure from institutional investors led to the instigation of a Study Group on Directors' Remuneration, chaired by Sir Richard Greenbury. This issue had been further highlighted by a study in 1994 of Britain's top 169 companies showing that between 1985 and 1990, while average earnings rose 17 percent, directors' pay had been increased by 77 percent.[4] The initiator and sponsor of this study group was CBI, the Confederation of British Industry. The terms of reference for this group were:

- To identify good practice in determining directors' remuneration and prepare a Code of such practice for use by UK PLCs.

The report of the Greenbury Study Group was presented in July 1995 responding '… to public and shareholder concerns about directors' remuneration.'[5] While the Cadbury Report was well accepted in wide circles and praised for its quality and constructive proposals, the Greenbury report was more controversial. It was criticised, not only for some of its recommendations, but also for its quality of work. Some critics pointed to the fact that the Study Group finalised its assignment only in a few months, while it had taken some eighteen months for the Cadbury Committee to make its landmark achievement.

Thus, in November 1995 a new corporate governance committee was set up on the initiative of the chairman of the Financial Reporting Council. Several sponsors were behind this committee, including LSE, CBI, the Institute of Directors, the Consultative Committee of Accountancy Bodies, the National Association of Pension Funds and the Association of British Insurers. This committee was chaired by Sir Ronald Hampel, chairman of ICI at the time, hence the Hampel Committee and Hampel Report.

The committee's terms of remit emphasised the importance of promoting 'high standards of corporate governance in the interests of investor protection and in order to preserve and enhance the standing of companies listed on the Stock Exchange'.[6] The Hampel Committee was asked to review the Cadbury code and its implementation as well as pursuing matters arising from the Greenbury Report. A general directive of the remit urged the committee 'to restrict the regulatory burden on companies, e.g. by substituting principles for detail wherever possible'.[7]

The Hampel Report was quoted at the beginning of this chapter as regards the dual purpose of corporate governance – accountability and business prosperity. The Hampel Committee on its part wanted to correct the balance, which had tipped in favour of accountability aspects in earlier corporate governance initiatives. While the Hampel Committee strongly endorsed accountability aspects, and recognised the contributions made by the Cadbury and Greenbury committees in that respect, it also voiced concerns that 'the emphasis on accountability aspects has tended to obscure a board's first responsibility – to enhance the prosperity of the business over time'.[8]

Against the background of this statement, it is no surprise to find that the Hampel Committee was entirely made up of directors and senior executives of British, mainly listed, companies. In the Hampel Report it is also explicitly stated that its perspective is different from that of the Cadbury and Greenbury predecessors. Both had been instigated by business failures and abuses of various kinds. The Hampel Committee had been equally concerned by business prosperity issues.

At the same time, the Hampel Committee recognised that business prosperity cannot be commanded. There is no single formula for how value can be created.

Thus, it was only to be expected, that the Hampel Committee favoured broad principles rather than detailed regulations and prescriptions about particular corporate governance structures.

Even as regards the matter of separation of the chairman and CEO positions, the Hampel Committee is more open to accepting exceptions from the basic principle of having the roles separated, than *the Combined Code* of June 1998. The Final Report of the Hampel Committee was delivered in January 1998. However, the committee continued its work, and after having integrated feedback from various quarters, in particular from the London Stock Exchange, it delivered what is referred to above as *The Combined Code*.[9]

WHAT HAS BEEN ACHIEVED SO FAR?

So, what has all this effort led to? Have the dual goals of improving both accountability aspects and business prosperity been achieved? For several reasons, it is much easier to review accountability aspects – changes and improvements in corporate governance standards – than changes in financial performance and long term business prosperity. First, it is already seven years since the Cadbury Report and recommendations – supported by the London Stock Exchange – were introduced. It is also fairly easy, although not without difficulties to judge the real quality of implementation, to check if companies comply with the Combined Code or not. Financial performance and, in particular, long-term business prosperity are affected by many other forces making it difficult to isolate the corporate governance impact. As far as it is known by the author, there is no study made in the UK similar to the Wilshire analysis of CalPERS' corporate governance programme in the USA referred earlier (Chapter 2). It should also be remembered that it was the Hampel Report that was the first of the *Code Committees* to emphasise the business prosperity aspect. So, if that has had any impact, 1999 will be the first full reporting year since the Hampel ideas were presented in 1998.

In reviewing achievements it is also important to recall who were the initiators and driving forces behind the development of the codes of corporate governance. It all started in the early 1990s with the Government threatening to take legislative measures unless private industry put its own house in order. A number of non-government institutions – including the LSE – took on this challenge. A first achievement to be recorded, then, is that the Government did not initiate any new legislation in this field. Even the Labour Government has refrained from this and stated that it liked the Hampel recommendations.

The institutional investors represent a major force behind the implementation of good corporate governance standards, in particular the domestic pension funds of which Hermes[10] is considered by many to be the most professional and active in corporate governance matters. The institutional investors are also strong drivers for financial performance and shareholder value. For some, the value creation aspect is at the forefront. This is especially the case for most of the foreign financial institutions.

The active role of the LSE is closely related to the emphasis the institutional investors – the dominating actors on the stock exchange – are putting on value creation and corporate governance standards. LSE has decided to use its power, in promoting good corporate governance standards, by requiring all listed companies to comply with the *Combined Code*. If any deviation from its principles and code of best practice is not explained satisfactorily by the company in question, it can be de-listed.

With such *strong teeth* present in the corporate governance arena it is not surprising that the *Combined Code* has been implemented in listed companies. Some eighty percent of all companies have separated the roles of Chairman and CEO, for instance. However, one must distinguish between *the letter* and *the spirit* of the *Combined Code*. Says Michelle Edkins, corporate governance executive of Hermes: 'Now it is too easy to comply with the letter of the Combined Code. That is why communication is so important so that the public can see if the company complies also with the spirit of the Combined Code'. So, when it comes to the actual quality of corporate governance standards, the situation varies from company to company and it is also more difficult to make an assessment.

One indication of the actual implementation of good corporate governance standards is to see what issues constitute the focus of corporate governance discussion:

- At the end of September 1999, LSE endorsed the *Internal Control: Guidance*

For Directors On The Combined Code produced by the Internal Control Working Party, chaired by Nigel Turnbull, of the Institute of Chartered Accountants in England & Wales (ICAEW). This will improve standards as regards risk management and internal control. The ICAEW Working Party was instigated against the background of the Barings showdown some years ago and similar control failures.

- Disclosure of director and executive remuneration has become more and more detailed due to pressure from institutional investors and compliance with the Combined Code. Some companies think that it has become too excessive: 'We are devoting nine pages of our annual report to providing details of director and executive pay – why all this detail, what do they need it for?' was the comment of one chairman the author spoke with.
- Disclosure of remuneration details has had the effect of increasing the whole level of total compensation. The level of pay is certainly an issue for other reasons as well, not least because of increasing globalisation. The much higher levels of remuneration in the USA is starting to have an impact in the UK, in particular in industries dominated by US companies, e.g. entertainment and media.
- In addition, it is not only the level of pay, which is in focus, but also its form. Stock options are being questioned. Hermes has reluctantly accepted stock options but prefers that directors be paid in stocks, so that at least half of the total compensation is paid in stocks. However, the US impact is increasingly governing the rules of the game in this respect too. Says Sir Dominic Cadbury, Chairman of Cadbury Schweppes:

Remuneration practices change all the time and it is necessary to remain competitive in an international context. Until recently executives who received share grants under the terms of an LTIP do not qualify for share options. Competitive pressure now make it necessary, particularly where US operations are involved, to award share options in addition to share grants as part of the total remuneration package.

- However, important the above mentioned issues are, the number one issue in the British corporate governance arena currently seems to be the *independence of non-executive directors*. It is a matter not only of being independent of management in a formal sense. What is really important, as one observer puts it: (is) 'that non-executive directors are experienced and competent enough so that they can fill their formal independence with content. We need to see increasing professionalism among non-executive directors both as regards their legal responsibility and their competence. It is not a soft option to be a director any longer'. One remedy is training programmes for directors, which are now being offered by various business schools. At the same time it should be recognised that the obvious need for further improvement should not belittle the progress already achieved. The old *crony* system is on retreat in favour of more professional ways of recruiting and assessing board candidates and directors.

- However, there are increasing difficulties in recruiting non-executive directors, which seem to have to do with more fundamental issues. Says Frances Cairncross, management editor of The Economist: 'There is now a struggle to define the role of the non-executive director. The trouble is that it seems to involve responsibility without real authority'. One Chairman the author talked to made the comment that: 'They (non-executive directors) get the same responsibility but they get much less pay than executive directors, and above all, they get much less information'.

- Although the problem of recruiting non-executive directors and the difficulties in providing reasonable prerequisites for them to carry out their responsibilities seem to have quite fundamental causes, most actors and observers believe that it will be possible to solve these problems within the existing board concept. 'It depends on how the chairman and the CEO can get along and how the chairman will get support from his non-executive directors. It is essential that the chairman knows when he should interfere and that he actually does it in such situations', says one commentator.

- Surprisingly enough, very few seem to question the British board concept of mixing executive and non-executive directors, and, as a consequence, also mix the role of the board as regards governance and executive matters, strategic and operative issues etc. For an outsider an obvious solution would be to simplify the role of the board to deal only with governance issues and staff it only with non-executive directors. As a consequence, additional issues of recruitment, remuneration and other current difficulties would be easier to deal with. The board could then manage with fewer meetings and the recruitment base could be enlarged with more overseas directors, thus enhancing the competence of the board as well. Among some ten people, including both senior directors, chairmen and CEOs as well as knowledgeable observers the author has met, only one person was in favour of such a solution. When the author asked for an explanation of his solitary view in this matter, his answer was: 'I am old enough to have that view – all the rest, who are younger than I, still have too big a stake in the current system'.

HOW ABOUT BUSINESS PROSPERITY IMPROVEMENTS?

One observation, worth mentioning in this context, is that with more non-executive directors on the boards, companies seem to have become more open and receptive to external bids. Thus, one could say that not only corporate governance and internal control have improved, but the market for corporate control (bids for whole or parts of companies) as well.[11]

A recent phenomenon is that in 1998 Hermes, a corporate governance leader among institutional investors, started a fund management entity 'based on relational shareholder activism' (Hermes Press Release, 13 March 1998). It was said to be the first of its kind in the UK and is a joint venture with US-based Lens Investments which has long experience of similar business in the US. This joint venture, called Hermes Lens Asset Management Ltd (HLAM), manages the Hermes UK Focus Fund where major UK and international institutions have been invited to invest. The UK focus fund 'will concentrate on mid to large capitalisation companies quoted on the London Stock Exchange'. Peter Butler, Corporate Focus Director of Hermes Investment Management and Chief Executive of HLAM, declared that: 'The creation of HLAM introduces the concept of *focused* investment to the mainstream institutional arena in the UK.' An additional statement by Mr. Butler clarifies the intent of the whole venture further:

- We are not interested in micro-managing businesses but our aim will be, wherever possible, to support management in the pursuit of improving long-term shareholder returns. The objective ..., is to stimulate change in companies in the top 350 with hidden shareholder value. We believe that considerable scope exists to generate above average growth for our investors.

The performance of HLAM so far (autumn 1999) seems to have met or even exceeded expectations: 'First year performance has been very good..., HLAM's largest client earned a time weighted return well in excess of the target of 5 percent over the benchmark FTSE All Share Total Return index (which was 23 percent)', announces a HLAM press release 22 November 1999. The HLAM investments include 12 companies and the fund under management has some ten participants, of which three are international – one US (CalPERS), one Canadian (OMERS) and one Swedish (SPP). Hermes itself, owning 75 percent of HLAM, seems to be very satisfied with HLAM's early development. Alistair Ross Goobey, chief executive of Hermes, has indicated that there are rich opportunities for further growth in the UK that needs to be taken care of, but also that there are additional opportunities in Europe: 'HLAM is growing so quickly ... must focus on opportunities in UK, and thereafter extending to Europe as a whole' (Press Release 22 November 1999).

It must be encouraging for anyone concerned with the renewal and future prospects of UK companies that a leading pension fund, such as Hermes, take steps to involve itself directly in making UK companies more agile and to improving their prerequisites for value creation. Furthermore, successful initiatives such as HLAM usually generate followers. Thus, the indirect effect may be far more important than what HLAM will be able to achieve in its target investments.

Although HLAM is an interesting and valuable initiative, particularly if it marks a new trend among traditional, institutional investors to become more active, it is still small scale – currently (early 2000) total assets under management amount to some GBP 400 million – in the overall context of renewing the UK economy. In that perspective, the UK venture capital industry is far more important. It is the second largest in the world, after the USA, accounting for about half of the total European venture capital market. The annual flow of UK venture capital investments amount to some GBP 5 billion (1998), of which some 75 percent are made in UK companies and the rest overseas. For the renewal and growth of the US economy, its venture capital industry has played a leading role. A similar pattern as witnessed in the USA is probably to be repeated in the UK. Venture capital investments have multiple effects on the renewal dynamics since they focus on and leverage some of the most crucial, fundamental forces of growth:

- Investments in start-ups and early stages of new companies; this is the largest category of UK venture capital investments in terms of number of companies.
- The industries of the new economy, high tech (largest sub-sector), biotech, and media, are dominating in the investment portfolios of UK venture capitalist companies, as is the case in the USA.
- MBOs (Management Buyouts) where the venture capitalist is instrumental in providing better growth prerequisites for a business than the former owner could. MBOs tend to have a double impact on growth dynamics: not only the MBO target entity will become more agile, so will also the company it is bought out from since it will become more focused on its core business. This is the largest category in terms of invested volume by UK venture capitalists.
- Venture capitalists do not only provide financial risk capital. Usually, they also bring in *brain capital*, experience and competence that will speed up growth and improve performance of investment targets. In this respect, the UK is likely to benefit from the fact that US venture capital sources provide larger funds – 28 percent compared to 27 percent of the total – than do UK sources.
- Thus, venture capital does not only boost the dynamics of economic and company renewal, it also improves the quality compared to other renewal efforts. BVCA (British Venture Capital Association) has shown (www.bvca.co.uk) that flotations backed by venture capital perform better than others.

Venture capital investments have expanded rapidly in the UK, more than twenty-fold over a fifteen-year period. The Government has supported it by introducing Venture Capital Trusts (VCTs), including tax incentives, (Financial Act of 1995) designed to encourage individuals to invest in small companies through such VCTs.

The impact of accelerating venture capital activities in the UK is already measurable. Venture capital backed companies have higher growth rates than the FTSE 100 and the same applies for exports, employment and profitability.

Thus, the dynamic venture capital market, HLAM, and other renewal initiatives might justify the conclusion that the business prosperity goal of corporate governance, which the Hampel Report so keenly emphasised, will hopefully start to be met.

Creating sustainable business prosperity is a long-term effort. Improving the current position requires in-depth changes and renewal of the artefacts of industries and company organisation as well as of culture and historically nurtured values.

Concerned about the latter aspect, Jonathan Charkham in his book, *Keeping Good Company*,[12] brings up the issue of the low status of the manufacturing industries in UK society, culture, and certain parts of the business community, in particular the City, the financial sector. Management guru Peter F. Drucker explains[13] how England lost its lead in the Industrial Revolution already by the middle of the 19th century, first to the United States and later also to Germany – for social reasons. While the key actors of the Industrial Revolution – the technologists and the manufacturing entrepreneurs – became social heroes in the United States and at least the technologists in Germany, they were never acknowledged as *gentlemen* in England. Now, when we have barely passed the threshold of the Information Revolution, will the same social values prevail in the UK concerning the key actors of this emerging revolution – the 'knowledge workers', to use Drucker's expression, and the entrepreneurs who will be needed to innovate the fundamental, sustainable value creation processes of the New Economy? More recent lessons in this respect are to be learnt from the USA. Some observers attribute the emergence and lasting success of Silicon Valley to the social values and rewards which engineers and entrepreneurial technologists were offered there compared to the *Old World Snobbery* in the East of the USA. In the latter culture an engineer is merely perceived as a *glorified manual laborer*.[14]

However relevant such questions and lessons are to understand impediments for change and future prosperity prospects in the UK, an assessment of these aspects are outside the scope and possibilities of this book.

SUMMING UP THE UK CORPORATE GOVERNANCE SITUATION

In comparing American and UK corporate governance activism, the club character of the British way is often emphasised. What is achieved most often happens behind closed doors and in a clubby atmosphere. This is probably both a strength and weakness of the British system. Its strength has been manifested in the way the corporate governance standards have been improved and the Combined Code has been developed and implemented. A plethora of industry associations and institutions participated in the effort or actively supported it. When the final proposal came it was already well anchored among all concerned. The weakness of such a *club* system is usually revealed when it comes to a situation where more radical change is required. Possibly, this situation is now emerging concerning the *impossible* role of the non-executive director, and, as a consequence, the whole issue of independent and competent boards. Will this issue be possible to resolve without fundamentally reforming the British board concept? If that is what will be required – who is going to stick their necks out from the club and do it? The British system, however clubby, has also generated some astoundingly audacious and often very successful mavericks. So, it might very well be a UK company pioneers this, but companies dominated by foreign owners could also do so, of course.

Germany – The Big Challenge

5

- '*Co-determination* is definitely not an export item!'
- 'Our legally prescribed, *collective leadership* is a formula for catastrophe!'
- 'In Germany the management structures are so complex that it should be obvious to everybody that profound change is needed badly.'
- 'We cannot go on mixing boards of banks and industrial companies – at least not in the long run.'
- 'German AGMs are a disaster where the principle of one share/one vote is mixed up with some strange idea of *shareholder democracy*'.

Rather drastic statements – such as the quotations above – are frequently encountered when discussing the German corporate governance situation with experienced and well informed people both within and outside Germany. These quotations indicate that Germany is both quite different from other corporate governance systems and that it is under pressure to change.

DISTINGUISHING FEATURES OF THE GERMAN SYSTEM AND THEIR HISTORICAL ROOTS

The traditional German system of corporate governance rests on three distinguishing features, namely:

- The stakeholder model – companies are not solely accountable to shareholders/owners.
- A limited role of the stock market in the total supply of risk capital.
- Collective leadership.

The first and second features have their roots in the 19th century while the third dates back to the reconstruction ideas after World War II.

The German stakeholder model

Today, the most pronounced feature of the German *stakeholder model* is that of *co-determination*, and its design. By law, employees are represented on the board of German corporations. In companies of more than 2000 employees, the parity principle applies meaning that fifty percent of the members of *Aufsichtsrat*, the supervisory board, should represent the employees. Since the law also prescribes a minimum number of board members depending on the size of the company, larger German corporations have very large boards.

By tradition, banks are also frequently represented on the boards of German companies. However, this is also because German banks still remain significant owners of German industrial companies.

At the start of Germany's industrialisation, German society was still heavily state controlled and regulated. The liberal reforms that were necessary to make industrialisation at all possible, were conditioned in various ways, one being that boards of companies at that time (*Verwaltungsrat*) were obliged to look after the interests of the state as well as of all major stakeholders – employees, creditors, suppliers etc. Later modernisation of German company boards – eventually leading to a two-tier structure – conserved the stakeholder concept. The *Aufsichtsrat* is based on co-determination and the banks are still frequently represented.

The *stakeholder model* was further reinforced by the traumatic developments of the 20th century – the two world wars, hyperinflation and currency reforms, and most recently the integration of East Germany. Collaboration and consensus became strong societal values in order to overcome post war crises and to succeed with the gargantuan task of reconstruction.

The German risk capital supply model

By all measures, the German stock exchanges are quite small. In all, there are eight[1] stock exchanges in Germany of which the one in Frankfurt, Deutsche Börse, is the dominating, accounting for some 80 percent of the total (Düsseldorf as number two accounts only for some 5–6 percent of the total). Deutsche Börse is less than half the size in market capitalisation value of the London Stock Exchange (LSE) and relative to Gross National Product it is less than one third of LSE – 51 percent versus 167 percent for LSE (1998). Instead, it is the banks that have played a leading role in financing German industry, including supplying risk capital.

This phenomenon also goes back to the industrialisation of Germany in the 19th century. The German industrialisation took place rather late but at an intensive pace around the middle of the 19th century. This is even referred to as *the big spurt* by economic historians[2] when in the 1840s and 1850s industrial production accelerated. The development of the capital market could not keep pace. Instead, the banks – based on the universal banking concept – came to play a crucial role. They supplied short and long term credit as well as risk capital, and in addition, developed important advisory, networking and even active owner functions. To illustrate this, let Peter Drucker[3] remind us of the historical connection between the largest German bank and the largest industrial corporation, Deutsche Bank and Siemens, respectively: 'Georg Siemens (1839–1901), the founder in 1870 of the Deutsche Bank ...save(d) the rapidly floundering Siemens Electric Company that his cousin Werner Siemens (1816–1892) had founded but had left leaderless at his death.'

To enable the German universal banks to absorb the risks involved and the inherent liquidity variations of playing these multiple roles, the *Reichsbank*, the German national bank, functioned as the lender of last resort to the banks and provided necessary liquidity guarantees. Thus, while this system functioned as a robust substitute for a stock market, it further re-enforced the semi-command character of the German economy and gave additional legitimacy to the *stakeholder model* of corporate governance.

Collective leadership

The executive management responsibility of a German corporation (*AG, Aktiengesellschaft*) is based on collective leadership. *Vorstand*, the management board of a German corporation, by law, is accountable as an organ for the operations of the company. Within itself, the *Vorstand* can appoint a chairman or, more frequently earlier, a *Sprecher* who represents the company externally. This person, whether called chairman or *Sprecher* is perceived as *primus inter pares* and also functions as the co-ordinator of the work of the *Vorstand*.

Thus, after World War II, the Germans shunned everything related to too powerful leaders. The concept of as well as the word *Geschäftsführer* were anathema – at least concerning large corporations (legal status of *AG, Aktiengesellschaft*). However, the *Geschäftsführer* concept – chief executive – and name are still used in smaller companies with limited liability status (*GmbH*).

CURRENT DYNAMICS OF GERMAN CORPORATE GOVERNANCE

Several forces, in particular the many facets of globalisation, have been driving through change and adaptation to international standards of corporate governance in Germany in recent years. To get access to international capital markets, e.g. through listings at the NYSE or LSE obviously requires adaptation to certain standards concerning transparency and disclosure. It also affects the German management structure in that the expectations regarding the person representing a company externally, formally the *Sprecher* or chairman of *Vorstand*, become very similar to those regarding a chief executive or chairman of an American or British corporation. Jurgen Schremp of Daimler Chrysler or Klaus Esser of Mannesmann earlier – who were both, when this was written (autumn 1999/early 2000), in the hot spot – are not perceived differently by international media and institutional investors than, say, Jack Welch of General Electric. And expectations very often also change the reality – it has been witnessed that Schremp and his fellow Spokesmen in Germany are starting to act more and more as chief executives, both externally and internally.

However, change is not only driven by such expectations and formal requirements from foreign stock exchanges. There are also more fundamental reasons for change, in particular that current governance and management structures slow down decision processes and severely reduce renewal capabilities of German companies. Concrete evidence of this can be found in how slowly Germany adapts to the new world of IT, mobile telephony and the Internet. Penetration of PCs, mobile telephones (currently, Germany has the same per capita penetration as Estonia), and Internet connections is far behind other technology oriented countries, e.g. the USA and the Scandinavian countries.[4]

The weakness of the German management structure is not only a matter of collective leadership – that 'formula for catastrophe', as one interview person expressed it. To an outsider, the whole concept of *Vorstand* seems strange and makes one wonder how it can work at all, in particular, in large, diversified corporations. The responsibility and the agenda of *Vorstand* seem far too complex to allow efficient decision-making:

- Still, *Vorstand* is the real power centre of the German corporation controlling both strategy and operations. *Aufsichtsrat* has been strengthened legally and the formal responsibility of *Aufsichtsrat* members has increased but, in substance, actual change seems to be limited.
- Meeting weekly or every second week, the agenda includes all kinds of decision items – from multi-billion dollar acquisitions to rather trivial operational issues.
- Possibilities for specialisation are limited because of the collective responsibility. Everybody must understand the implication of all decisions regardless of whether it concerns a large and complex investment project or a minor issue, and irrespective of the business, market or technology in a highly diversified corporation (still not uncommon in Germany).
- Many *Vorstands* have become quite large – average figures ranging between 3.4 and 7.1 have been reported from recent studies[5] – thus slowing down decision-making processes even further.

It is impossible to give a comprehensive picture of the current dynamics of the German corporate governance arena within the scope of this book. However, it is obvious also from a limited number of interviews and a sample of secondary sources that changes are taking place and many key actors in German industry want to see more change. At the same time there are also powerful status quo forces. Since impediments to change are legal in such crucial issues as collective leadership and co-determination, further change is a matter of federal politics involving very powerful spheres of influence and stakeholders. 'Proposing to abolish *co-determination* would be perceived as a declaration of war (by the trade unions)', as one interviewee expressed. *Aufsichtsrat* membership represents – in addition to the possibility of exerting an influence on policies and decision-making – a source of income for the trade unions. Part of the fee to the individual employee members of *Aufsichtsrat* is transferred to a powerful foundation – the Hans-Böckler-Stiftung – controlled by the unions.

Keeping *co-determination* – at least in its present, rigid form – will make it difficult to give *Aufsichtsrat* a more powerful role in the governance of German corporations. *Aufsichtsrat*s are currently too big to be efficient decision making bodies, particularly since size is more a matter of manpower than the extent of competence. What seems to be even more serious is that *Aufsichtsrat* meetings are rather formal and are not used for real discussions and problem solving. Instead, they are preceded by informal, separate gatherings where employee representatives and AGM elected members, respectively, acquaint themselves with the subject matter and take their stand.

Serious as this may seem, it should also be mentioned that there are top leaders in German industry who see less of a problem in current governance and management structures than in some of the overriding features of the German economy and institutional settings. They argue that despite *collective leadership* and *co-determination* it has been possible to achieve quite impressive change and renewal. One example mentioned is how the steel industry has been drastically restructured so that today only three blast-furnaces produce more than what twenty did not too long ago. In addition, many earlier independent companies have disappeared – without too much fuss. Another example is how traditional steel and engineering conglomerates such as Mannesmann have been transformed into international growth leaders in new telecoms markets. What worries these commentators more is the lack of deregulation and reforms as regards pension systems, social welfare programmes and health care. Germany and its Social Democratic Party are lagging far behind Mr. Blair's UK in this respect, creating future competitive disadvantages for Germany.

THE LBO MARKET HAS NOT TAKEN OFF AS EXPECTED

Although there are examples showing that impressive restructuring have taken place in Germany, much – maybe most – remain to be done. A few years ago international private equity firms focusing on the LBO/MBO market set up business in Germany in expectation of a booming deal flow in the late 1990s. So far these expectations have not been met. Germany is lagging far behind several other European countries. Total venture capital investments in Germany – although second largest in Europe – are only 27 percent (1998) of those of the UK. Furthermore, the MBO/LBO part makes up merely 29 percent of total venture capital investments (1998),[6] among the lowest in Europe. On the other hand, Germany takes a top position as regards the proportion of venture capital investments going into companies in the start-up and seed money phases. This is also reflected in the following phenomenon.

NEUER MARKT – A NEW RENEWAL FORCE

Started in March 1997, the Neuer Markt of Deutsche Börse in Frankfurt has grown rapidly to become a new force of economic renewal. In 1999, this new stock exchange accounted for almost one hundred and forty of the one hundred and sixty IPOs in Germany, adding as many new companies to its total list of more than two hundred. By the end of 1999 the total market capitalisation of Neuer Markt exceeded 85 billion Euro making it the largest in Europe. This is encouraging for the renewal of the sluggish German economy, particularly since the Neuer Markt so clearly signifies the future. It is dominated by the young generation in all respects: the companies listed are predominantly emerging out of the new economy – IT, Internet, biotech etc; very often the entrepreneurs are young and the risk capital provided come from domestic sources of younger generations. The dynamic of an emerging German risk capital market is further enhanced by rapidly growing flows of savings being channelled into mutual funds. In 1999 a doubling was recorded compared to the previous year.

Thus, the Neuer Markt also seems to mark the beginning of something Germany, together with many other European countries, lacks: pension savings funds. They are essential, not only for the benefit of future retirees, but also for a well functioning equity market.

In the Neuer Markt, some 80 percent of listed companies as well as of trading volume are domestic. The international trading volume as well as the number of non-German IPOs are increasing, though, further enhancing its leading role in the European new economy.

SUMMING UP: THE GERMAN CORPORATE GOVERNANCE SITUATION TEACHES US ALL SOMETHING ABOUT GLOBALISATION

The decade of the 1990s can be seen as a first phase of the new globalisation era. It is true that international competition is not new and it has intensified successively over a long period of time. But what really transformed that development into something entirely different – as regards intensity, speed, and scope – thus justifying the term *globalisation* – were two new phenomena, namely the fall of communism and the new technologies of IT, telecommunications and internet. The open world market has not only become much larger. Competition is now reaching every *corner* of the national economies. Monopolies as well as dictatorships crumble. (More about this in Chapter 9.)

The German corporate governance situation and challenges must be seen against this tremendous change. The globalisation of markets, including capital markets and flows, has forced every nation with *an economic survival instinct* to curb inflation and maintain macro economic stability. Many other nations have learnt to do what Germany used to be best in class at. They have also learnt what could be called the first globalisation lesson. So, what will be the next lesson of globalisation and the next step in the escalation of the global competitive race between nations and regions? And what will this imply for Germany?

To try to come up with an answer to that, will require at least that the following two aspects be taken into account:

1. Nations and regions do not compete directly – any longer (if we assume that wars and colonialism are things of the past, at least as regards modern democratic states). Instead, they compete indirectly. The *wealth of nations* today depends on what prosperous and competitive companies, having their resource base in a particular country, are doing in the global battlefield. Companies in turn are dependent upon how advantageous and rich their local environment is in providing the best possible business environment – institutional settings as well as quality of resources, clusters of competence etc.

2. A second aspect of importance is something of a paradox as regards globalisation: the more developed globalisation becomes, the more important the local business environment of companies will be! It is true, that globalisation to a large extent is driven by developed companies who outsource and move some parts of their activities to emerging markets in order to get access to lower factor costs and in that way become more cost effective. However, such opportunities are open to all companies and are thus not enough to make a distinctive difference to creating a strategic advantage.

Thus, the current and potential competitiveness of a company in the global market place is to a large extent a function of the local business environment. So, much more will be required, both now and in the future, than just macro economic stability. This is what the next lesson in globalisation is all about.

The best-in class-position that Germany has held in macro economic stability has been very much a function of the same forces and values that also shaped its system of corporate governance, namely consensus and collaboration. This system has served the German economy well in the past – or, at least this *formula* has not created too many *catastrophes*, it seems. However, the situation will change. To create the best possible prerequisites for German companies to compete globally, and thereby boosting German economic development at large, should not one key step include the reformation of the corporate governance system, notably modernising *co-determination* and abolishing mandatory, *collective management*?

The Germans' answer to that question in reality is currently written in the stars. The battle between forces of change and status quo is played out in the open. Private industry has demonstrated that it wants change and wants to play by the rules of the international capital markets. A watershed case in this respect was the way Klaus Esser of Mannesmann worked to fight off Vodafone's hostile bid. He was trying to convince international stockholders to support his line of an independent Mannesmann. Mr. Esser did not run for cover with the help of traditional German *poison pills* as has been the case so frequently in the past. But the political side, represented by Mr. Schröder, the German chancellor, made public appearances, denouncing the hostile bid. Furthermore, this was not an isolated case. Shortly before the Mannesmann case, he took the initiative to have the Government to bail out Holzmann, a giant German building contractor, from bankruptcy. These actions on the part of the Social Democratic Government indicate that the legal reforms required to develop German corporate governance are not imminent. How private industry will be able to live with this situation and find practical solutions is illustrated by the Daimler Chrysler case, which will be reviewed in an analysis of cross border mergers in Chapter 8.

However, also without changes of these corporate governance fundamentals, legal reforms – particularly in corporate taxation – could radically improve prerequisites to boost restructuring of many too diversified German corporations. For example, one significant factor inhibiting the LBO/MBO market is the prevailing capital gains tax of divestments done by corporations. Still, when this is written (early 2000), political status quo forces have managed to stall the enactment of such a proposed reform.

France: Le Corporate Governance – Now's the Time?

6

As shown earlier in this chapter, each country is different and has its own particular characteristics of corporate governance as regards formalities and substance. When it comes to France there is a temptation to exclaim: the French corporate governance system is the most different of all. Although the original – and still dominating – corporate governance system was modelled on the British company structure back in the middle of the nineteenth century, the French variant has its own quite distinct features. The distinguishing characteristics of the French system remained even after the German system inspired French legislators to introduce an alternative two-tier company structure in the middle of the 1960s. In effect, the core of the French system has been far from what modern corporate governance is all about – transparency, accountability and concern for all shareholders. Now, that corporate governance is being reformed in France – to a large extent driven by influences and forces from the outside – it is time, perhaps, to also adopt the substance and fundamental ideas of corporate governance as they are understood outside France.

CHARACTERISTICS OF THE FRENCH SYSTEM OF CORPORATE GOVERNANCE

There are two systems of corporate governance in France, sometimes referred to as *System I* and *System II*.[1] The former is the dominating traditional system based on a unitary board (*le conseil d'administration*)but with a uniquely powerful French version of a combined chairman/CEO, the *PDG* (*Président Directeur Générale*). Until recently, the *PDG*'s role has been prescribed by law. In *System I* the roles of chairman and chief executive cannot be split. The latter, *System II*, has a two-tier governance structure with a supervisory board (*conseil de surveillance*) and a management board (*le directoire*). This alternative system, however, has not been widely used, accounting only for a couple of percentages of the total.

Furthermore, in order to characterise the traditional French system of governance, the following fundamental features – all with a common thread – need to be highlighted:

- While the Germans have been shunning strong leaders and building formal obstacles to prevent such roles and positions, the French have nurtured their preferences for power centralised in a strong leader or in an institution. This tradition dates back to de Gaulle, Napoleon and further back in history. Thus, the PDG function and role epitomise this tradition. (However, The *PDG* represents also a more recent brand of devotion for one strong leader. The *PDG* function was enacted by the Vichy Government in the early 1940s). In *System II, le directoire* seems to have taken this power position. So, in that respect it is not different to the German system.
- The state has played a conspicuous and dominating role in French industry – both through direct ownership of many of the largest companies in manufacturing, utilities and various service businesses and by other means. State ownership goes back a long time, in particular in what is often referred to as *natural monopolies*, e.g. electricity utilities, and railways. Additional state ownership is a result of spates of nationalisations at various points in time, the latest being in the early 1980s when Mr. Mitterand came to power.
- A third distinguishing feature is the French elite system where the top leaders of both industry and government are recruited from the same top schools. This elite system is further strengthened by a rotation of top leaders between industry and government service. Given the size of France, its tight circle of elite members is quite remarkable. One has to compare societies and countries of only a fraction of the size of France to find something similar.
- Furthermore, among large privately controlled companies, frequent cross-ownerships have reinforced the traditional character of a tightly controlled and centralised governance system.

SOME MAJOR CHANGES OF THE FRENCH BUSINESS ENVIRONMENT

Several of the traditional features of the French business environment are undergoing major changes. Developments seem to be accelerating in recent years, having started already in the 1980s in some fields. Some of the most significant changes have occurred in the following three areas: privatisation of state holdings; international integration of the French capital market; and, in corporate governance.

Privatisation

One such area of quite dramatic change is in privatisation. This was origin-

Table 6.1   French privatisation[a]

Government	Companies revenue for the state (in billions of francs)		Total
Chirac	Societe Generale	17.2	
(1986–1988)	Suez	14.9	
	Parabas	12.8	
	Others	25.6	70.5
Beregovoy	Rhone-Poulenc	3	
(1992–1993)	Total	9.5	12.5
Baladur	Elf Aquitaine	33.4	
(1993–1995)	BNP	27.3	
	UAP	17.9	
	Others	28.7	107.3
Juppe	Usinor	10.1	
(1995–1997)	Others	15.3	25.4
Jospin	France Telecom	76.5	
(1997–...)	Aerospatiale	12	
	Others	24.8	113.3
	Overall total		329

[a] Source: Adapted from *Le Figaro*.

ally triggered by some problems and disappointments as regards the results of the nationalisations done in the early 1980s. President Mitterand's reaction was to introduce what came to be called the *ni–ni* policy of neither additional nationalisation, nor any privatisation. However, when Mr. Chirac became prime minister his bourgeois government initiated massive privatisation during its term (1986–88), and this policy was resumed when a new bourgeois government was elected in 1993. This development is perhaps less surprising than the fact that the current socialist government under Mr. Jospin (1997–...) has been the record performer, in terms of total privatisation revenues, since Mr. Chirac initiated this policy in 1986. Le Figaro published an overview of this development in February 1999[2] as summarised in Table 6.1.

Does this imply that the French socialists have learnt from the fall of communism and have envisioned liberal reforms to promote prosperity? It should be remembered that a contributing factor to this apparent change of world view might have been some domestically created problems and consequences of the concentration of power in the French system of state ownership, close ties between government and business, and lack of corporate governance. A series of business scandals emerged during the Mitterand years and culminated in 1996, the year of his death, when more than a dozen chief executives of the top 40 companies in France were under investigation for criminal offences (fraud, corruption etc) or were already serving sentences. There were also rather blunt reasons for this socialist turn-around to continue privatisation. Poor corporate governance allowing mis-management of state controlled companies and banks caused huge losses and ensuing bailout costs, e.g. concerning Credit Lyonnais. The European Commission has estimated these costs at Ffr 145–190 bn making it the world's largest bailout operation, accounting for 1.5 percent of the French GDP.[3] In addition, it improved the financial situation of the state and thus supported efforts to achieve convergence criteria in preparation for EMU. However, even after the massive privatisations since 1986, the French government sector is huge in terms of business ownership. Furthermore, when privatisation was done, the almighty state – even with a bourgeois government at the helm – did not let go unconditionally. In many cases a *golden share* was retained, meaning that the government imposed certain constraints or veto rights, limiting the scope of actions that could be taken by the company concerned. A case in point was the intended merger of Volvo, the then Swedish car and truck maker, and Renault, its French Government owned counterpart. What finally stopped the merger was the intent of the French government/owner to impose such a *golden share* requirement on the merged company. Another French *specialty* in this context was to stage the privatisation by organising a *noyau dur,* a group of companies which took the controlling majority of the privatised company.

International integration

Considerable change has also taken place as regards the integration of the French business sector with that of the outside world. Globalisation has become sharply visible in *Corporate France,* not least in the capital markets and in international restructuring of ownership.

- France has become one of the leading countries of direct investments, both as regards outflows and inflows of investments. In 1998, France ranked third after the USA and the UK as regards inflows. Concerning outflows, France came fourth, after Germany. This pattern was also consistent for the accumulated flows of the 1990–98 period.[4] The accelerated participation in international restructuring by French companies has been preceded by a similar process domestically. Not surprisingly, the pioneers in this development were mavericks – entrepreneurial individuals outside the top elite – such as Mr. Pinault and *Crocodile Claude.*[5] Mr. Pinault started as a timber importer and merchant in Bretagne and has skilfully built up a vast holding in retail and other industries. Since he did not have the elite schooling he never become part of the French top echelon. Claude Bébéar, on the other hand graduated from one of the elite

schools, but instead of entering one of the *turbo careers* leading to a predes-
tined top elite position, he preferred to start at the bottom in a small
insurance company in Normandy. When he eventually reached the position of chief executive, he transformed this small insurance company and
used it as a platform to acquire and revitalise other poorly managed
French companies and, when strong enough, also foreign ones. *Crocodile
Claude* is claimed to be the first to have tried and succeeded in carrying out
a hostile takeover in France when he made his first acquisition in 1983.
Starting out as number 17 among French insurers, Mr. Bébéar has made
AXA the largest insurance company in the world in terms of premium
volume.[6]

- Overall foreign ownership of French companies has increased significantly as well. Some 35 percent of all listed companies are today owned
  by foreign investors.[7] Among the *CAC-40* there are companies with up to
  50 percent foreign ownership currently.

- So, globalisation has hit the French economy and companies have to play
  the global competitive game if they want to survive. As one *PDG* and
  early mover mockingly predicted the end of some of his *CAC-40 PDG*
  colleagues' survival formula in 1995 during his speech at a forum of
  partners at Groupe Bossard, the leading French management consultancy
  at the time: 'it will no longer be of any avail to run down the corridors of
  the Elysee Palace.'[8]

- An important explanation of this heavy dependence on foreign investors,
  in particular institutional ones such as pension and mutual funds, and at
  the same time a major weakness of the French economy, is the lack of
  domestic pension funds. France is not in a uniquely weak position in this
  respect. Germany has about the same low (less than six per cent of GDP)
  pension fund assets. This represent only a fraction of the pension assets of
  countries such as the USA (58 percent), the UK (75 percent), Canada (43
  percent), and not to speak of rich neighbours such as Holland (87 percent),
  and Switzerland (117 percent).[9]

Le corporate governance

As this title indicates there is no purely French term for corporate governance – at least not in frequent use. However, it is not only the linguistic
influence that comes from the Anglo–American sphere. It can be argued
that the ideas about corporate governance developed in the USA and the
UK have had considerable impact in France, not least the Cadbury Report,
which triggered the initiation of what became the *Rapport Vienot*. Furthermore, Anglo-American corporate governance standards and requirements
have had their way in connection with listings on the American bourses and

the LSE. Institutional investors, e.g. American ones such as CalPERS, TIAA-CREF and Franklin Mutual have introduced their practices in France.

In reviewing some of the important features of French corporate governance, Mr. Marc Vienot is a recurring and probably the best known name associated with French corporate governance. Mr. Vienot was the *PDG*, now retired, of the big French bank Société Generale and the chairman of an unofficial working group commissioned by the National Board of French Employers (CNPF) and the Association of French Private Companies (AFEP).[10] Its first report was presented in 1995, followed by a second report in 1999. This initiative and the *Rapport Vienot* marked the beginning of a serious corporate governance discussion in France. It came in the wake of quite a few, conspicuous scandals, mentioned above. Compared to the Cadbury Report and the Combined Code in the UK, the Vienot recommendations were quite modest. However, they focused on some of the critical shortcomings of French corporate governance:

- One of these shortcomings was the frequent cross-shareholdings between French companies and cross-directorships among a tight elite establishment.
- In addition, there were recommendations as regards board committees for nomination of directors, for compensation, and for auditing.
- Vienot also recommended that a company board should have a minimum of two independent directors, or a sufficiently larger number in order to constitute at least one third of the board.
- In the second report, Vienot proposed a change in legislation to give a company board (*Conseil d'administration*) the option of splitting the *PDG* function into a separate, non-executive, chairman and a chief executive officer.
- Concerning disclosure of director and executive pay, Vienot recommended that the total amount, broken down in fixed and incentive based pay, as well as the incentive formula it is based on, should be reported. Individual compensation should not be disclosed, as is the case in *Corporate Anglo-America*.

There have been other initiatives concerning corporate governance, e.g. one launched by the French Management Association (Association Francaise de la Gestion) which submitted its report in 1998. In this, the role of the AGM was highlighted and the responsibility of institutional investors to use their voting power was emphasised. The report went on to say that asset management firms should develop guidelines regarding the use of their voting power. The report is a bit tougher when it comes to executive compensation compared to Vienot. It recommends full disclosure.

CORPORATE GOVERNANCE COMPLIANCE

It is difficult to acquire a comprehensive view of how corporate governance compliance recommendations have developed. This is partly because the various recommendations were only recently published. There are also differing results reported from the various systematic studies that have been undertaken. One international comparison[11] ranks France number 3 as regards corporate governance. Another study, carried out by the Association of Financial Management, AFG-ASFFI, concludes that French *CAC-40* companies are failing to meet certain standards of corporate governance. Such shortcomings include retaining *poison pills* and too frequent multiple directorships. French listed companies are still too slow to publish year-end and interim results.

One fresh initiative taken this new millennium is worth mentioning in this context. The Président of CGIP, a French, family controlled investment company, and also chairman of Medef, the confederation of French employers, M. Ernest Antoine Seillière in March 2000 disclosed his remuneration as head of CGIP. This will probably be followed by others voluntarily or forced by possible legislation in this matter.

SUMMING UP

There seems to be a new vitality in the French economy. The Paris Bourse is the largest in continental Europe (marginally larger than the Deutsche Börse) and if an aggressive privatisation programme is continued, then there would be market capitalisation potential solely in the big government sector. Currently (end of 1999/early 2000) the Paris stock exchange is expanding rapidly both in turnover and value. IPO's and start-ups are also mushrooming and France has started to catch up with international developments in Internet connections. However, Minitel, the early French web variant, seems to have blocked an Internet breakthrough for a long time, and it is still difficult to register strong progress over a longer period. Quoting a Mr. Bavarez, economic historian and writer, Wall Street Journal (991202) claims 'that France has not created a single net job in the 1990s'. The European Venture Capital Association is a bit negative as well when reporting[12] that France falls behind Germany in venture capital investments and accounts merely for some 25 percent (1998) of the size of the UK in this respect.

Maybe, both pictures reflect reality. Current dynamics are a recent phenomenon and it will take time to actually produce fundamental results. If this is true, what explains the recent dynamics? Are they driven by an accelerated general business boom in Europe or do corporate governance reforms have anything to do with it?

It is outside the scope of this brief review of French corporate governance to be able to give a just answer to that question. It is true that the European business cycle is accelerating upwards, but it is also evident that corporate governance has gone beyond mere talk. The progress observed in France as regards a new vitality of the forces creating business prosperity is probably more a result of competition becoming globalised than effective reforms of corporate governance. Some of the *PDGs*, still within traditional corporate governance structures, have been more agile than others in exploiting the new opportunities of global competition and border-less markets.

To really improve corporate governance in France – in addition to whatever small progress that currently have been achieved – quite radical structural changes seem to be required that would improve some fundamental prerequisites, e.g.:

- The government needs to withdraw from direct involvement in the business sector by privatising everything that can be exposed to market competition. In addition to enhanced market dynamics and prospects for economic growth, an immediate strengthening of state finances would follow.
- The government should also withdraw from the business sector by reducing its *dirigisme* and focus more on measures and institutions that would enhance and safeguard competition in all sectors of the economy. France, together with Germany as the two dominating continental economies, has a particular responsibility in EU in this respect.
- A serious shortcoming is the lack of pension funds in France – not only for safeguarding future pensions but also for the functioning of corporate governance and the stock market as well as for supplying a potentially accelerating demand for risk capital. Of course, if the supply will not appear there will be less growth, start-ups, IPOs and consequently less demand for risk capital. Thus, the end result would be a lower welfare level.
- France has among the highest saving quotas (17 percent of GDP) in the industrialised world but French households own less shares than those of most other developed countries – about 15 percent of French households compared to some 60 percent in the USA and about the same in Sweden. The latter comparison is quite relevant since widespread share ownership has emerged in Sweden despite an even larger Government sector in relative terms compared to France. The combination of a dearth of domestic pension funds and low household direct investments in the stock market have made France, needless to say, extremely dependent on foreign institutional investors. *Le défi américain*[13] seems to have reappeared in a new disguise!

When trying to predict what will happen in France, the outside observer is confronted with a similar dilemma to the German situation. There are both change and status quo forces in both countries. The critical issues are very much related to the political sphere while at the same time the party in government mainly belongs to the status quo camp. The business sector in both countries is ambivalent, possibly a bit more change oriented in Germany than in France. As regards the political sector it is probably the other way around – based on the assumption that national pride will be at work in France to fight the American challenge. On the other hand, it is difficult for an outsider to conceptualise how the French socialists, by reducing the maximum workweek to 35 hours will be able to mobilise resources to build up pension funds and achieve a cultural change in favour of making every household capitalistic enough to transform its savings into risk capital on the Paris Bourse and Le Nouveau Marché.

Japan – A New Restoration in the Offing?   7

JAPANESE IDIOSYNCRASIES – WHAT LIES BEHIND?

Why did 94 percent of all publicly traded Japanese companies (1766 out of a total of 1884) hold AGMs on exactly the same day in June 1996?[1] This was by no means an exceptional occurrence but a repeated pattern from one year to the next, although the percentage of AGMs on the same day is not exactly the same. Furthermore, the same study reported that the average length of these AGMs was 26 minutes. A reasonable explanation to this awkward expression of *efficiency* may have been that in 86 percent of all AGMs not a single question was asked by participating shareholders and their representatives.

Obviously, a coincidence rate of 94 percent is not a chance occurrence; it is the result of deliberate co-ordination – and the question is why? The explanation has to do with some unique features of Japanese society, and, in particular, its system of corporate governance. Holding AGMs on the same day is simply a defence against the so-called *sokaiya*. While Corporate America used to suffer from *greenmail*(a combination of *green money* and *blackmail*), a kind of legal abuse of shareholder rights by incumbent boards/executive management, many large Japanese companies are the targets of real blackmail and sheer extortion by such *sokaiya*. Unless the targeted company pays a *fair* (as defined by the extortionist) amount of money (multi-million dollars and more have been involved) the *sokaiya* threaten to not only disrupt the AGMs but also disclose corporate misdeeds. However, this phenomenon not only relates to the *sokaiya*, who are usually affiliated to gangster syndicates, exploiting isolated misdeeds by management of some companies. This appalling traffic is systemic and thereby a symptom of severe shortcomings and dysfunctions of the Japanese corporate governance system and corporate management structures. Holding almost all AGMs on the same day spreads the *sokaiya* thin on the ground and, as a consequence, the board and corporate management of a company can at least avoid *losing face* at the AGM. This does not remedy the extortion but the pay off can be carried out secretly and the misdeeds remain undiscovered. So, this short-cut solution to a very serious problem reveals something more about the Japanese system – it seems to be extremely averse to change, it shuns alternative solutions aimed at the root causes of what is seen at the surface. The Japanese government seems to be part of the problem as well. Although the Commercial Code of Japan was amended in the early 1980s to make payoffs to *sokaiya* illegal, the actual enforcement of this law has been too lax.

ORIGINS AND KEY FEATURES OF JAPANESE CORPORATE GOVERNANCE

After World War II, SCAP – the Supreme Command of the Allied Powers (lasted until 1952) – under General Douglas MacArthur set out to establish a constitutional democracy and imposed institutions aiming at an open society of free markets and competition. Applying the American *trust-busting* experience, one important focus of SCAP reforms was the large and family controlled conglomerates – called *zaibatsu* – were broken up. The family-controlled holding companies at the top of each zaibatsu were dissolved and ownership of the individual companies was distributed among the general public. As a consequence private ownership of the large corporations was well spread and accounted for some 70 percent of the listed companies at the end of the 1940s.[2] However, a decline of this share soon started; by 1970 it was down to some 30 percent and today it is already below 20 percent. Private ownership has been replaced by institutional owners: banks and other financial institutions as well as business corporations. Foreign ownership is still quite limited accounting for some 13 percent (1997).[3]

An immediate reason why this started to happen was that the reforms initiated by SCAP were not followed up wholeheartedly. The Communist revolution in China (1949) and the Korean conflict (1950) profoundly changed the geopolitical prerequisites in East Asia. US priorities in the area changed accordingly. Furthermore, General MacArthur was also appointed supreme commander of the UN forces in Korea.

However, to understand the forces at work in the Japanese economy and society after the initial SCAP reforms and what has shaped the current structure of industry, ownership, corporate governance – or lack thereof – and management, we have to seek explanations in history by reviewing some additional critical events since the middle of the 19th century.

- For several hundred years, Japan had been secluded from the outside world when the US Commodore Matthew Perry in 1853 anchored in Tokyo Bay. Backed by four 'ominously black warships'[4] Commodore Perry requested services, e.g. refuelling, for US ships passing Japan. The concessions Commodore Perry eventually achieved after long and tough negotiations became a precedent for similar agreements with several other nations (Britain, the Netherlands, Russia). Thus, this effectively ended Japan's seclusion policy.

- The opening up of Japan had vast political and economic consequences for further development in Japan. In 1868 an overthrow of the old *shogunate*, known as the *Meiji restoration*, took place. This feudal system whereby Japan had been divided into a number of quite independent regions was replaced by a state, centrally controlled by an oligarchy under the newly reinstated emperor. The new regime was obsessed with the idea of creating a strong state. Technology and know-how were imported from Western countries and a rapid industrialisation process of Japan was set in motion.

- The transformation and rapid industrialisation of Japan was proven – much to the surprise of Western nations – in 1905 when the Japanese navy defeated the Russian navy in the Russo–Japanese war. However, this also marked the beginning of internal power struggles within Japan. The oligarchy that had overthrown the old *shogunate* in 1868 had not prepared for the transfer of central power and a sense of fellowship to a new generation of leaders. Instead the leaders of powerful institutions such as the Army, the Navy, the Ministry of Foreign Affairs, and the Ministry of Finance identified primarily with their respective institution rather than seeing themselves accountable to a superior government of Japan.

- The industrialisation process also saw the emergence of a number of powerful, family controlled conglomerates – *zaibatsus* – many with well-known names, e.g. Mitsubishi, Mitsui and Sumitomo. The *zaibatsus* controlled the productive resources and thus became an important countervailing power to the Ministry of Finance and other strong government institutions. However, at state level, the power struggle dashed all hopes of democratisation and while the military progressively gained control, the Army and the Navy – reporting independently and directly to the emperor – were not on speaking terms with each other. Thus, a process of dissipation of central power was set in motion that eventually enabled military fanatics to occupy Manchuria in the early 1930s and later make the fatal mistake of attacking Pearl Harbour, engaging Japan in war with a nation ten times the industrial capacity of Japan.

- Concerning the balance of power between the government institutions and the *zaibatsus*, some of the former, in particular the Ministry of Finance being responsible for resource allocation in the war efforts in Manchuria and in World War II, learnt that their power position vis-à-vis the *zaibatsus* was enhanced in industries which were particularly crucial for the war machine.

SUMMING UP SOME KEY FEATURES OF THE CURRENT STRUCTURE

The historical review above, provides input and background for a list of the most important features of Japanese society and the economic system.

1. The Japanese government is more of a federation of ministries and various agencies than a cohesive, co-ordinated national government to which these ministries and agencies are accountable. As a national entity, Japan has retained weak leadership since the early part of the 20th century. This is evidenced by Japan's difficulties to deal with domestic crises, e.g. the current record-long recession as well as the frustration many other countries have experienced in trying to negotiate sustainable agreements with Japan.

2. The lasting effects of SCAP's dissolving of the *zaibatsu* holding companies were two-fold – both presumably unintentional.

   • It shifted the balance of power between the *zaibatsus* and the state bureaucrats in favour of the latter. Thus, these bureaucrats could apply the same type of wartime economic policy and resource allocation in the post-war development. In particular, the Ministry of Finance, MOF, became the real power-house of *Japan Inc.*

   • The *zaibatsus* were reborn, now renamed *gurupu*(groups) or more common *keiretsu* in most cases recognised by their old *zaibatsu* names: Mitsui, Mitsubishi, Sumitomo etc. The old holding companies were wound up but the reborn versions were organised around a trading company, several manufacturing companies and – most important – a bank. These banks, the so-called *City banks* or main banks came to play a crucial role in the economic policy of Japan.

3. Since World War II, the economic policy of Japan has been to expand its manufacturing base, particularly of mass-market products for export markets. The key elements of this policy are as follows:

   • The main vehicles were the manufacturing companies of the *keiretsus*, all of which had to specialise in certain technologies and products.

   • The financing of the expansion of these companies and *keiretsus* was done through the City banks mentioned above. Starting in the early 1950s, the restructuring of the ownership of the operating companies was financed by these banks – directly and indirectly. The general public had rather limited financial capacity to take part in new issues of shares. And even if they had the financial means, in many cases, they were not invited to take part. Instead, the banks became direct owners but also financed cross-ownership between operating companies. Furthermore, equity financing – once a stable, mutual ownership had been established – became less and less important. By the end of the 1980s, before the financial bubble burst, bank financing accounted for some 80 percent of most companies.

- To make this financing model viable, the government came to play an all- important role – directly as well as indirectly. The City banks could refinance themselves – at very low interest rates – in the central bank, the Bank of Japan (BOJ) which was subordinate to MOF, the Ministry of Finance. This eventually led to BOJ attaining a unique global position by being the only net lender of all central banks in the developed world. Indirectly, the government has been equally important for this financial model by providing full deposit guarantees to all banks. This system of government guarantees is sometimes referred to as *the convoy system*. All are protected, no single bank will be left to go under because of poor judgement of risk or mismanagement. Since the Japanese in general are big savers and their favourite assets are bank deposits, these guarantees have been further fuelling the credit expansion of the banks.
- The current industry structure of Japan is, to a large extent, a result of the economic policy where controlled competition has been a key element. By allocating specialisation focus for the various manufacturing companies and by providing cheap financing, the export companies could develop their export market competitiveness through economies of scale and competitive pricing. The domestic market has effectively been protected from external competition. The leading operating companies of the *keiretsus* constitute a prioritised echelon of resources in the dual structure of the Japanese economy. Business cycle variations and other economic disturbances are absorbed by several layers of suppliers and sub-suppliers to a leading *keiretsu* company. These constitute a sort of lower level part of the dual structure, often small and medium sized, family owned companies providing flexibility to the overall quite rigid structure. Another typical feature of this *keiretsu* centred manufacturing focus is that the distribution – wholesaling as well as retailing – is organised in vertical structures tied to each *keiretsu*. This has been a very effective means in controlling foreign as well as domestic competition.
- The Japanese financial sector is also very much the design of state bureaucrats. A key feature has been compartmentalisation where a few licensed actors have been allowed in each field – banks for traditional banking, security houses to deal in securities etc.

4. Finally, some brief comments about a major topic – Japanese culture and its core values: (a) The Japanese culture is collectivist rather than individualistic. One political outgrowth of this is what seems to be the primary

overriding goal for economic policy, namely full employment. One observer[5] makes a striking comparison between Japan and the USA in this
respect. In 1998, the two countries had the same unemployment rate –
4.1 percent. İn Japan that was the worst figure since 1956 while in the USA
this was perceived as one of the best achievements ever. At the same time,
such a comparison is a mere curiosity unless other costs and benefits are
taken into account. What is perceived as a low figure in the USA is an
additional benefit of a record long business boom, fundamental renewal
of the economy at large, and creation of new growth with long-term
potential. The same unemployment figure in Japan is a fundamental failure of *Japan Inc.* and an unacceptable cost unless it is an indication of rapid
restructuring and renewal of the traditional model. (b) Appearance is
often more important than actual content. Although this might have
obvious negative effects, it could also explain why Japan has practically
eliminated street crime. At the same time, crime is *big business* in Japan,
carried out by other means and directed at other targets than what is
common in other countries, as the *sokaiya* extortion referred to initially.
(c) Risk aversion is generally strong making the Japanese less entrepreneurial than desired when renewal is required. Thus, overall social
change is hard to achieve. On the other hand, if it happens it involves
more or less everyone at the same time. Historical cases in point include
the *Meiji restoration* when Japan was transformed from a closed feudal
society to a rapidly industrialising economy in about ten years as well as
how quickly social and economic reconstruction took off after World War
II.

THE JAPANESE STAKEHOLDER CONCEPT

Although the Japanese Company Act states that companies are controlled by
their owners, the fact of the matter is that the Japanese corporate governance
system is very different to the Anglo-American concept. Institutional
owners, who are mutually dependent through cross-holdings and inter-
business transactions, dominate. Bottom-line orientation is weak. It is rather
a matter of absolute size and market share as first hand goals.

Employees constitute an important stakeholder body, which is evident
through the lifetime employment institution. Thus, absolute growth to
support lifetime employment has been prioritised before profitability.

Bank financing has been a major source of funds as explained above. Since
interest rates have been kept low, this has further weakened the profitability
motive. The main bank exercised some kind of corporate governance in
relation to its keiretsu companies. Links between the main bank and the
company have also been strengthened through an arrangement whereby

following retirement, senior bank officials made a second career with the company.

However, after the big banking crisis that followed the real estate speculation crash and financial bubble in the late 1980s, many of the traditional links to one main bank have started to deteriorate. Bank financing for a certain company or keiretsu is now more evenly spread among several banks. As a whole, bank financing remains the major source of funding, although reduced, accounting for some 60 percent of corporate financing.

The Japanese board

Japan applies the unitary board concept – but in its own way. One scholar (Kanda, see Hopt et al.) characterises the traditional board of the large companies as homogenous: all men, all over 50 years of age, and all internally recruited. In addition, a common feature is that the board is big, often consisting of some 50 directors. The board is recruited among loyal and senior officers of the company and is regarded as a reward for services rendered. The strongman of the board is the president of the company who is also the main decision-maker when it comes to board recruitment. Even the chairman is perceived as being below the president. The recruitment of a new chairman is often a matter of the president, because of age, finding it appropriate to step down in his active presidential role to continue in the more laid-back role as chairman. It is obvious that a board of that size and composition can neither function as a decision-making body, nor as a strong corporate governance agent vis-à-vis executive management. Thus, the function of the board, as well as that of the AGM, tends to be merely ceremonial.

Statutory auditors

In addition to accounting auditors who are elected among professional CPAs, the AGM of a Japanese company elects statutory auditors (*kansayaku*) who are supposed to monitor management performance. These auditors are not required to be professionally trained and are in most cases recruited internally. Mostly, they seem to have played a rather passive role.

SUMMING UP THE CORPORATE GOVERNANCE SITUATION IN JAPAN

It is obvious that corporate governance as applied in Japan bears limited resemblance to corporate governance as understood by Western countries – an appearance at best without much substance. At the same time it should be acknowledged that the Japanese growth formula has been extremely successful for a long period. Japan became prosperous and its economy grew to become the second largest in the world. Does this mean that corporate governance has no significance?

First of all, there are exceptions in the general pattern of how companies are governed or not governed in Japan. Some of the really successful companies have been controlled by private owners. A notable case in point is Sony which very early on (1958) adopted an international name (the founding name of the company was TokyoTsushin Kogyo K.K. – Tokyo Telecommunications Engineering Corporation) and already in 1960 established Sony Corporation of America. Sony became a truly international Japanese company, not least because one of its two founding owners, the late Dr. Akio Morita, moved to live in the United States when Sony was established there in 1960. Sony issued ADRs (American Depository Receipts) on the New York Stock Exchange as early as 1961. Thus, it was exposed to the expectations and profitability requirements from one of the most demanding equity markets in the world from the very outset of entering international competition.

However, most Japanese companies have not had such exposure to a truly international business culture and to Western capital markets as Sony and a few others. Many became successful within the Japanese corporate governance system. One possible explanation is that the overall success of *Japan Inc.* represents a specific paradigm where most technologies – process as well as product technologies – were imported and the Japanese contribution above all was a superior skill in improving and applying these technologies to manufacture useful and cost effective products for world markets. If this is so, then it is natural to ask the following question: does the lingering crisis – the longest recession since World War II – indicate that this paradigm has come to the end of the road?

THE NEW PREREQUISITES

The short answer to the question above is: yes! However, reviewing the four aspects below – each representing a tough challenge to the existing 'prisoners of success'(see next section!) – will qualify this answer further.

1. Ever since they entered international export markets, Japanese companies have been exposed to international competition. However, for a long period this competition came primarily from companies in the Western markets, who were less cost efficient than the Japanese exporters. The process of globalisation that started to gain momentum in the 1980s and after the collapse of the communist command economy regimes in the early 1990s seems to progress at lightning speed, further fuelled by the new technologies, has dramatically changed the strategic position of

many *Japan Inc.*-players. Many Western companies have outsourced large parts of their processing and manufacturing to low cost producing countries and in that way neutralised earlier cost disadvantages. Furthermore, many Asian and East European companies have followed in the footsteps of Japan and by exploiting superior factor cost advantages have managed to out-compete their old master. Maybe, more Japanese chief executives and boards should have listened to the chairman of Toyota, Mr. Hiroshi Okuda when he stated: 'Do not be a prisoner of success. The worst thing is not to change.'[6] More fundamental renewal might be required.

2. A core competence of *Japan Inc.* has been its manufacturing prowess at turning out mass-market products – hardware. This seems to be a key success factor for companies such as Honda, Toyota and Sony. However, to create new growth and value added output, the Japanese economy through existing companies as well as start-ups would need to embrace the logic of the new technologies – software, simply put – on a grand scale. Are the prerequisites available to achieve that? Are there enough software engineers who not only have the technical skills but are also entrepreneurial and innovative enough to achieve a major impact? Will they get the necessary support, e.g. from risk capitalists or the traditional financial sources in Japan? Not to mention other aspects, e.g. to what extent is the Japanese written language a drawback for this renewal.

3. The changing demographics of Japan represent another major challenge. The population will successively grow older, increasing the pension and health care burden of a shrinking percentage of the active population. Japan shares this challenge with several other countries, e.g. Germany, France, and Italy in particular among the larger European countries. However, Japan is worse off since its total population is expected to decrease, thus automatically reducing GDP growth unless this is compensated for by giant leaps of productivity improvement. A common feature of Japan and these countries is that pay-as-you-go systems dominate the social welfare systems. Thus, this is a matter of public finances and the development of the GDP in each country. The problem in Japan is aggravated by several factors. Life expectancy is the highest in the world making pension schemes and most probably health care provision more expensive. As one counter measure, Japan has already decided to increase the retirement age from 60 to 65 in the next two decades. The Japanese government is already struggling with budget deficits and increasing public debt, the latter being one of the largest in the developed world. Additional costs for pension and health care programmes will further amplify the vicious circle of debt servicing, increasing budget deficits and accumulating debts. Reducing public pension benefits – which would be one way of getting out of this problem – would make private pension schemes and asset accumulation crucial to safeguarding indivi-

dual retirement subsistence. This brings yet another challenge to the surface. As mentioned earlier, people at large in Japan are big savers (the rate is substantially higher than the OECD average) but they prefer to allocate most of their financial assets to bank deposits. The appalling fact is that many of these banks would have to file for bankruptcy if the government would terminate its *convoy system* of deposit guarantees.

4. It should be obvious from the analysis presented earlier in this paper that the *Japan Inc* model has run out of steam. The government cannot go on subsidising large parts of the economy by offering low interest rates to refinance further expansion of insolvent banks. The cheap money growth model has gone to the wall. The only way out is fundamental restructuring to restore the health of the financial sector as well as improving profitability in industry at large, and thereby paving the way for a more genuine renewal of the economy.

A NEW RESTORATION ON ITS WAY?

For some years now an increasing awareness has emerged in Japan that the problems the economy is facing will not go away with the upturn of the general business cycle. This has also resulted in reforms and change initiatives at various levels of the economy. Since the government plays such an important and active role in the economy, and since the regulatory structure was built up to support the traditional *Japan Inc.* model, a crucial prerequisite for further change is massive deregulation and liberalisation. Furthermore, a redefinition of the role of the government and its withdrawal from too much micro-management of the financial and business sectors will be necessary. Without such fundamental changes it is not very useful to discuss or initiate improvements of corporate governance in most Japanese companies.

Japan's Big Bang

Some twenty years after the USA and ten years after the UK, the Japanese government in late 1996 launched reforms aiming at deregulating and liberalising the financial sector in Japan. The Japanese version of big bang is actually not one big bang. Instead, it is supposed to be implemented in steps over several years, and, as it has turned out, over a longer period than originally planned. One of the most important reforms of the whole package – the termination of *the convoy system*, government bank deposit guarantees – which was initially supposed to begin in 2001 has been postponed for a year. It remains to be seen if this will hold since a very powerful lobby of LDP (Liberal Democratic Party – currently in government) politicians has been formed to resist this crucial reform.

The overall goals of the big bang in Japan have been summarised in three words: Free, Fair, and Global. These words refer to the purposes of establishing a free market for financial services with open entry, free pricing, product differentiation etc. Furthermore, to make it fair and transparent for all actors involved as well as adapting practices to be consistent with a globalised financial market.

So far (through fiscal 1999) concrete reforms have included removal of barriers between different types of financial service providers to enter each others' markets. Banks can now issue bonds, sell their own mutual funds etc. Securities firms are now allowed to offer derivatives and other types of new investment products. Brokerage commissions are no longer regulated. The Ministry of Finance has been stripped of some of its earlier powers and has partly been replaced by a new regulatory and monitoring agency for the financial sector. The Bank of Japan achieved a more independent status and clearer responsibility for monetary policy. Currency regulations have been abolished and anyone can now open foreign currency accounts anywhere. Foreign financial firms can establish themselves and operate without special permits and so forth. Insurance companies will be included in these reforms and be free to enter the banking market. Earlier barriers between life insurance and casualty and property assurance have been dismantled.

Nonetheless, important reforms aiming to achieve the overall goals of big bang and adapt to international standards – in addition to the termination of *the convoy system* mentioned above – are missing. The government is still a dominating actor in the savings market by owning The Postal Savings System, which controls one third of the market, not least because of a favoured competitive position (no profitability or dividend payments requirements). Transparency and disclosure are still far below international standards. It was discovered that the banks that finally had to file for bankruptcy had been able to hide huge losses on bad loans – in one case amounting to USD three billion.

Thus, the Japanese government has numerous demanding decisions to get through the political machinery as well as reforms to implement, before the necessary prerequisites for good corporate governance are in place. However, significant change has taken place in the financial markets as well as in the business sector indicating moves in the right direction.

Unleashed dynamics in the financial sector

Although the big bang is still a long way from being completely implemented, what has been done so far has been enough to ignite a chain reaction of changes. Some of the most important include:

- Major foreign banks and financial services firms have entered the Japanese market. Merrill Lynch is building up operations by acquiring the resources and a network of branches from the failed Yamaichi Securities. An American group, Ripplewood Holdings, is attempting to take over LTCB, Long Term Credit Bank of Japan, which was nationalised because of imminent failure due to bad loans. Several joint ventures between international financial service companies and Japanese counterparts, e.g. between Salomon Smith Barney and Nikko Securities, between Dai-Ichi Kangyo Bank and J.P. Morgan, and between Merrill Lynch and Sumitomo Bank.

- Several quite spectacular mergers between domestic banks have taken place. Fuji Bank and Dai-Ichi Kangyo Bank have merged, including also state owned Industrial Bank of Japan. Other mergers include those between Tokai Bank and Asahi Bank, and Sumitomo Bank and Sakura Bank to form the world's second largest bank (asset size). One result of the ongoing merger mania is that the so-called *City banks* have been reduced from nine to six. There are rumours that this merger activity between domestic banks and other financial firms has been driven by the government, anxious not to let foreign banks take the lead in Japan. In a report[7] this aspect was highlighted by an analogy with Great Britain's Wimbledon tennis tournament: although it is arranged by the English and takes place in London, it has come to be dominated by non-British players. Another concern of the Japanese government has also been that – due to the extended recession and the vulnerable position of the Japanese banks – Japan's financial role has drastically diminished in East Asia.

- In the traditional financial structure of the Japanese economy, the stock exchange was merely a stage for speculation. Any additional roles were limited. With big bang and foreign influence as well as the Japanese government's ambition to make Tokyo a financial centre in Asia – in competition with Singapore and Hong Kong, in particular – changes have started to happen. Two new stock exchanges for high tech companies/start-ups have been established. The Tokyo Stock Exchange has started *Mothers* (of *Internet babies*) and NASDAQ has set up a similar stock exchange in a joint venture with the Osaka Stock Exchange.

New economy and Japan

As a Swede, the author is surprised not to have seen an onslaught of Japanese invaders into the rapidly growing mobile telephone market, e.g. by Japanese electronics giants Sony and Matsushita. The pattern from earlier waves of consumer electronics products has not been repeated, at least so far. The rapid technology development, e.g. WAP (Wireless Application Protocol) for Internet, and various synergies with mobile telephony systems seem to have helped the top three companies – Ericsson, Nokia and Motorola – to stay ahead. Is this an indication that the so-called new economy has not caught on yet in Japan?

In Japan, Internet penetration is still quite low, compared to the USA, Sweden and Finland, comprising some 13 percent of Japanese households in 1999. However, mobile telephones are much more frequent and the leading operator, Docomo, is expanding rapidly. Its share has skyrocketed since it was listed in 1998.

In the burgeoning e-commerce phenomenon, the driving forces in Japan seem to be foreign entrants while domestic companies are constrained by the traditional distribution and retailing structure.

As regards Japan and the new economy at large Business Week[8] quotes the president of Toshiba Corporation, Mr. Taizo Nishimuro: 'I think there will be a New Economy, (but) it won't be the same as the US.'

Historically, the Japanese have repeatedly demonstrated that they are quick learners and that they can rapidly adapt to new prerequisites. It remains to be seen if the cultural drawbacks to entrepreneurship, risk taking, and genuine innovation will stall the renewal process this time. In addition, there is the shortage of engineers with adequate Internet and software competence that will remain a bottleneck in the short and medium term, at least.

Corporate governance reforms and improvements

Keidanren, the powerful *Japanese Federation of Economic Organisations*, launched *Urgent Recommendations Concerning Corporate Governance* in 1997 which mainly include some suggestions to sharpen corporate governance as regards the function of the auditors. Keidanren perceives the necessity of improving corporate governance arguing that: 'in order to maintain and strengthen their international competitiveness into the twenty-first century in the context of an age of *mega-competition*, Japanese businesses must realise a form of corporate governance that meets global standards'. In this perspective, Keidanren also urges corporations to formulate their own guidelines as well as take measures to invigorate the functioning of the board of directors. Keidanren itself stated that it 'will continue to consider the following issues:

1. The proper functioning of the board of directors;
2. Review of the operation of general meetings of shareholders; and
3. Positioning of other stakeholders vis-à-vis each other and shareholders; and measures to improve disclosure.'

Thus, this clearly demonstrates complete awareness of what some of the critically important corporate governance issues are all about. However since then, Keidanren has not presented any progress on these issues. On the other hand, Keidanren seems to have focused on important prerequisites for good corporate governance by repeatedly urging the government to initiate structural reforms.

Another constellation, *Corporate Governance Forum of Japan* (its members comprise business executives as well as institutional investors, and academics) set up a Corporate Governance Committee that presented its Final Report in May 1998: *Corporate Governance Principles – A Japanese View*. The international inspiration and model for this report seems to be the Cadbury Report and the *Combined Code* of the UK, in particular. However, its concrete recommendations are rather modest in that perspective. The 1998 report includes two sets of principles: *Step A Principles* for immediate adoption and *Step B Principles* requiring 'legal reforms on a grand scale'. In addition it is said that: 'Ultimately, the Committee intends to develop the Principles into a *Code of Best Practise*'. The overall ambition of this *Forum* is explained as follows: 'Our aim is to establish an independent system of outside directors in Japan, and by establishing a market for independent directors to promote the transferability of corporate executives between companies. Also we will endeavour to have these Principles adopted as part of the requirements for Initial Public Offerings.'

No doubt, this declared aim reflects well some fundamental weaknesses of the Japanese system of corporate governance. As regards examples of concrete recommendations, one includes the issue of CEO (*shacho*) and chairman. The principle says that the two roles should be separate but if such separation is not implemented, 'an explanation should be offered to the shareholders.'

Other urgent issues of Japanese corporate governance are treated rather vaguely in this report, e.g. the one concerning board size. For an outsider it is obvious that Japanese boards are far too big and need to be drastically reduced from current numbers of 50–60 directors to, say, ten.

The Corporate Governance Forum merely states that the board should have an appropriate size.

In that context some individual companies have been bolder, notably Sony Corporation where a board of ten directors has replaced the earlier *crowd* of some fifty directors. A couple of other internationalised Japanese corporations have followed Sony's example.

CONCLUSION

It should be clear from the analysis presented here that Japan is changing and opening up to the outside world. Whether this ultimately will lead to a corporate governance system comparable – in substance – with that of the USA and UK is more doubtful. Certain scepticism is also justified when considering whether the indications of a new openness are genuine enough to allow free competition – for domestic as well as for foreign companies. Is a comparison with the *Meiji Restoration* in the 19th century very relevant? What happened then was that Japan opened to the outside world but the massive inflow of ideas, know-how, raw materials and processed goods that followed was controlled by the Japanese. Only some changes within the internal Japanese power structure took place after that. According to Mr. van Wolferen's analysis, SCAP made changes only to favour the state bureaucrats.

Will these bureaucrats have to yield now because the changes taking place herald a new paradigm? In a globalised world of 'an age of *mega-competition*', to use the words of Keidanren, national governments will have to yield to forces beyond their direct control. Japanese companies will have to comply with international standards of corporate governance if they are going to maintain their standing with customers, their credibility with investors and their legitimacy with local communities around the globe. Successively, the rules of the remaining domestic economic *games* will have to be adapted if the Japanese should continue to prosper and some of the big Japanese issues, in particular *the greying of Japan* should be dealt with successfully.

Convergence or Confusion? Summing up Country Analyses 8

The preceding review of the corporate governance situation in the five countries – the USA, the UK, Germany, France, and Japan – has provided a panorama of various issues and suggestions for possible improvement. While corporate governance, no doubt, is seen as an important aspect in all the five countries, the concrete corporate governance agenda differs from one country to the next.

TWO CATEGORIES

The analysis of the corporate governance situation and agenda for action in each country have highlighted the importance of the historical background, the institutional setting specific to each country, the initiation and progress of corporate governance so far etc. No wonder, then, that the concluding result differs between the five countries.

However, recognising the unique situation in each country, it is still possible to distinguish two categories of countries as regards what needs to be done and by whom. One category includes the USA and the UK while Germany, France and Japan belong to the other.

- In the UK and the USA, important corporate governance issues are of concern mainly to the actors directly involved, i.e. the institutional investors and other actors on the *owner side* and those accountable for the corporations – boards of directors and executive management – on the *corporate side*. However, one exception to this general state of affairs should not be forgotten. US legislation need to become more 'owner friendly', referring to Dr. Crist's statement in Chapter 3.
- An uniting feature for France, Germany, and Japan is that further development and diffusion of good corporate governance principles will require massive political reform. However, the content of such political reform varies widely between the three countries. In France, the most pressing reforms include privatisation and withdrawal of the state from direct involvement and *dirigisme* of economic life, to enhance institutions that will safeguard open competition, for example. In Germany, it is mainly a matter of changing laws in order to dismantle an outdated

Table 8.1 The relative importance of stock markets

Country	USA	UK	France	Germany	Japan
Market cap./GDP (%)	184	200	100	62	111

stakeholder model, abandon collective management, and introduce taxation structures (e.g. reduce or eliminate capital gains tax) that would stimulate rather than impede industry restructuring. In Japan, the scope of political reform needed is the most far-reaching – in essence, dismantling the whole concept of *Japan Inc.* A good start would be to fully implement, the *big bang* of financial and banking reform. All three countries share the need for decisive action in one particular area, i.e. pension reform.

So, what is the fundamental divide between the two categories? Peter F. Drucker, the management guru, offers one convincing answer to that question when he observes that it is only in the USA and the UK, among larger nations at least, that corporations are 'run for the benefit of their shareholders'.[1] This means that the dominating performance criterion for American and British corporations is shareholder value. In the countries of the second category, stakeholders other than the owners, e.g. the government, the employees, and the unions – are applying additional performance criteria: life-long employment, regional policy aspects etc.

This basic difference includes a number of other distinguishing features, not least the liquidity of the equity capital markets and the importance of the stock exchange in the total economy of each country as the figures in Table 8.1 illustrate.[2]

Thus, the two categories of these five countries are also distinguishable as regards the financial significance of the domestic stock markets.

THE EMERGENCE OF A NEW LOGIC

However, globalisation is bringing a new logic to the corporate governance arena. Corporations are no longer solely subject to the prioritised performance criteria of their country of origin and registration. Sony of Japan, Daimler Chrysler of Germany, and Schneider of France, for example, together with a host of other internationalised corporations have to perform in accordance with the expectations of Anglo–American institutional investors, the main suppliers of funds, if they want access to international capital. Thus, these corporations have to deliver shareholder value, but increasingly they are also scrutinised from the perspective of activist Anglo–American institutional investors applying their corporate governance standards.

Global convergence?

Does this mean that we are witnessing a globalisation of corporate governance principles that, eventually, will result in one *Combined Code* for a homo-
genised global corporate governance arena?

Several forces are at play driving development towards globalised capital
markets, and as a consequence, also working in the direction of homogenis-
ing corporate governance standards, for example:

- Corporations seeking international capital have to comply with standards
  set by the financial centres of the world, particularly New York and
  London. Such standards include certain requirements concerning
  accounting and overall transparency. In addition, attractiveness in the
  eyes of activist investors is enhanced if the company conforms with
  their corporate governance standards. It has also been indicated that
  companies with good corporate governance practices are valued at a
  premium compared to companies lacking such practices.
- The big institutional investors, including American activists such as
  CalPERS and TIAA-CREF, are increasing their proportions and absolute
  amounts of foreign investments, followed by activism focused on local
  companies as well. CalPERS has outlined and adopted corporate governance policies for its investments in the UK, France, Germany, and Japan
  for example. As far as TIAA-CREF is concerned, one spectacular case
  occurred in France when it took action against Eramet, a government
  dominated company. The French government tried – abusing the rights
  of other owners – to use company assets to achieve certain political goals.
- The deteriorating government-backed pension systems in many countries
  have stimulated the growth of private solutions. Big actors in this field
  include mainly Anglo–American financial services companies, which are
  growing rapidly in undeveloped pension savings markets such as France,
  Germany, and Japan. However, that is not the only consequence. Propor-
  tionately more of the placements of collected funds are channelled to
  liquid markets, i.e. the financial centres of the world, than to the country
  of the future retiree. Thus, the pressure on companies to migrate to the big
  liquid stock exchanges increases, as well as on local governments and
  bourses to adopt international standards.
- The stock exchanges themselves are internationalising through alliances –
  albeit with varying success – and joint ventures, e.g. NASDAQ which is
  entering European and Japanese joint ventures. Cross-border trading of
  shares is also being facilitated by new actors, e.g. Jiway, the joint venture
  between OM of Sweden and Morgan Stanley Dean Witter. These movements will tend to support further diffusion of international (=Anglo–
  American) corporate governance standards.
- Other financial services actors, e.g. banks, credit rating institutes as well

as the World Bank are also promoting good corporate governance standards. Even some big buyers of goods and services have included corporate governance aspects in their assessment of the reliability of potential suppliers.

- There is a lively international debate of corporate governance issues, promoted by voluntary organisations, e.g. the International Corporate Governance Network (ICGN), and International Bar Association (IBA), Section on Business Law, as well as by organisations such as the OECD.

Status quo forces

Although forces driving globalisation of capital markets and corporate governance standards are strong, and a certain degree of homogenisation has already occurred, there is still a long way to go in the countries reviewed. The conclusion stands even if the analysis had included additional countries to the five largest economies of the world reviewed here. Several obstacles and countervailing forces, making changes difficult and time consuming, can be identified, e.g.:

- Peter Drucker's observation, referred to above, indicates that changes will involve fundamental aspects of political ideology and ideas about society. Experience tells us that such change is likely to be slow. The inherent logic of the stakeholder model is one of status quo forces resisting change. Acknowledging shareholder prerogative would require other stakeholders to yield their interests, at least in their own eyes, and, obviously in some cases, their formal power, e.g. as regards the German unions. But would they be worse off in reality? We shall come to this issue in Chapter 12 when the fundamental philosophy of the stakeholder model will be discussed.
- Since many of the obstacles regarding change of corporate governance practices are legal, the political decision machinery in the countries concerned needs to be mobilised. In that usually time consuming process, resistance from stakeholders and vested interests of various kinds must be eliminated.
- Many of the large Anglo–American financial services companies and institutional investors operating internationally are primarily, and very often solely, interested in the return on their money. If one holding looks less promising, they simply divest it. Alternatively, they just follow the index movements. Thus, for this type of investor, corporate governance aspects are less relevant, and there is no ambition to become active as regards the fundamental performance of the portfolio companies. Indirectly, it could be argued, that the investment practices of this type of investor have disciplining effects on companies. However, these investors

represent less of a pressure on companies and countries to improve their corporate governance standards.

- Among American activist type of institutional investors there is also a concern not to appear as the *ugly American*, telling other countries and foreign companies to do things the American way.

One common denominator

Regardless of all the differences among the five countries in focus here, not to mention the rest of the world, and a fairly slow convergence process, most serious actors involved seem to have a shared view concerning one crucial corporate governance issue:

the importance of an independent (and competent) board.

Of course, there are differences regarding the seriousness of various parties when it comes to concrete action. However, that should not deflate the value of having a common starting point for further discussions. We will come back to the importance of the board in later chapters, but before terminating the discussion at this point, two aspects will be covered here, namely:

- Perceptions of the unitary and two-tier board concepts.
- A brief review of chosen board concepts in cross-border mergers.

SOME CONFUSION CONCERNING DIFFERENT BOARD CONCEPTS

In discussing and comparing different board concepts, the most common distinction is that of unitary and two-tier board structures, respectively. This is confusing since it is not always clear whether it is the formal aspect of different, legally provided, board concepts that is being referred to or the actual division of tasks – strategic/governance issues and executive/operational matters – and balance of power between the board/non-executive directors on the one hand and executive management on the other. A summary review of the situation in the five countries will clarify this point further.

The US board

The US corporation has a unitary board. Predominatingly, the Chairman and CEO roles are performed by the same person. This person and his/her combined function are thus very powerful, rendering it difficult to separate the strategic governance role of the board and the executive duties of management as well as to establish a healthy balance of power. There are also additional executive directors on the board of a US corporation, further aggravating this issue. Steps have been taken to improve this situation: the number of executive directors is being reduced; a non-executive, lead director is being appointed in more and more companies; a brave minority is arguing for a separation of the chairman and CEO roles.

The UK board

The UK board is unitary, not only formally, but also, perhaps more than in any other country with unitary boards, concerning integration of strategic governance and executive/operational matters. There are several, sometimes even a majority of executive directors on the board enhancing the integrated character of the UK board to handle both strategic governance issues and operational matters. A big leap has been taken, though, in the direction of splitting tasks and improving the balance of power by the separation of chairman and CEO roles in most large corporations. However, a significant symptom of the *impossible* situation of the UK board concept is the difficulties in recruiting good non-executive directors.

The German board

The large German corporations (legal entity *AG, Aktiengesellschaft*) have two-tier boards: a supervisory board, *Aufsichtsrat*, and a management board, *Vorstand*. The actual role of *Aufsichtsrat* has been and to a large extent still is ceremonial, leaving the centre stage of power to *Vorstand*. This structure gives the German board concept, in its actual performance, a unitary character. However, the whole system is suffering from two major shortcomings, further enhancing the power position and role of *Vorstand*: *co-determination* and *collective management*. *Co-determination* tends to make *Aufsichtsrat* impotent or a mere nuisance. With half of *Aufsichtsrat*'s members elected by the unions and employees, the supervisory board becomes far too big to function as a problem-solving and decision-making body. Worse still, it does not offer a climate for open discussions. Meetings tend be a mere formality where the two stakeholder parties have taken their stands prior to the meeting.

Attempts have been made to strengthen the actual role of *Aufsichtsrat* and some companies seem to have made progress in this matter.

The French boards

French law lays down two types of boards. The dominating one is a unitary board (*System I*), until last year requiring that its *PDG*(*Président Directeur*

Générale) performed the combined duties of chairman of the board and CEO. The traditional *PDG* role and power position is uniquely strong. Thus, the role of the board to perform a governance function has been negligible. The option introduced last year to separate the functions of chairman and CEO within the unitary system should improve the board's prospects of exercising governance.

The alternative board concept (*System II*) is a copy of the German two-tier system. It is much less frequent and considered to be similar to the German governance system in its actual performance by making the management board (*le directoire*) the dominating body.

The Japanese board

Japanese law provides the unitary board concept. In real life the Japanese corporate board seems to be a long way from exercising any governance duties. Recruited internally, including some fifty members or more, and with the president as the strongman of a Japanese corporation, it merely fulfils a ceremonial function. Japanese corporate governance committees have recommended the introduction of external board members. However, there seems to be slow progress in this respect, except for a few Japanese multinational corporations. Sony pioneered reform by reducing its board size to ten as well as by electing non-Japanese and external directors. A couple of other Japanese corporations have followed Sony's example.

IS THE FORMAL CONCEPT IRRELEVANT FOR THE ACTUAL GOVERNANCE ROLE OF BOARDS?

The summary review of the situation in the five countries above indicates that the legal provision does not guarantee a clear separation of the actual governance role from that of executive management. The two-tier German and French versions do not seem to support the governance role better than the unitary concepts in the USA, the UK, Japan, and France. Furthermore, this conclusion is corroborated by the Swedish experience. The unitary board, provided by law, is clearly *two-tier* in its actual performance in most Swedish corporations. The typical Swedish board is made up of non-executive directors with the exception of the CEO. There is also a tradition of combining a strong non-executive chairman with that of a strong CEO (Chapter 10 will explain how this tradition emerged within the model Wallenberg sphere). However, attempts are made in several countries to strengthen the governance role of boards, irrespective of whether a unitary or two-tier system is applied.

The four-field chart in Figure 8.1 offers an overview of the formal and actual board concepts in the six countries reviewed as well as of movements

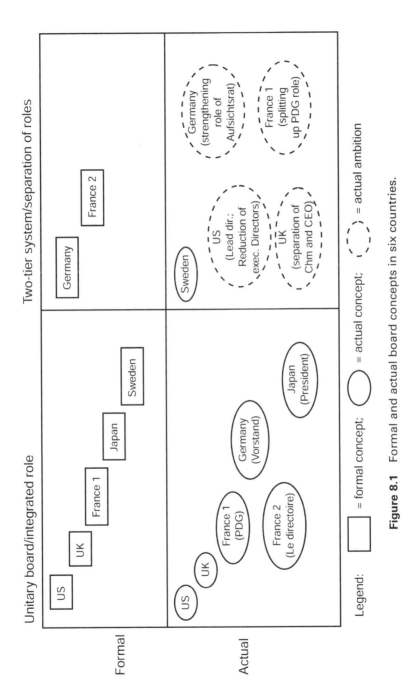

Figure 8.1 Formal and actual board concepts in six countries.

to create an actual two-tier system (= separation of the governance and executive roles, respectively).

CROSS-BORDER MERGERS – VANGUARD OF INTERNATIONAL CORPORATE GOVERNANCE CONVERGENCE?

Do cross-border mergers of large listed corporations, done on an equal basis, serve as a vanguard of international convergence of corporate governance standards? There are complications when trying to identify intentions to include such features since the merged entity is subject to legal requirements of its country of registration even if the merger has been based on equal terms. Furthermore, in the short and medium terms, one will often find temporary solutions of people issues affecting the composition of the board, e.g. the nomination of chairman and CEO.

Out of a sample of five cross-border mergers – AstraZeneca, Aventis, BP Amoco, Daimler Chrysler, and Pharmacia & Upjohn – three seem to have included features beyond what is legally provided or of a mere temporary nature. These corporations include Aventis, Daimler Chrysler and Pharmacia & Upjohn.

Aventis

Aventis SA – registered in Strasbourg, France – is the merged entity of Hoechst, Germany and Rhône-Poulenc, France. In this case, corporate governance features have been included which go beyond what is required in France. The intention seems to have been to integrate some typical German features into the new corporate governance structure. Hence, Aventis has a two-tier board while the original board of Rhône-Poulenc was unitary. Furthermore, there are plans to include employee representatives in the supervisory board, which is not provided by French law. However, unlike the German procedure, the employee representative(s) will be appointed and granted discharge by the AGM.

Daimler Chrysler

Unsuccessful attempts were made to have a unitary board to govern this mega corporation, the merged entity of German Daimler–Benz and American Chrysler Corporation. Instead, the new entity had to comply with the law of its country of registration, Germany. However, to overcome all the shortcomings of the German corporate governance structure, an informal board – a *shareholder committee*– was initiated by the German chairman (of the supervisory board) and his American counterpart. This informal board includes the two chairmen of the board of management (*Vorstand*) – Herr

Schremp and Mr. Eaton – as well as the chairman of the supervisory board (*Aufsichtsrat*) – Herr Kopper. This informal board is said to work as an ordinary American board.

As a gesture of goodwill, the German unions have given one of their seats on the supervisory board to a representative of the American employees. At the same time, this highlights the misfit of German corporate governance idiosyncrasies in a globalised business world since the American employees outnumber the German ones, not to mention all the other nationalities in this giant corporation.

Pharmacia & Upjohn

Swedish Pharmacia and Upjohn of the USA, two pharmaceutical companies merged in 1996 to form Pharmacia & Upjohn, registered in the USA. The board of the company has borrowed features from both corporate governance cultures. The overall board concept is Swedish in the sense that all the directors are non-executive, including the chairman, except the President and CEO of the company. The American character of the board is to be found in its committee structure, which is similar to other US boards.

Currently (early 2000), it seems that this structure will change. The company is in the process of merging with Monsanto, the American pharmaceutical and agrochemical company, to form the Pharmacia Corporation. The current President and CEO of P&U, Mr. Hassan will hold the same position in the new company while Mr. Shapiro, Chairman and CEO of Monsanto will become full time chairman in the Pharmacia Corporation. When Mr. Shapiro retires next year (2001), Mr. Hassan will become Chairman and CEO. Thus, the conventional American order will be re-established.

AstraZeneca and BP Amoco

The two remaining companies of the sample of five examined in this context, do not deviate from what is expected of a company registered in the UK. Astra, the Swedish pharmaceutical company, which joined forces with British Zeneca, gave up its board concept of just having non-executive directors on its board. AstraZeneca has a typically British board with a non-executive chairman – Mr. Barnevik in this case – and with several executive directors.

In the case of BP Amoco there seems to be a temporary arrangement with two co-chairmen. One is British, non-executive co-chairman, Mr. Sutherland, former non-executive chairman of BP. The other co-chairman is full time, former Amoco Chairman and CEO, Mr. Fuller. The temporary character of Mr. Fuller's duties is indicated in the corporate governance statement of the new company, which says that Mr. Fuller's key responsibilities are to work with the CEO on the merger transition process.

CONCLUDING REMARKS ON THE CROSS-BORDER MERGER CASES

It may be possible to find other, more exciting cases of creative and lasting examples of corporate governance arrangements than the five looked at here. Hopefully, such findings would include merged entities with corporate governance arrangements that go beyond the shortcomings of the country where a cross-border merged company happens to be registered. However, among the five cases, special credit should be given to Daimler Chrysler for trying to beat the constraining German corporate governance system.

Returning to the initial question of this section: can we conclude that cross-border mergers serve as a vanguard in an international convergence process of corporate governance standards? The preceding review indicates that the answer could be both yes and no. Such mergers have to accommodate the differences of corporate governance between the parties involved, at least if they are supposed to be *a merger of equals*. At the same time, such a merger and new entity is subject to the corporate governance rules – legal and/or conventional – of its country of registration. How much easier it would be if there was an international *Combined Code* to refer to! At the least, cross-border mergers help us see the need for an adaptation of corporate governance rules and institutions to the globalised world we are part of.

Corporate Governance – Where Will it Go? 9

Is there a future for corporate governance and if so, what will it look like? Or is the corporate governance movement that started in the mid-1980s in the USA and got its breakthrough in the first half of the 1990s now on the wane? Is it just another of these fads that come and go in the corporate world, and the world of business buzzwords? After all, one key driving force behind the emergence of the corporate governance movement as well as an instrumental reason why CalPERS and others managed to get an impact in the boardrooms of Corporate America and elsewhere, was poor financial performance. Who needs corporate governance now, some may argue, when stock markets are soaring and *the new economy* will take us to the *Promised Land*?

Confronted with such difficult questions and seductive arguments, it might be useful to take a more detached view, e.g. by trying to answer the following: how can we fit corporate governance into a longer historical perspective? What is the historical significance of this corporate governance movement?

To get additional ideas about what will happen to corporate governance in the future, let us then try to sum up some key features of the turbulent 1990s, a decade that probably will go down as one of the most dramatic and decisive in the annals of mankind.

WHY DID EXECUTUVE MANAGEMENT BECOME SO POWERFUL?

If the corporate governance movement was a shareholder reaction to poor financial performance and managements' abuse of shareholder rights, why had the incumbent management of many companies become so powerful and arrogant that they did not care. 'Mind your own business!', as Roger Smith, Chairman and CEO of General Motors at the time, said to CalPERS when they asked for a meeting to discuss GM's paltry performance. How come that the shareholders – the owners and suppliers of risk capital – could be neglected and dismissed like that?

To find an explanation to this phenomenon, the following simple figure (Figure 9.1) will help us shed some light on this paradoxical and sometimes appalling behaviour.

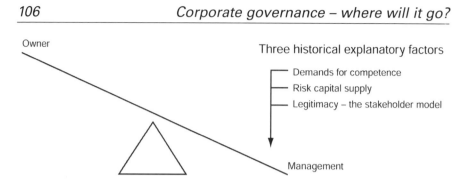

Figure 9.1   Three factors have tipped the balance of power.

The management revolution

The three factors listed on the management side of the seesaw in the figure above all reinforce one another and resulted in what is commonly referred to as *the management revolution*. A brief review of each factor is given below.

Demand for competence

Peter F. Drucker, the prolific writer on management and economic issues, suggested[1] that the economic progress since the breakthrough of industrialisation can be explained by three knowledge revolutions:

- *Knowledge about* **technology**: we learnt to command technology scientifically and could make the breakthrough from handicraft to engineering and industrial production.
- *Knowledge about* **work**: systematic study of work and application of *scientific management*, pioneered by Frederick W. Taylor, boosted productivity and laid down important organisational principles.
- *Knowledge about* **knowledge**:Drucker's concept of the large organisation is that it is based on management's ability to organise and co-ordinate different types of knowledge, e.g. various types of technical and functional knowledge. It was the emergence of the large railway companies in the USA, in particular, that triggered and necessitated the development of systematic organisation and management structures. The rapidly growing new industries, e.g. chemicals and automobiles, generated new challenges for organisational innovation and management competence. Du Pont and General Motors introduced new means of control (the so-called Du Pont diagram) and the divisionalised organisation, to mention two early pioneering achievements. Early *manifestos* on the new issues of management and organisation included Taylor's *Scientific Management* and *Industrial and Public Administration* by the Belgian mining engineer and general manager, Henri Fayol. In this book, published in 1916, Fayol

distinguishes the various functions of an industrial operation, and he is the first to put a particular emphasis on the importance of the administrative function or process which he divides into five parts: planning, organizing, managing and giving orders, co-ordinating, and finally checking. This was the beginning of what later, particularly after World War II, became a major university discipline and growth basis for numerous business schools – management. A landmark in this development, by the way, was Drucker's study of General Motors in the 1940s, and book *The Concept of the Corporation* (1946).

The key message, conveyed by reviewing three types of knowledge, is that the running of a business in the industrial era required a plethora of highly trained engineers, experts, and specialists, including professional managers. What used to be owned and run by the same people had to be separated into those owning a business and those experts and professional managers running it. The professional management of a company based its role – and power position – on its professional skill to manage and create value by means of an organisation of various experts and scientific methods to use resources productively. Through the increasing complexity of prerequisites for business operations, the demand for more sophisticated management skills grew, and the power platform of executive management became ever more enhanced.

Supply of risk capital

The formidable economic development that was made possible by the industrial revolution offered unprecedented growth opportunities for companies. These growth opportunities were far beyond what most private owners could finance. Furthermore, entrepreneurs who started companies were mostly people without wealth. We have seen earlier in this chapter that in Germany, the universal banks came in as the principal financier of companies. In other countries, and in the USA in particular, the stock market came to play a crucial role in corporate financing. Ownership became dispersed among many relatively small owners in each company. This pattern was further enhanced by the growth of pension funds and other financial institutions, a phenomenon observed as early as the beginning of the 1930s by Berle and Means in their now classic book, *The Modern Corporation and Private Property*.[2] The ensuing fragmentation of ownership and the new logic of raising risk capital further enhanced the power position of the executive management of corporations. As a consequence, the board of directors of corporations came under the control of the incumbent management and became integrated with executive management by way of executive directors and the combined role of chairman and CEO. Ownership was further alienated from decision making in and governance of the corporations.

The stakeholder model – a philosophy for management supremacy

We have seen how legislation and external forces, particularly in some countries outside Anglo-America, still apply other performance criteria to corporations than shareholder value. Owners are just one of several legitimate stakeholders.

The implicit corporate governance view of this model has also served the interests of incumbent management. In fact, the stakeholder model has provided a philosophy of legitimising management as holding the superior position of functioning as the independent arbitrator between conflicting demands of various stakeholders. Thus, owners are just shareholders, one of several stakeholders, who will get their fair return, subject to other stakeholders' legitimate demands being adequately satisfied, and to what is best for the company as a whole. And who would know better what is best for the company than the incumbent management.

The stakeholder concept has also been popular among organisational researchers, ever since Barnard first outlined this model in the late 1930s.[3] This concept will be further discussed in Chapter 12.

A governance model, unchallenged as long as it delivered

This governance model of strong, unopposed executive management remained unchallenged until many companies started to encounter growth and profitability problems as a consequence of the oil crises and the aftermath of these in the 1970s and early 1980s. After World War II and throughout the 1950s and 1960s there was strong overall growth, companies thrived, salaries increased rapidly, and the demographics were favourable. The workforce, as a percentage of the total population, increased during this golden era. Few seemed to have worried about future pensions.

In this perspective, it is hardly surprising to find that the pension systems established at that time in many of the European countries, mostly dominated by socialistic governments, were of the pay-as-you-go type and government financed. At that time there were no problems in paying for the limited number of pensioners, the total tax burden was still modest, and strong economic growth generated automatic increases of government tax revenues. In contrast to this, *après moi le deluge*-attitude of problem solving, General Motors, a pioneer of the corporate pension system in the 1950s, set another trend in the USA, that of fund-based pensions.

Economic stagnation, companies forced to restructure and lay off staff under pressure from foreign competition, and increasing numbers of people approaching retirement age raised the awareness of the importance of returns on pension funds. This should be recognised as a significant background for the emergence of corporate governance in the 1980s and that challenging the supremacy of incumbent management successively gained momentum.

MANAGEMENT IS CHALLENGED BUT FIGHTS BACK

However, before this, other important changes had taken place and introduced new 'rules of the game' to the incumbent management of a company, and, in the end, also a threat to its supreme power: the emergence of – to use Alfred D. Chandler's term – an *institutionalised market for corporate control*.[4]

Another significant separation

Chandler (1990) points out that during the 1960s, large diversified corporations started to separate corporate management from that of operational management for the first time. Instead of seeing itself as part of daily management and decision making, corporate management started to define its role as owner and manager of a portfolio of business entities. Furthermore, corporate management defined its competence in very general terms, which triggered the conglomerate phenomenon. Corporations diversified by acquiring businesses, unrelated to their existing ones, and thus entered industries where they had no prior experience. The fundamental driving forces behind the conglomerate wave were a surplus of financial resources since many of the corporations experienced maturing markets in their traditional businesses, and, for the same reason, a need to find new growth opportunities.

The creation of an institutionalised market for corporate control

The conglomerate wave faded away – more or less abruptly from one conglomerate corporation to the next – but in the process, a new market and service industry had emerged. Acquiring business units meant that other corporations or owners had to put business units up for sale. This took off rapidly, creating a market for the trading of business units. Many market makers, brokers, facilitators, advisors etc emerged in the process. A whole, new service industry of investment bankers and their entourage of lawyers, due diligence specialists, valuation experts etc saw the light of day and grew rapidly in the 1970s and beyond.

The diversification wave of the 1960s was also followed by a wave of divestitures during the 1970s among the large corporations. This was in turn followed by yet another phenomenon, the corporate raider. The market for corporate control that had been created made low performing corporations open to acquisition attempts by a new type of owner specialist, the corporate raider. After gaining control, such raiders restructured the acquired company, sold off assets and businesses, cut corporate overheads, but also, many times, R&D expenditure and similar long term commitments to jack up profitability and improve cash flow in the short term.

At least, Chandler (1990) is quite negative as regards the effects on capital-intensive industries of the emergence of the *institutionalised market for corporate control* in the United States when he concludes that 'long-term investment may have been sacrificed for short-term gain'.

CONCLUSION – OWNERSHIP HAS GAINED A LITTLE MORE WEIGHT

Our brief historical analysis has brought us to the point where the corporate governance movement took off. Not only as regards the point in time, but also as regards its triggers. Corporate raiders showed the way, by directing attention to low-performing corporations, and by demonstrating the power of ownership. It was also one of the means through which incumbent management tried to stave off raider attacks, so-called greenmail, which triggered the reaction of Jesse Unruh, and the start of CalPERS programme of corporate governance and owner activism.

This brief historical review also highlighted another significant split – after the decisive separation of ownership and executive management earlier – namely the one in the 1960s between corporate management and operational management. Should this be interpreted as a step towards the profession-alisation of ownership?

We come back to this issue in Part III, Chapters 12 and 13. However, one conclusion about ownership can be drawn already at this point. What happened during the 1960s, 1970s and throughout the 1980s, showed that ownership, and eventually also corporate governance, matters. The seesaw still tipped much lower on the management side, but the ownership side had started to put their act together and gained enough weight to begin to coun-ter-balance executive management.

Previously, we have shown, how corporate governance got its break-through in the first half of the 1990s in the USA, followed by the UK a few years later, and how it had become a hot topic as well as an area of reform in many other countries in the late 1990s. Let us now review some of the key events of the 1990s to see what the implications are for ownership and corporate governance in the longer perspective.

THE 1990s – A DECADE OF PARADIGMATIC CHANGE

The start of the 1990s was marked by the bursting of the world economy bubble, due to the inflationary and other economic excesses of the 1980s. Property values plunged and left huge voids on the asset side of many banks and financial institutions. The USA experienced this first, followed by a succession of other countries. Some countries confronted this crisis promptly and resolutely. In others appropriate measures have been a long time coming, notably in Japan, where much dragging of feet is still impeding a healthy recovery.

The deep recession that followed brought about unprecedented pressure on companies in all industries to call their operations into question. Harsh measures were applied, using new or re-invented rationalisation methods, audacious turn-around efforts by unsentimental, *take-no-prisoner* type CEOs for hire, and shareholder value demands from the stock market. We included a new set of buzzwords in our vocabulary: *delayering, business process engineering (BPR)* to mention a couple of examples.

A string of irreversible changes

However deep, the challenging situation facing companies and whole economies was not solely caused by the recession. There was no return to business-as-usual when the business cycle turned upwards after a deep trough. The 1990s saw one irreversible change after the other justifying the conclusion – if it ever needed to be justified – that, together they resulted in paradigmatic change. Doing business in the new millennium after what happened during the 1990s is radically different from the 1980s and earlier. Before summing up the new business logic and implications for corporate governance, we should remind ourselves of some of the structural changes that took place.

Fall of Communism forced market capitalism to show its hand.

With the collapse of Communism, the globalisation process, with its long historical roots, took off apace. The effects of this were not only that a number of earlier command economies of the Comecon system opened up for integration into the open world economy. In the short term they did not have much direct impact on world demand. However, the fall of Communism also completely changed the rules of the game in countries that traditionally considered themselves part of the open market economy.

The end of the cold war that followed the dismantling of the USSR, brought a lot of politically protected and obscure business arrangements out into the open. Market competition started to reach all corners of the world. The consequences of this were most clearly visible in countries which used to be semi-integrated into Comecon, e.g. Finland and India, as well as in countries of big Communist parties, e.g. Italy, but also in places where dictatorships had been protected by Western powers for geopolitical reasons.

The fall of Communism, finally, also started to change the politics of several western socialist parties. Privatisation of state owned companies took off, following the example set by Mrs. Thatcher in the 1980s. Whether this change of policy took place as an expression of a change of heart or as tactically justified *realpolitik* is debatable. Still, there is an active hard core of traditional socialists in power in some countries, e.g. in this author's own country, who have entrenched themselves defending old ideas, such as state control of the housing sector, government health care monopolies etc. At the time of writing (early 2000) there is a *chicken race* between Sweden and Albania to see which one will be last to start (!) privatising its former state telecommunications monopoly.

New technological breakthroughs generate unlimited opportunities: The new economy

What seems to have happened during the 1990s is that – in several technologies, e.g. in IT, telecommunications, and the bio-sciences – research and development, that had been going on for a long time, suddenly reached some kind of critical mass or breakthrough. Suddenly, a whole new world of eliminated constraints and new opportunities was opened up, through a combination of these technologies and some new application device.

- Obviously, the really *new, new thing* (referring to the title of a book about an outstanding Silicon Valley entrepreneur/inventor, Jim Clark, creator of Silicon Graphics and Netscape), for example[5] is the Internet. The basic concept originated more than 30 years ago. Important milestones can be identified in the early 1980s when the TCP/IP protocols were introduced making the Internet practically available for non-military use. Then a successive development of communication capacity, e.g. fibre optics, computer capacity, and PC market penetration, brought the Internet to a point where a real breakthrough was imminent. However, the missing link making the Internet available to a mass market had still not been attained. It came in 1995 with the introduction of Netscape, the first easy-to-use tool for Internet browsing.
- The Internet is a sweeping invention and innovation, for which it is difficult to find comparable analogies in the past. Peter F. Drucker makes the analogy with the railways – for e-commerce. But, however sweeping the consequences of e-commerce will be, it is just one application of the Internet.
- Another crucial application of the Internet is as a research tool, e.g. in the bio-sciences, where it is boosting research productivity to make quantum leaps possible. Global availability, thanks to the Internet, has been a prerequisite for the speed of progress in the global *HGP* project, initiated in

1989, for instance. (*HGP* stands for *Human Genome Project*, a large project mapping the human set of genes). The accelerating pace of development is illustrated by the foundation of Celera in 1997, a company stating its mission '..to become the definitive source of genomic and related medical and agricultural information.', and which in three years has completed a total mapping of the human genome. Celera seems to have outpaced HGP by a more skilful exploitation of the latest available information technologies.

• Other breakthroughs in the bio-sciences have also been prolific thanks to progress in several technological fields. One example is how the multiplied capacity to handle large amounts of data has made it possible to apply holistic research methodologies to studying living systems, instead of the traditional reductionist correlation methods. The precision in drugs engineering, for instance, will reach another order of magnitude, thanks to this.

Changing demographics is causing a tidal wave in stock markets.

This is something of a paradox. Demographic changes are foreseeable a long time in advance and they are not irreversible, although it takes time and is not easy to counteract. Suddenly during the 1990s (and for many, not least politicians, rather late in the 1990s) everyone became aware, from government planners to private individuals, that the population was getting older in most developed countries. Furthermore, in several developed countries, the population was decreasing. So, not only would the number and proportion of retired people increase. The total size of the workforce would be smaller, and its share of the population would suffer a double hit. The situation differs a lot between countries. Japan and Germany seem to be the worst hit, while the USA is significantly better off. One obvious consequence of this, that should have been realised earlier, is that the *pay-as-you-go* systems for pensions, social welfare etc will not be possible to sustain in the future. Governments are delaying with the instigation of reforms necessary to deal with this in several countries, as we have pointed out earlier. However, private individuals have taken action themselves. Pension savings-products have suddenly become a hot market in many countries and funds are flowing into stock markets in ever-increasing volumes. This is, of course, a tidal wave. When these eager savers will reach their retirement age, the tide is likely to turn.

EMERGING BUSINESS LOGIC OF THE NEW ECONOMY

The dramatic changes and *the new, new things* that appeared during the 1990s gave rise to a radically new business environment for companies. Some important features of the emerging, new business logic include:

- A single global economy is already a reality. The globalisation process has been going on for a long time. We are now beyond that in the sense that the Internet, not least, makes the world one global market. What separates reality from the virtual reality of a global market are impediments, mainly of a regulatory nature. What will happen to such regulations seems to be decided by the outcome of regulatory/political competition between countries, and between individual countries and international bodies. However, private individuals are no longer at the mercy of either. It has become extremely difficult to control cross-border trade, e.g. via the Internet. Savings funds are flowing out of Japan as long as actors on the Japanese investment market are not offered the same prerequisites as in alternative markets. Lack of political support is impossible to hide any longer, e.g. as the Swedish Government is experiencing when it is trying to prolong its temporary agreement with the EU concerning rather drastic limitations of private importation of wine and spirits. The EU commissioner in charge of the matter has received e-mails from thousands of Swedes telling a different story to that of the Swedish Government. National boundaries are eroding and people are developing loyalties to a host of other communities than the territorial nation.
- The Internet and the rich variety of emerging new technologies are likely to generate a huge, secular growth wave. More and more economists, analysts, and decision makers in high places witness about their belief in the new economy, that the Internet and other new technologies, together with global competition, have already boosted productivity. The proof is in the unprecedented length of the boom of the US economy, and particularly, that such high growth rates and employment levels have been possible with contained inflation. However, the new economy is not only a matter of enhanced productivity. There is also new growth, and new products and services are continuously being offered creating new value and additional employment.
- We seem to have entered a new *Gründerzeit* of start-ups galore and mushrooming entrepreneurship. While most students graduating from business schools and technical universities in the mid 1990s preferred future careers in large and well-established corporation, today their younger counterparts go for start-ups and new companies. There, they think, that they can make a difference from the start – and, in most cases it seems, they aim to become multi-millionaires before 30. That is encouraging and contributes to boosting this growth mechanism further by increasing overall risk taking in the economy.
- However, the new economy is not solely materialising in the form of start-ups. There are also vast opportunities to re-invent, to renew the old companies in a fundamental way by applying new technologies. In e-commerce so far, we have heard mostly of the early start-ups, Amazon.-

com and the like. Now, new acronyms are coming into use, e.g. *B2B*, denoting business-to-business e-commerce. The big automobile corporations have announced the setting up of a new mega site for all sub-suppliers. It sounds like a giant supply-chain rationalisation project. And, it probably is, but it might also spawn completely new ways of organizing the value creation process of offering cars to end customers. Very often a new technology keeps inventing itself and continues innovating its own value and use.

- We will have to manage an increasing flow of risk capital seeking promising investment opportunities. At least as long as the tidal wave, mentioned above, remains in full flow. Basically this will come from two sources, one primary and one secondary. The primary source is the one mentioned already, individual savers who want to safeguard their income and affluence when retired. The secondary source is generated by companies of *the old economy*, who do not see the new opportunities, or do not dare to invest in *the new economy*. As their business stagnates, if managed carefully, they will be able to free capital tied up in their traditional business.

- It seems that stock markets are also strongly indicating the arrival of a new logic. Market valuation of start-ups and IPOs are incomprehensible for all of us brought up in the old economy. It is a matter of mass-market psychology, many argue. However, the new trend was created when Netscape was listed in 1995. It was the first IPO that was launched without showing four consecutive quarters of net earnings, which were the established criteria at the time. Netscape was still in an early loss-making phase. At the point of taking the decision to go for the IPO, there were only professional market makers involved, and, a priori, no market hysteria. However, Netscape became an immediate success on the stock market and its share price went through the roof. After that the floodgates opened for the big hype. One start-up after the other has been launched, where the imagined logic seems to be: the bigger the loss, the higher the future value creation potential.

- One significant consequence of the hyped-up values of the companies of the new economy, is the enormous financial power by which these companies are endowed. Issuing new shares is a cheap way, at least in the short run, to finance big acquisitions. Cisco Systems, the networking equipment company and highest valued of all companies of the new economy, has used this high-powered tool to finance its rapid and successful growth, to mention one outstanding example. In fact, the merger boom of recent years differs significantly from that of the late 1980s. In 1998, 67 percent of all mergers were financed by shares compared to merely 7 percent ten years earlier (Fortune, January 11, 1999, referring to a study by J P Morgan). If the valuation superiority over companies of the old economy were to remain, the new economy companies would have the upper hand in future integration of the old and new economies. If this would be good or bad probably varies with the situation. However, it will certainly add future challenges to the function of ownership.

THE NEW ECONOMY, THE MORAL OF CORPORATE GOVERNANCE AND THE FUNCTION AND ROLE OF OWNERSHIP

It should be obvious that the new economy of mounting dynamics of ample opportunities for start-ups and fundamental renewal of old companies on the one hand, and the increasing supply of risk capital on the other, will create an unprecedented market for ownership. A huge and differentiated mediating function between these two supply sides – one of risk capital and the other of promising but uncertain investment projects, start-ups etc – will be called for.

Thus, the dynamics of the new economy further highlight the fundamental moral of the corporate governance movement: the indispensable function and role of conscientious, competent, and value creation focused owners.

This is not only essential in the micro perspective – for the viability and success of the individual company or the small shareholders in that company. It is of fundamental importance to the whole market economy.

Chandler (1990) suggests that the *modern corporation* is perhaps the most important social innovation of the twentieth century. He contends that this innovation has made it possible to exploit global advantages of *scale and scope*. (The *modern corporation* does not necessarily have to be a mega corporation to exploit global *scale and scope*. The size needed depends on the size of the global market segment.)

Furthermore, this social invention, the greatest of the twentieth century, according to Chandler, in combination with one of the greatest social inventions of the nineteenth century – the joint-stock company as a well defined legal entity, extending the scope for risk-taking by separating private capital and payment liability from the legal entity, the company[6] – represents an enormously powerful mechanism for economic growth. Its potential is taking on unprecedented proportions with the emergence of a globalised and liquid risk capital market channelling funds to new start-ups as well as to the renewal of old companies no matter where the source is and where the investment target happens to be located.

It is obvious how vital it is for this important institution, or systems of institutions, to work well. The corporate governance movement can be seen as a reaction to the shortcomings in the workings of this system of institutions, imperfections in how the accountability aspect as well as how the prosperity, or value creation, aspect were cared for.

However, it is even more important, now that the corporate governance agenda also includes pro-active ideas and measures on how to enhance accountability and value creation in situations where not all the mistakes have been made. After all, we are only at the beginning of the new economy.

Before discussing the implications of this for the function and role of ownership further, we should benefit from a review of what ownership is all about, and what competence is required to succeed as an active owner. The next section of the book, *Part II. Ownership Makes A Difference*, will offer an opportunity to learn from a successful owner – with almost 150 years of experience of earlier *new economies*, several generations of start-ups, and repeated rounds of renewals of old companies – the Wallenberg sphere of Sweden.

PART II

Ownership Makes a Difference

A Case Study of the Wallenberg Sphere

Ownership Makes a Difference

10

PURPOSE AND CONTENT OF THIS CHAPTER

The purpose of Part II (Chapters 10 and 11 as well as Appendix 3) is to explore and illustrate what owner value creation is all about and what kind of competence is required to become successful in the role of being an active owner. Since a good starting point for such a journey of discovery must be proven success in real life, this study will focus on one such case, namely what will be referred to as the Wallenberg sphere of Sweden. Swedish industry is dominated by a few, large multinational corporations – ABB, Ericsson, Electrolux, StoraEnso, Volvo etc. Many of these successful companies are part of the Wallenberg sphere and have long historical links to it. Representatives of the Wallenberg dynasty have made significant contributions and played leading roles as active owners of these companies. The fifth generation of this dynasty, which dates back to the middle of the 19th century when their great great grandfather started a bank, Stockholms Enskilda Bank,[1] has just taken leading positions in this sphere.

What lies behind the Wallenberg success, which has been admired and envied, not only in Swedish industry but also internationally, as something unique? What does the Wallenberg sphere's distinctive ownership skills consist of?

Illustration of important aspects of owner competence

This study will not have the whole answer to these questions. It would take a very detailed analysis, if indeed it were at all possible. The aim of this presentation is more limited – it illustrates some important aspects of owner competence as a basis for our continuing analysis of the role of ownership and the kind of competence it requires. The aim is further facilitated by the fact that the Wallenberg sphere as a whole, or member companies of the group, have been studied by several prominent economic historians and researchers for example, Christer Danielsson, Torsten Gårdlund, Olle Gasslander, Jan Glete, Håkan Lindgren and Ulf Olsson.[2] This together with what the author has been able to observe and capture in conversations with representatives of the group and with outsiders – critics as well as admirers and neutral assessors – makes it possible to try and structure and exemplify the distinctive Wallenberg ownership skills. To this end it is important to identify patterns of success and the critical factors which can be distinguished therein, as well as examples of failure where they have entered into business outside their own field of competence.

Summary of contents

This chapter will start by reviewing the scope and financial success of the Wallenberg sphere. Its historical development will be analysed from the perspective of its active ownership in order to identify patterns of success and the key factors of competence explaining its financial success. A separate appendix includes additional background data on the historical roots of the Wallenberg sphere, some critical events that have formed its development as well as examples of how its active ownership has been exercised in a couple of its strategic holdings. The appendix, which should be useful to read in parallel with this chapter, starts with a brief review of the portfolio of Investor and its core holdings.

The next chapter will give a brief review of the present situation and key challenges as well as how they are being dealt with by those at the helm today. First of all, by Percy Barnevik chairman and Marcus Wallenberg CEO, respectively, of Investor, the investment company and key active owner instrument of the Wallenberg sphere, and by Jacob Wallenberg, cousin of Marcus and the same age, chairman of SEB, the former family bank, and vice chairman of Investor.

Conclusion in two steps

The conclusion of the analysis of the success of the Wallenberg sphere will be summed up in two steps. The first (Figure 10.1) constitutes what can be called the core competence elements of the success formula of the Wallenberg sphere's active ownership. In a second step at the end of this chapter, another vital part will be added (Figure 10.5) to present the complete concept of the sphere's success formula or *distinctive competence of active ownership* of the Wallenberg sphere.

INTRODUCTION OF THE WALLENBERG SPHERE AND DYNASTY

In the business world and in the community of large multinational corporations Sweden stands out by being over-represented by its number of companies on the Fortune 500 list (size by revenue) as well as on the FT (Financial Times) 500 list (size by market capitalisation) – especially if one includes corporations which today are registered elsewhere but with a Swedish origin

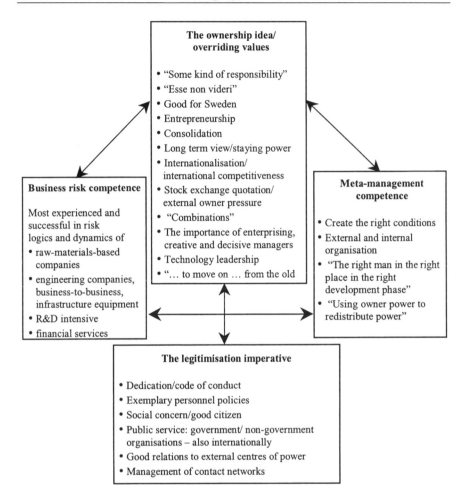

Figure 10.1 Core competence elements in the active owner value-creation success formula of the Wallenberg sphere.

(e.g. ABB). The first list includes eight such companies and the second list ten. On a per capita basis, Sweden in these respects ranks number 8 and 5, respectively. Among smaller nations only Switzerland and Holland have larger corporations on a relative basis.

Some of these companies are household names, e.g. Electrolux, Ericsson, Volvo, while others are better known in the business-to-business world, e.g. ABB, Astra(Zeneca) and Stora Enso. In addition to the top 500 companies there are several Swedish companies which are global or top ranking in their respective fields, e.g. Atlas Copco, Sandvik, SKF, SAAB and Scania.

Wallenberg – a name of international fame

As well-known as these companies are in the international business community there is also another Swedish name – The Wallenbergs. The target of frequent cover stories in leading business magazines (e.g. Business Week, European Edition/October 20, 1997, and the Institutional Investor of October 1999) and less spectacular articles there is also an awareness that many of the leading Swedish corporations are part of what is often referred to as the Wallenberg sphere of interest. In fact, out of the total market capitalisation of companies listed on the Stockholm Stock Exchange, the Wallenberg sphere has a decisive influence in companies accounting for some 50 percent of that value (end of 1999). So, the Wallenberg sphere should be able to take some of the credit for the finding of a recent study, namely that Sweden was the most successful stock market of the 20th century.[3]

A dynasty of five generations

> My own introduction into the sphere and its affairs happened early and spontaneously. I took an interest in these matters at an early age, listening to and discussing with my father (who died when Marcus Wallenberg was 15). My grandfather (Marcus Wallenberg, Jr. 1899–1982) was also a teacher from my early youth. Being with him was always a way to get acquainted to the sphere. Whatever he did outside the office – sailing, hunting, or whenever I had a chance to be with him – my grandfather always lived with the sphere and its current issues. There were always key people from the sphere companies taking part in these sailing trips, hunting parties etc. Thus, I was – from my boyhood years and onwards – in the midst of a constant flush of information about the sphere.
>
> *Marcus Wallenberg, CEO of Investor*[4]

A conspicuous theme of recent cover stories and media attention has been the fact that the fifth generation of the Wallenberg family has recently started to take leading positions within the sphere – the two cousins, Jacob Wallenberg as chairman of SEB (originally the family bank, founded in 1856 and the first of the formidable Wallenberg achievements) and Marcus Wallenberg as CEO of Investor, the investment company that successively has become the leading owner instrument of the whole sphere. Thus, the Wallenbergs are admired widely for their achievements as owners of leading Swedish corporations, their extensive global network of business partners and contacts as well as for their staying power, now spanning over five generations. Table 10.1 includes the succession of key figure-heads over these five generations and their formal roles in the Wallenberg sphere (in Enskilda/S E-Banken[5]/SEB and Investor, respectively). The quotation above gives a hint

Table 10.1 Five generations of the Wallenberg dynasty and sphere

		Formal position
1.	A.O. Wallenberg (AOW) 1816–1886	CEO of Enskilda 1856–86
2a.	K.A. Wallenberg (KAW) 1853–1938 (son of AOW)	CEO of Enskilda 1886–1911 Chairman of Enskilda 1911–1938
2b.	Marcus Wallenberg, Sr. (MW Sr.) 1864–1943) (son of AOW, half-brother of KAW)	CEO of Enskilda 1911–1920 Chairman of Enskilda 1938–1943
3a.	Jacob Wallenberg (JW) 1892–1980 (son of MW Sr.)	CEO of Enskilda 1927–1946 Chairman of Enskilda 1949–1969 Chairman of Investor and Providentia 1946–1978
3b.	Marcus Wallenberg Jr. (MW) 1899–1982 (son of MW Sr.)	CEO of Enskilda 1946–1958 Chairman of Enskilda 1969–1971/ and of S E-Banken 1972–1976 Chairman of Investor 1978–1982
4a.	Marc Wallenberg (Marc W) 1924–1971 (son of MW)	CEO of Enskilda 1958–1971
4b.	Peter Wallenberg (PW) 1926– (son of MW)	Chairman of Investor 1982–1997 Honorary chairman of Investor 1997–
5a.	Marcus Wallenberg 1956– (son of Marc W)	CEO of Investor 1999–
5b.	Jacob Wallenberg 1956– (son of PW)	Chairman of SEB 1997–

about how the traditions and responsibilities of the Wallenberg sphere were handed down from one generation to the next. This ability as well as a set of other key features and strengths of the Wallenberg sphere will be discussed in-depth later in this chapter.

The fifth generation still has to prove itself

Of course, the success of the fifth generation is still an open issue since the young Wallenbergs have only recently taken over and the fourth generation, Peter Wallenberg, the father and uncle of Jacob and Marcus, respectively, is still active first of all as chairman of the Wallenberg foundations, the holder and administrator of earlier family fortunes and also as honorary chairman of Investor and the undisputed head of the family. Moreover, the Investor share has under-performed since mid 1998, lagging far behind the general index of the Stockholm Stock Exchange. The so-called investment company discount (for an explanation of this phenomenon, see note 4, page 167) is currently (early 2000) much higher than it has been for many years – oscillating around 35 percent.

Extraordinary performance

Historically, however, the performance has been extraordinary. One Swedish krona invested in Investor at its start in 1916 has multiplied to SEK 3500 by the end of 1999 which outperforms the general index of the Stockholm Stock Exchange by more than a factor of three. Also, in the last 20 years, annual returns have exceeded the general index of the Stockholm Stock Exchange by a couple of percentage points. This modest outperformance is caused by developments during 1998 and 1999, in particular. Investor's share price sank by one percent in 1998 due to an increase in the investment company discount. In 1999 although Investor's market capitalisation increased by some quite remarkable 30 percent, the extremely bullish Stockholm Stock Exchange doubled that. The investment company discount increased further during 1999. This recent, relatively poor performance also places Investor a few percentage points behind another legendary investor, Warren Buffett and his Berkshire Hathaway during the same period in terms of average annual performance.

Spectacular international growth of industrial holdings

This quite remarkable financial performance historically has been paralleled by the spectacular growth of the Wallenberg sphere companies.

Figure 10.2 has been taken from one[6] of several studies of the sphere made by distinguished Swedish scholars of economic history. It shows the number of employees in the companies which constitute the ten biggest Wallenberg holdings, at four different times from the mid-1920s to 1990. Thus defined, the number of employees in the sphere has therefore increased thirty-six fold during these 65 years, all employed by well-known international companies.

And even more spectacular growth of value

The growth of managed assets has been even more spectacular as shown in Figure 10.3. The three years shown have been selected to reflect the total scope of the Wallenberg sphere. At the end of the turbulent 1920s almost all major holdings, except Enskilda (the family bank) were concentrated in the portfolio of Investor. Earlier some of them were also owned by the bank. During a long period between 1929 and 1992, the Wallenberg sphere used several investment and holding companies to control the whole group. In 1992 and 1994 a restructuring took place where all holdings were concentrated in Investor. The

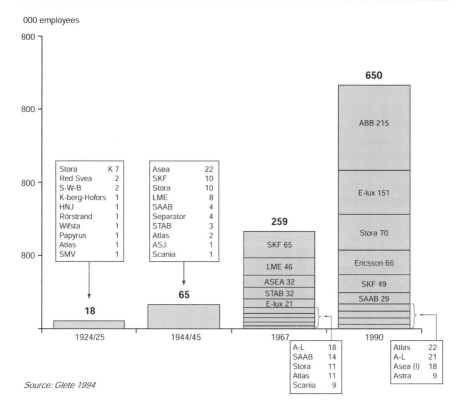

000 employees

Figure 10.2 The Wallenberg sphere, 1924–1990: number of employees (in thousands) in the ten biggest holdings.

balance sheet at the end of 1998 is the last one before Investor and the Wallenberg sphere enter a new phase of intensive restructuring under new management. Percy Barnevik became chairman in 1997 and Marcus Wallenberg CEO in 1999 replacing Peter Wallenberg and Claes Dahlbäck, respectively.

THE WALLENBERG SPHERE – WHAT IS IT?

> ... the term *Wallenberg sphere* refers to a group of firms in which the Wallenberg family has exercised some form of active ownership.[7]

Professor Lindgren, economic historian at the Stockholm School of Economics, defines this commonly used term in his monography of Investor, the Wallenberg dominated investment company. It is appropriate to talk about a sphere (of influence) rather than a group since the Wallenberg sphere is kept together not by a mostly formal owner majority but by a variety of means –

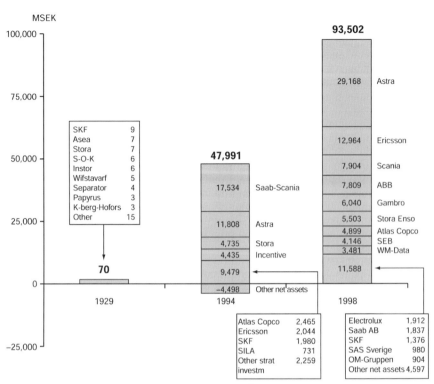

MSEK

1929	**1994: 47,991**	**1998: 93,502**	

1929 portfolio:
SKF	9
Asea	7
Stora	7
S-O-K	6
Instor	6
Wifstavarf	5
Separator	4
Papyrus	3
K-berg-Hofors	3
Other	15

70

1994 portfolio:
17,534	Saab-Scania
11,808	Astra
4,735	Stora
4,435	Incentive
9,479	
−4,498	Other net assets

Atlas Copco	2,465
Ericsson	2,044
SKF	1,980
SILA	731
Other strat investm	2,259

1998 portfolio:
29,168	Astra
12,964	Ericsson
7,904	Scania
7,809	ABB
6,040	Gambro
5,503	Stora Enso
4,899	Atlas Copco
4,146	SEB
3,481	WM-Data
11,588	

Electrolux	1,912
Saab AB	1,837
SKF	1,376
SAS Sverige	980
OM-Gruppen	904
Other net assets	4,597

Source: Lindgren 1994, Annual reports of Investor AB

Figure 10.3   Investor's share portfolio 1929–1998.

pyramid constructions, differentiated voting rights as well as by tradition and competence. However, the actual ownership power is considerable and based in a set of foundations and beneficiary funds, which have been instigated by earlier generations and their endowments. The current ownership structure, including major holdings in the portfolio of Investor is as follows (Figure 10.4).

FOUR DIMENSIONS OF THE WALLENBERG SYSTEM FOR SUCCESS

The analysis of the Wallenberg system for success will start by a review of the four competence elements presented in Figure 10.1.

What can we learn from the review of the historical development of the Wallenberg sphere? What are the critical factors explaining the undisputable successes the sphere has fostered?

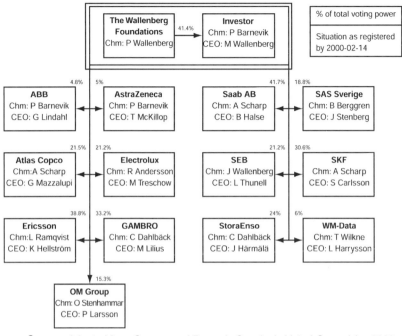

Source: *Adapted from Owners and Power in Sweden's Listed Companies 2000 by Sundin, Anneli and Sundqvist, Sven-Ivan*

Figure 10.4 The Wallenberg sphere of core holdings[8]

To analyse these questions further it will be useful to break them down to four dimensions, the concluding answers to which are summarised in Figure 10.1.

- Are there certain types of business where the sphere has been more successful? Has a pattern of specialisation emerged? In that case – what patterns can we distinguish, what historical driving forces explain them, and what characterise these businesses?
- How has the sphere organised and managed its relations with the individual companies? What characterise the interventions of the sphere representatives? In other words, how does its corporate governance system look like and what experience explains it?
- What has been the external relations policy of the sphere? How has it legitimised itself in the business community in Sweden as well as internationally – and in society at large? How has it managed its various stakeholders?
- What is the philosophy behind the formation of the sphere? What are the

values that have been guiding the actions taken? Could one distinguish a basic owner idea that has propelled and directed all the sphere's energetic efforts?

Business specialisation and competence

If we look at Investor's current portfolio of strategic holdings, the companies dating back to before World War II can be sorted into three basic categories:

- Engineering industry companies: Scania (heavy trucks), ABB, Atlas Copco, SKF and Saab AB.
- Raw material based/forest products: Stora Enso.
- Financial services: SEB.

Engineering industry companies

Historically the first category included several additional, and what was then regarded as strategic holdings, e.g. Alfa-Laval. This company was divested during the financial squeeze which Investor and the sphere faced in the early 1990s. The appendix includes a review of the history of active ownership in three of the core holdings in this category: ABB (Asea), Saab, and Scania (for some 25 years the latter two formed one group, Saab-Scania). In the past, Ericsson was also regarded as a mechanical engineering company. However, the technological revolution that Ericsson itself has been a key force in furthering has justified a re-categorisation of that company.

Several raw material-based companies became one pulp and paper holding

The raw material-based category today only includes one strategic holding, Stora Enso, entirely focused on forest products, pulp and paper. This company is the current result of a long transformation and specialisation process on the Swedish side where Stora became the restructuring vehicle of the Wallenberg sphere. Stora, earlier called Stora Kopparbergs Bergslags AB[9], owned several steel mills which were all divested in the 1970s. In the forest products/pulp and paper industry the Wallenberg sphere controlled several other, separately managed companies. A few years before MW's death in 1982 these had been restructured into two groups, namely Papyrus which acquired three other sphere companies Nymölla, Hylte, Kopparfors, as well as Stora which acquired Bergvik and Ala. Subsequently, Stora, with PW as chairman and Bo Berggren as CEO, merged not only the Stora and

Papyrus Groups but also restructured the entire Swedish and core parts of the European pulp and paper industry as well. Stora acquired the Billerud-Uddeholm Group and the largest German company, Feldmühle. These actions triggered further industry restructuring both in Sweden and in the rest of Europe (where the major Nordic companies – one Swedish/Finnish (Stora Enso), two Finnish, three Swedish and one Norwegian – currently dominate the entire European pulp and paper industry with the exception of a few of other major players, e.g. AWA, Jefferson Smurfit and International Paper.

When this book is being finished (early 2000), Stora Enso is in the process of acquiring its first, major US company, Consolidated Paper, further enhancing its leading position in the global pulp and paper industry.

Banking – the origin of all categories

The third category, financial services, is more or less self evident through Enskilda, the origin of it all. However, it should be mentioned that a lot of new initiatives in financial services were started within Enskilda, later becoming independently managed companies, e.g. Eurocard. When S E-Banken was a non-strategic interest of the Wallenberg sphere (after MW's death and until the banking crisis in the early 1990s) Investor was seriously considering going into investment banking and the OM company – which claims to be the first for-profit stock exchange in the world and which also acquired the Stockholm Stock Exchange in 1998 – was started during this period. OM introduced derivatives on the Swedish market and became very successful. Later it has developed other types of exchanges, based on its own technology, e.g. for electrical power where OM is expanding internationally.

In the beginning of this year (2000), OM announced a new pioneering initiative: direct cross border trade of stocks on line. The new company, Jiway, is a joint venture with Morgan Stanley Dean Witter, the US investment bank and financial services firm.

Successive specialisation

All three categories reflect the early formative period of the sphere when Enskilda was at the centre of Swedish industrialisation. It was the natural resource based companies and the mechanical engineering industries that were driving industrialisation by also providing competitive and valued products on the export markets. Well-functioning financial services, not least with institutions having access to foreign capital markets, were an important prerequisite for the whole industrialisation process.

Although many of the present strategic holdings originated in this early phase of development that is not the whole story. They also represent a successive owner specialisation by the Wallenberg sphere. All core holdings today are international corporations addressing global markets. In the early phases of development the sphere had substantial holdings in companies primarily addressing the domestic market, e.g. infrastructure companies in transportation such as railway operators as well as retail operations. Today, only SAS, which was created to provide international flight connections, remains. The first SAS flight took place in 1946 between Stockholm and New York. Now, although officially presented as a strategic holding, it can be argued – pre-empting a discussion of future issues in the next chapter – that in reality it is a financial investment awaiting future restructuring and value creation opportunities. SAS is operated as a consortium under one management in which three national holding companies – owned 50/50 by each government and private interests – have a stake: the Swedish 3/7 and the Danish and Norwegian ones has 2/7 each. Since the Wallenberg sphere is the largest private owner of the Swedish holding company and since SAS was initiated by MW the active ownership of SAS has traditionally been exercised by the Wallenberg sphere. As long as both international and domestic air traffic were heavily regulated it was possible to do what was needed as an active owner. It was even a strength to be backed up by the Scandinavian national governments in certain matters. Now, the present owner structure is both obsolete and obstructive. SAS has joined the Star Alliance – another consortium. As deregulation advances further, SAS would need to be incorporated as one entity and floated on the stock exchange to be able to take part in further international restructuring. It is unlikely that the Wallenberg sphere would then remain as owner but would plan for an elegant exit. Originally, however, SAS fitted the Wallenberg sphere and it represented renewal, i.e. moving away from the railway technology towards the modern and internationally oriented aviation technology.

International competitiveness

Thus, an early common characteristic, with the exceptions mentioned above, of strategic holdings was international focus and competitiveness: exports was the natural start, but followed by internationalisation quite early on in most companies. Stora Enso, Ericsson, and the engineering companies – ABB, Atlas Copco, Scania, and SKF – are all currently in the top league of their global markets, not least because of early internationalisation.

The raw materials based companies – now concentrated in Stora Enso – mark the very first industry experience of the sphere. Thus, the international focus was a key feature from the very outset. In his first banking operation in Sundsvall that preceded the foundation of Enskilda in 1856, AOW financed the export trade of forest and steel products. After Enskilda was established the first industrial holding was Hofors ('acquired' when the company went bankrupt and Enskilda had its shares as collateral for loans), a traditional 'bruk' (land holding with forests, agricultural land, hydropower potential etc) where the sphere became involved in one of its first major industrial investments – in pulp production for export markets.

Capital intensive and financially demanding business

Few industries require more long-term commitment than the forest based industry, especially in the Nordic countries where trees are cycled over a period of 60–100 years. What is also typical is the high capital intensity of processing investments, especially in pulp and paper. In addition, considering that the timing of such investments is critical for success and that profitability can vary dramatically over the business cycle it is obvious that a company in this industry must have financial resilience and its owners must be able to bring financial clout to the table.

Moreover, the mechanical engineering companies also comprise demanding financial issues. Their typical markets of business-to-business, large infrastructure and industry investment projects have complex financial aspects. Such large investment projects will not happen in the first place unless the long-term financing is solved and someone is willing to absorb the risks involved. Secondly, there is the matter of short-term financing of the construction and commissioning phases. Thirdly, there is the cash management issue where traditionally advance payments are made that generate a positive cash flow for the supplier.

Other strategic holdings – what business competence?

What about strategic holdings falling outside of the three main types? Do they also represent another business logic requiring different types of business competence? Such holdings include:

- Pharmaceuticals/Health Care: Astra(Zeneca), Gambro.
- Engineering: Electrolux.
- IT/Telecoms: Ericsson, WM-data.

Ericsson, as mentioned earlier, has made a remarkable transition from a mechanical engineering/traditional telecoms company to global leadership in digital and mobile telephony. Thus, it is one of the best examples and proofs of the renewal competence of the Wallenberg sphere. Several aspects of this will be discussed later. WM-data, is a fairly recent core holding and represents one of Investor's most recent renewal effort, which will be discussed later.

Electrolux reveals the sphere's strength and weakness

Electrolux is another matter, since its origin in the sphere dates back to the 1950s. Electrolux's business is dominated by consumer capital goods – white and brown goods, household vacuum cleaners etc, outdoor products such as lawn mowers etc. There are some business-to-business products, e.g. industrial kitchen equipment, chain saws for professional use etc but they are relatively small in the overall picture. Thus, Electrolux falls outside the *business logic mainstream* of the Wallenberg sphere. However, there are two basic explanations as to why Electrolux has remained in the sphere, namely:

ASEA (now ABB) diversified early into all kinds of electrical household appliances with mixed success. When an opportunity to acquire Electrolux appeared in the late 1950s MW did not hesitate to take this opportunity arguing that Electrolux was needed to co-ordinate all the ASEA companies in this field.[10] The ambition of MW and the Wallenberg sphere seems to have been to get ASEA to focus on power equipment, emerging industrial automation, process control focus, and the business-to-business market. Thus, this master move was done in the best tradition of its active ownership, highlighting its industry restructuring competence.

Electrolux had a very consumer-oriented culture at this time – its growth success had, to a large extent, been based on direct sales of vacuum cleaners to housewives by *knocking on doors*. Another early success product was refrigerators based on a Swedish invention in the early 1920s. -By acquiring Electrolux, the Wallenberg sphere got competence and critical mass to 'co-ordinate ASEA's companies' in this field.

The second reason is that Electrolux – especially during the 1970s and 1980s –was driven by an ambition to achieve a leading global position through acquisitions and industry restructuring. Thus Electrolux was applying a strategy where the financial skills and the extensive international network of the Wallenberg sphere were key success factors supporting an extremely well-fitted and dynamic executive management which will be discussed later.

However, when this skilfully engineered expansion and restructuring phase was over, the shortcomings of the Wallenberg sphere as regards consumer products and markets were once again revealed. Electrolux' performance stagnated during most of the 1990s and has improved only recently.

Pharmaceuticals and health care – a demonstration of renewal and perseverance

The two strategic holdings in pharmaceuticals and health care, Astra(Zeneca) and Gambro have different origins but common threads of active ownership – renewal and perseverance. Astra was already acquired in the mid 1920s as a private venture capital initiative by JW and a handful of his business partners. At that time Astra was still a loss-making small subsidiary of the state wine and spirits monopoly. Astra did not get its first real break-through until 1948 when Xylocain, a dental anaesthetic, was launched. Astra was listed on the Stockholm Stock Exchange in the mid-1950s when it also became a strategic holding of Investor. Astra at that time represented the new spectacularly growing chemical industry. Astra also diversified outside pharmaceuticals in the 1950s and 1960s both through acquisitions of several companies and through R&D projects. In addition to attractive opportunities in the chemicals market, there were also political risks driving this diversi-fication. The Swedish leftist government at the time harboured plans to nationalise the pharmaceutical industry. Astra's diversification strategy went on until 1977 when a refocusing on pharmaceuticals took place.

A success called Losec

The decision to turn *back to basics* was not taken only because of a relaxed nationalisation threat. Pharmaceutical research in one of Astra's subsidi-aries, Gothenburg-based Astra Hässle AB, had started to generate some very interesting new drugs. A new methodology and competence base for research and development, introduced in the late 1950s and early 1960s, began to generate interesting products already in the 1960s, but its first market success occurred in the early 1970s, Seloken, a cardiac drug. Astra Hässle had started an elaborate collaboration with university clinics which also led to a refocus of pharmaceutical R&D. Instead of only being based on its chemistry competence, the biological mechanisms of the human body became the new focus in the early 1960s. In retrospect it may be of some interest to note that ICI's pharmaceuticals, later to be spun off renamed Zeneca and merged with Astra, chose the same focus about the same time. However, ICI managed to get its first product launched, based on this focus, some 18 months before Astra Hässle in 1966.

What was to become the formidable success of Losec (this brand name is an abbreviation of *low sec*retion), the ulcer treatment drug, started as a devel-opment project based on the same paradigm in the mid-1960s. It took more than twenty years to reach market launch in 1988. However, when Astra decided to concentrate on pharmaceuticals in 1977, the Losec project was a close down candidate. The project had encountered repeated difficulties but survived thanks to one man, in particular, the now legendary R&D chief of Astra Hässle, Ivan Östholm. Recruited in the mid-1950s, he built up Astra Hässle's new R&D department, introduced the new methodology and research focus. He initiated, in addition to a host of other projects, the Losec project and – above all – he repeatedly rescued and protected the

Losec project until his retirement in 1983. In 1977, the new Astra CEO at the time offered Dr. Östholm early retirement which would have eliminated all serious resistance to close the project, but Dr. Östholm simply turned down the very generous pre-retirement terms that he was offered.

Thanks to Dr. Östholm's entrepreneurial spirit and stubbornness the Losec project overcame all difficulties – including management's distrust – which no less than five times confronted the project with the risk of termination. At the same time this also tells something about what kind of organisational principles that were applied within the Wallenberg sphere. This will be discussed further in a following section of this chapter covering that aspect.[11]

As a consequence of Losec becoming the world's best selling drug, Astra's value increased rapidly and became Investor's heaviest holding ever (until the fourth quarter of 1999 when Ericsson's market capitalisation outperformed all other core holdings in Investor's portfolio), accounting for more than 40 percent of the total portfolio in the early 1990s.

Gambro/Incentive – a double loop renewal

Gambro, which originally introduced the artificial kidney, a Swedish innovation, has now broadened its range of medical equipment but its foremost growth area is in a variety of health services. Its main business in health services is a chain of dialysis clinics where Gambro is number two after global leader Fresenius, the German Group. Gambro is quite new in the Investor portfolio and was the final outcome of a complete restructuring of the Incentive Group. In that way it can be argued that Gambro is an expression of 'double loop' renewal on the part of the Wallenberg sphere. In the 1960s, Incentive was initiated by MW to function as a kind of venture capital/development company which was supposed 'to participate in companies with an intrinsic growth potential and facilitate their further development'.[12] To some extent this idea was practised – including also investments in medical equipment and other new technology companies – but successively Incentive became a kind of 'assembly point' for companies that didn't fit anywhere else in the Wallenberg sphere. This character was further emphasised when Incentive picked up what was called 'rest-ASEA', the part of the ASEA Group that was not merged with Brown Boveri, to become ABB. After an intensive restructuring of the Incentive group during the early 1990s all but one of its diverse holdings were divested or listed as independent companies. A new focus was decided upon – medical technology and health care – where the recently acquired Gambro (as part of the Cardo Group, earlier controlled by Volvo) was to become the nucleus for future growth and also the new name of the Group. Thus, a second loop of renewal was completed and the Wallenberg sphere had entered a new type of business.

Health care – proven success and new challenge

Astra (Zeneca) has been in the Wallenberg sphere for a long time, first privately owned by JW (and other private partners) and since the mid-1950s as part of Investor's portfolio, but has remained a solitary case in a sphere dominated by mechanical engineering and raw materials-based companies. At the same time, there are similar features of business logics that explain Astra's success as those of, for example ABB, Ericsson and Atlas Copco: heavy R&D – although the element of uncontrollable chance is quite specific to medical R&D – and technological renewal as well as patience and perseverance to let entrepreneurial processes (e g as in the case of Losec) come to fruition.

Gambro fits well into this pattern, at least as regards its medical equipment business. Health care services is more of a new challenge. However, Gambro shares the ambition to grow in service business with many of the other mechanical engineering companies. Their growth opportunities are to a large extent in the market for business-to-business services. This has been a priority growth direction of ABB for a long time. Atlas Copco, to take another example, has recently made major acquisitions to support such growth.

Summary of business specialisation and competence

Historically the Wallenberg sphere has successively focused on and been most successful in fostering successes and creating value in business characterised by the following features. As a corollary, these also reflect the active ownership competence profile of the sphere.

- Business-to-business, infrastructure and industrial investments' markets.
- International/global competition.
- Raw material processing, horizontal and vertical integration.
- Technology dependent, major R&D investments for renewal and growth.
- Capital intensity.
- Project financing/overall financial ingenuity and close collaboration bank/company.

The Wallenberg sphere and its individual holdings: the meta-management relation

First the captain...

Prior to KAW luring his younger brother away from his legal career to start working in the bank MW Sr. sent a letter (1887) with a recommendation about what should be done about the problematic Hofors company. His first recommendation was to replace the chief executive since that person was 'an impediment to our economic progress'. This marked the beginning of what was to become a key feature of the type of active ownership of the Wallenberg sphere, that particularly MW Sr., and his son MW and his grandson PW, exercised in its individual holdings. The key thing was to have good management and most importantly, a chief executive who was a driving force, competent, trustworthy and fitted the specific situation. MW Sr. emphasised particularly a certain quality of what he thought was necessary to make a chief executive successful. The expression he used for this could be translated to 'constructive acquisitiveness'[13] by which he meant a strong thrust to develop and grow a business profitably. Several candidates were rejected and already employed chief executives were replaced for lack of this quality. It was not the ambition or the task of the owners to try to micromanage a specific company. Instead they wanted to manage through managers to apply what in this book is called *meta-management*.

Thus, the first checkpoint was always the chief executive – to find the right man for the job. Nurturing strong naval traditions within the family, a typical expression to denote this wisdom was: 'First the captain and then the ship'. There are numerous examples of the efforts spent to find the right person to be chief executive, e.g. when Sigfrid Edström finally was persuaded to take on the turn-around candidate ASEA in the early 1900s after long negotiations (see appendix!). When Percy Barnevik was selected for the same job in 1980 it was also only after quite a diligent search process. Following in the tradition of his father, MW, in particular, developed profound skills in achieving a fit between the development situation of a company on the one hand and the competence profile and personality of a chief executive on the other. An illustrative case is MW's long involvement in Ericsson (director of the board from 1932, vice chairman 1946, chairman 1952–76) and his instrumental role in appointing new CEOs to fit the situation each time. Table 10.2 of CEO successions at Ericsson makes this point clear.

As can be seen, MW's tradition of finding well-fitting CEOs continued after his death in 1982. Lars Ramqvist who was CEO between 1990 and 1997 seems to have been the right choice to maintain and further enhance Ericsson's global leadership in mobile telephony.

Close contact without interference

Selecting and replacing CEOs to fit the development situation and challenges of a corporation is one thing. Quite another is the on-going relation between the Wallenberg sphere as active owner and the CEO of a company. A lot has been written and witnessed about both MW Sr. and MW in this respect. CEOs who have worked under MW give a similar picture with three features in particular:

Table 10.2 CEO successions at Ericsson - the man to fit the situation

Year	Key issue	CEO	Key strengths
1932	Restructuring after the Kreuger crash	Holm	Rationaliser, profit improvement expert
World War II	Only domestic market accessible	Ericsson	Recruited from Swedish Telecom - basically the only customer
1946–1963	Re-internationalisation, global exploitation of a superior electro-mechanical switch	Åberg	Long career within Ericsson's international sales organisation
1964–77	Achieving technology breakthrough of digital switching (AXE)	Lundwall[a]	Supertechnician of new telecoms technologies
1977–90	Complete breakthrough and commercialisation of AXE	Svedberg	Earlier project manager of AXE
1990–97	Commercial breakthrough and global leadership in mobile telephony	Ramqvist	Earlier head of mobile telephony division

[a] Became chairman after MW.

- Hard and tough performance pressure – carried out and followed-up in an intensive on-going dialogue. The telephone was his favourite instrument for frequent contacts. The following quotation probably expresses the experience of many CEOs who worked under MW. 'Dodde's (Dodde was a pet name used by people in his closest circle of associates) knowledge of Papyrus was not limited to the overall structure of the company. He was thoroughly knowledgeable of the details. He knew by what speed the various paper machines operated, he knew the purchase prices of ground wood pulp, as well as the name of the chief controller's next man and the fill-up level of the water reservoir of the company's hydro power station. (As CEO), it was a matter of knowing all such details and to come up with an answer when Dodde was on the phone. There he was often. Morning and night. Weekdays and Sundays. He wanted to keep himself informed. In addition, he wanted to find out if the CEO was as alert as Dodde thought he ought to be.'[14]
- 'Borderless' collection of information from external sources as well as internally from the company and not only through the CEO. MW knew people at many levels of the organisation. He spontaneously and easily communicated with white collar as well as blue collar people when he

walked around the premises of a company he visited. This was one of his ways of always keeping himself extremely well informed and he had a good memory, also for details. At the same time, it should be emphasised, MW strictly kept to the formal structure as regards division of roles and responsibilities. He was as anxious not to infringe upon the authority and responsibility of the CEO as he was in frequently reminding the CEO of these duties.

- Generous with his support in times of difficulty – provided the CEO did not try to hide anything – and when asked for. For instance, nobody could match his access to and handling of high level contacts around the world.

MW and JW – different styles but same basic principles

MW became the pacesetter – he developed what his father had started to perfection. He not only dominated the main part of the Wallenberg sphere (MW and his brother JW had divided the responsibility of the sphere as regards major holdings). He had an enormous impact on Swedish industry and the business culture at large for a long time.

His brother, JW, has been described as having another style and way of managing his relations to the chief executives of his sub-sphere of companies. He was not as intense on a day-to-day basis in his dialogue with the management of a company as his brother. There was more leeway but not less interest, and certainly not less accountability. Ivan Östholm, the legendary R&D head of Astra Hässle emphasises the importance of JW's involvement as active owner and chairman of the company: 'I was impressed by JW's great interest in the research of the Astra group and his dedication to make long term commitments. Despite his own owner interests in the company, as chairman he wanted to limit dividends to what was absolutely necessary. As much as possible of profits should be redeployed in long-term investments in the company. R&D had highest priority when he was around.'[15]

Thus, JW as well as MW practised the principle of decentralisation of responsibility to chief executives and their management teams.

All the elements of meta-management that characterised the third generation of the Wallenberg sphere were still in place during PW's reign but he seems to have had a different management style – more peer-like – and during his time Investor developed its staff and capacity to collect and analyse information in addition to personal channels.

Active ownership through the chairman and the board

The formal platform from which to exercise the ownership of the Wallenberg sphere was usually that MW – as well as his father, brother and son – was chairman of the company concerned.

In the early phases, additional directors of the board included other investment partners in the company concerned. This was the case both in the bank from the beginning and in the industrial ventures. MW Sr. changed the character of the boards he chaired, both as regards the bank and in the industrial companies to become less executive than they used to be. MW developed the boards further to include CEOs from other companies. In Investor he even brought in many of the CEOs of the Investor holdings to the board. This practice continued during PW's reign but successively CEOs were replaced by persons who at the same time were chairman of one or several holdings. The motive for bringing in CEOs, presumably, was to improve the information basis as well as the quality of board discussions. There was no doubt who had the final say in all matters when MW was in charge. PW, later, continued in this tradition. He has been quoted saying: 'the buck stops here', which must be interpreted as a clear signal of who is the real decision maker. MW, himself, was chairman of some thirty companies. He was succeeded, not only by PW, but by several trusted, non-family, close associates.

CEOs retire early to become professional chairmen and directors

Particularly since PW came to power, there has been a systematic effort to have CEOs of sphere companies leave their executive role in their mid-50s to be available for directorships instead. In most cases such a person has been both a director of Investor and chairman of one or several sphere companies, e.g. (in seniority order):

Hans Werthén:	† 2000-01-01, Chairman, until retirement, of Electrolux and Ericsson (former CEO of Electrolux).
Curt Nicolin:	Chairman, now retired, of ABB (earlier ASEA), SAS and other companies; (former CEO of ASEA, SAS).
Anders Scharp:	Chairman of Atlas Copco, Scania, Saab, SKF, retired chairman of Electrolux and retired vice chairman of Investor; director of Investor; (former CEO of Electrolux).
Bo Berggren:	Chairman of SAS, retired chairman of Astra, Stora, retired vice chairman of Investor; (former CEO of Stora, Incentive).
Björn Svedberg:	Chairman of Ericsson, now retired; director of Investor; (former CEO of Ericsson, SEB).
Percy Barnevik:	Chairman of Investor, ABB, AstraZeneca; (former CEO of ABB, ASEA).
Claes Dahlbäck:	Chairman of Stora Enso, Gambro, vice chairman of Investor and SEB; (former CEO of Investor).

The wide scope of active ownership

The active ownership of the Wallenberg sphere has included much more than management of CEOs and staffing of boards. Of key concern has always been the development of the business of each holding: is the sustainable value creation potential being achieved?, is the pace of renewal going fast enough and in the most promising direction?, is the business supported by the best possible structure?, etc. Questions of this type have been in focus and have generated initiatives and direct involvement by representatives of the sphere. MW engineered consolidation of ownership in ASEA and Ericsson by buying back shares from GE and ITT, respectively. The appendix to this chapter outlines the many restructuring, merger and de-merger initiatives in Electrolux, ASEA, ABB and Saab–Scania to take a few examples. In the long history of Ericsson's many radical steps of renewal, the Wallenberg sphere seems to have been not only the driving force in most cases but also in good collaboration with the other major owner, the Handelsbanken/Industrivärden sphere. The change of top management to fit the challenges at various stages of the development of a company was highlighted earlier. In addition, MW took the initiative to form a joint venture (Ellemtel) with the Swedish State Telecom Agency (called Telia today) which resulted in AXE, the first commercially successful digital switch which later also became a critical part of Ericsson's mobile telephony systems. When further development of the latter was in a critical phase in the early 1990s, the Wallenberg sphere in parallel with the Handelsbanken/Industrivärden sphere decided to support a massive R&D effort, which had a dramatic negative effect on short-term earnings, to achieve a new technological breakthrough (the digital mobile telephony systems and terminals), which later paid off handsomely.

'Mobilising power to change power'

In managing its relations to its holdings, the Wallenberg sphere has never hesitated to use its power to change and renew, which also lead to a change in the power structure of the company concerned. This prompts another definition of meta-management: 'mobilising power to redistribute power'.[16] Since such interventions and initiatives have been based on a thorough understanding of the situation in each case they also created added value.

Key levers of meta-management – a summary

Summing up, the key levers of the Wallenberg sphere in exercising meta-management include:

- Finding the best CEO to fit the specific situation of the company concerned. Never hesitating to replace a CEO who fails to achieve or if a new situation so requires.
- The on-going relationship between the leadership of the sphere/chairman of the company concerned and its CEO could be summed up by the following sequence: Tough, intensive demand dialogue – superior information – generous support.
- Systematic development of a cadre of very competent and loyal general managers for CEO, director and chairman positions in the sphere. For a selected few of trusted associates, the final phase of this systematic development includes membership of the board of Investor.
- Governance of holdings through the chairman and additional directors representing the Wallenberg sphere. The chairman of the board has a strong position in the companies of the sphere. This was of course evident when the chairman was a senior member of the dynasty. When non-Wallenbergs have become more frequent as chairmen during PW's reign they have successively become more powerful. While the important governance dialogue earlier took place between, e.g. MW and the CEO of the company it is now between Investor/the leadership of the sphere and the chairman (always non-executive, but for very exceptional cases) on the one hand and the CEO on the other. This also means that the board as a whole has become more important in the governance of the sphere holdings.
- In the old days the so-called Statistical department of Enskilda and a network of experts and advisors supplied the top representatives of the Wallenberg sphere with information, analyses and similar support. Over the last twenty years, Investor has developed resources and competence to provide this type of assistance in-house. In recent years this support has been organised in what is called business teams for each strategic holding. Such a business team is headed by one of Investor's senior investment officers who sometimes also serves on the board of the company concerned. Thus, the professional chairmen and directors of the Wallenberg sphere have more support, probably of a higher quality, than directors in general are used to.
- The idea of 'first the captain…', the strong belief in the importance of the individual initiative, entrepreneurship and 'constructive acquisitiveness' have had their corollary in the decentralisation principle.
- Making sure that each company has the appropriate internal and external organisation. While internal organisation is part of the dialogue with the board/CEO of every company, the external organisation has invariably been an important agenda item in the Wallenberg sphere. Frequent initiatives – mergers, acquisitions, divestments, partnerships – have also been taken both with and without the board's/executive management's collaboration.

- Overall one could say that meta-management aims at *creating the best possible conditions* for a company to prosper as well as for the board and management to be effective and efficient. As outlined above, this could involve many different aspects in the Wallenberg sphere.
- Finally, the Wallenberg sphere has been skilful in 'mobilising power to redistribute power', nota bene, based on an in-depth understanding of the situation and issues in focus. Applying its owner power in this way generated a virtuous circle: sustainable value was created while the competence and credibility the sphere acquired in that process further enhanced its position of power and its radius of impact.

Managing the Wallenberg sphere's relation to the environment: Legitimisation and institutionalisation

A helping hand from the King

In his biography of AOW, professor Göran B. Nilsson tells the story about how AOW during the crisis of the late 1870s got help from King Oscar II. Rumours about bad loans and that Enskilda was going to be squeezed by an imminent liquidity crisis made many customers nervous enough to start withdrawing their deposits. The acute situation was dramatically improved by the King let it be known that he had deposited a large sum of money in the bank. The actual sum was 10,000 kronor, a sizeable amount at that time, but rumour had it that it was many times higher. (Professor Nilsson also refers to King Oscar's autobiography where the King recalled the story and rejoiced at the exaggerated rumour). Thus, the King himself demonstrated, further amplified by that exaggerated rumour, that he had confidence in the bank. The sceptics regained their faith in Enskilda and a potentially devastating run on the bank could be avoided.

An elaborate legitimisation policy ...

From the very start, the Wallenberg sphere displayed conscious efforts to legitimise itself by developing its relations to external centres of power such as the story about the King above indicates.

In addition to creating wealth by managing the bank and its other holdings successfully, the Wallenberg sphere has developed a whole range of ways and means to legitimise itself, not only in the eyes of kings, other potentates and governments, but also in the business community and in society at large. Such ways and means are summarised in:

- An uncompromising dedication to the responsibility of developing the sphere of companies for sustainable success but also with an eye for the interests of the wider community.

- A strict code of conduct – both in how it runs its business and as regards personal behaviour. The Wallenberg dynasty has not included any robber barons, neither any jet set playboys. The most controversial of the Wallenberg figure-heads was KAW. Some of his private financial deals were criticised for being too *creative*. If KAW had any resemblance to the American robber barons in his business dealings, he also followed their example to improve his reputation. Childless, he and his wife donated their entire fortune to a new foundation, The Knut and Alice Wallenberg Foundation, by far the largest of all the Wallenberg foundations.
- Well looked after personnel – from top management down. Good performance has been rewarded, but even people who have failed, if they have done their best, have been treated well. At layoffs, severance pay has historically been quite generous.
- Most of the wealth of the sphere is today controlled by the Wallenberg foundations which are the biggest donors to research institutions and universities. The Stockholm School of Economics, one of Europe's oldest business school, was also initiated by the Wallenbergs in 1903 (opened in 1909).
- Several initiatives by the sphere to establish non-governmental organisations to promote good practice and high ethics in industry – both in Sweden (e.g. Industriförbundet, the Confederation of Swedish Industry as well as SAF, the Confederation of Swedish Employers) and internationally. The Wallenberg sphere has been a major driving force in the development of ICC – the International Chamber of Commerce where both MW and PW have served as chairmen.
- In Sweden, two leading figures of the sphere have recently been or still are chairmen of Industriförbundet and SAF, respectively, namely Dr. Bo Berggren and Mr. Anders Scharp. Earlier another key figure of the sphere, Dr. Curt Nicolin was chairman of SAF (the Swedish Employers Confederation).
- KAW as well as MW Sr., JW and MW all served the Swedish government in various ways. KAW was foreign secretary during the Great War. The others have, among other things, greatly contributed to international negotiations drawing upon their negotiation skills and extensive network of contacts around the globe.
- Internationally, the involvement in ICC was preceded by other engagements for government and non-government organisation. In particular, MW Sr. was widely respected for his involvement in the post-war negotiations of Germany's war reparations and as chairman of the Finance Committee of the League of Nations.

... has contributed to the business success of the sphere companies

This institutionalisation policy has served the Wallenberg sphere well. The doors of the mighty have always been open for the leading figures of the sphere. This has not only lent prestige and legitimacy to the sphere and their representatives. It has been most valuable for business operations. PW in his role both as head of the sphere and as chairman of ICC has had access to the US Administration, including the US president. PW also opened doors in China for Ericsson which nobody else would have been capable of.

A trend setter

As a result of its long-term performance and a conscious legitimisation policy the Wallenberg sphere has become an institution in Swedish business life. Its impact has reached beyond its own sphere of holdings. The sphere has been a trend setter as regards international orientation and growth as well as work ethics, for a long time offering the most prestigious careers in the private industry and so forth.

One serious offence

Seldom has its credibility and good faith been questioned, except on a couple of occasions, namely:

* The Bosch Deal.
* A popular target for various types of assaults and slander campaigns launched by marxists/left wing extremists.

The latter point was more prevalent in the late 1960s and throughout most of the 1970s. All private interests were attacked during this period. The only special feature of the Wallenberg sphere in this context was its position as the largest and most powerful of all the private groups.

Out of favour with the American authorities

The first point is more complicated and concerned Nazi Germany. While MW had excellent contacts in the Anglo-American sphere, JW had better contacts in Germany. However, it turned out that his closest personal contacts were with people who belonged to the group that tried to assassinate Hitler in 1943–44. One of these, Dr. Goerdeler, was actually executed for his participation in the conspiracy. However, what really caused problems for the Wallenberg sphere, especially in the US, was a deal with the Bosch family, a fictitious agreement where JW bought Bosch's foreign holdings with a binding buy back clause. The purpose of the deal was to protect this property from confiscation by the enemy powers during the war. This secret agreement was revealed by the American forces through documents found in Bosch headquarters after the war. The American authorities blocked all the Wallenberg sphere's property in the US. However, MW eventually managed to sort out the problem with the Americans and the ban was lifted.

The idea of ownership and overriding values

What drives individuals, whole families, generation after generation as in the case of the Wallenbergs, to set up companies and continue investing in them and to developing them? Many entrepreneurs and owners are satisfied to have set up a business and reached a certain level. They don't want the worry of further growth. Is it an inordinate desire for wealth, to become *stinking rich*? Not in the Wallenbergs' case. Naturally, the representatives of the different generations have had considerable personal fortunes. But their magnitude is still relatively modest for the representatives of the current generation, compared both with other Swedish fortunes and with what earlier generations of Wallenberg generated, but placed in foundations which are inaccessible for private consumption. Many people have pointed out how small the family fortune is in relation to the total wealth represented by all the companies within the Wallenberg sphere. During Peter Wallenberg's chairmanship of Investor, for example, the material value of Investor increased from around 2 billion kronor at the beginning of the 1980s to around 75 billion kronor in the autumn of 1996 while during the same period the private family fortune remained more or less stagnant around SEK 300–500 million.[17] Thus there must be other driving forces, apart from the purely pecuniary ones, which continue to be the guiding star for developing the Wallenberg sphere.

Esse non videri

The illustration in Figure 10.1 includes some quotations from members of the Wallenberg family. A recurring expression which Marcus Wallenberg (MW) often used is 'some kind of responsibility'. The active generation which is involved in administering the assets of the sphere and managing its companies has to be reminded of, and remind itself of, the responsibility it has towards the earlier generations, the companies which it has been involved in developing, for their continuance and for other implications which may be covered in this expression. MW Sr. used the motto – *esse non videri* [18] – which emphasises the significance of what one achieves rather than the quest for public notability or conspicuous consumption.

Patriotism and globalisation

The ownership idea has also included a strong feeling for Sweden as a nation and as a territorial base for the Wallenberg interests. This value was not only expressed in the fact that they saw themselves as developers of Swedish industry and Swedish companies, where they were also anxious to safeguard Swedish ownership, but also meant that they gave direct and active support to the state and to the public as mentioned earlier. One might ask oneself if this value is still as strong as it was in earlier decades. Globalisation has gained momentum and the prerequisites for success have changed dramatically for many industries and companies over the last 10–15 years.

A value creating symbiosis

Globalisation has also changed the prerequisites for what used to be a kind of symbiosis between the Wallenberg sphere of powerful, export-oriented companies and the Social Democratic government. The Wallenberg sphere, representing the backbone of companies generating export-led, economic growth, offered increasing employment and incomes and a growing tax base in exchange for political and labour market stability. In addition, the government sector was also a strategically important customer for several breakthrough innovations of the sphere companies in infrastructure-related technologies. Railway and hydropower investments were mainly done and financed by the government. This was important for ASEA and Atlas Copco. Telecoms investments where Swedish infrastructure used to be at the forefront have been all-important for Ericsson's technological leadership until the 1990s. Sweden's foreign policy of neutrality and staying out of military alliances boosted an indigenous defence industry where SAAB was the monopoly supplier of airplanes etc. The Social Democratic government on its part got the prerequisites for an expanding welfare state and was anxious to keep their part of the bargain. This symbiosis peaked in the period from World War II and until the end of the 1960s. During large parts of this period, the Social Democrats had the same minister of finance, Gunnar Sträng while MW was the dominant leader of the Wallenberg sphere. Many claimed – including these two figure-heads themselves – that Sweden was *run* by the two of them during this period. One could often hear statements from one or the other that 'I'll call Sträng' or 'I'll call Wallenberg' to get something important settled quickly and easily.

Now, a value of less value?

The foundations of this symbiosis started to deteriorate when traditional industry companies stopped growing in Sweden, particularly as regards employment in their Swedish production units – the core constituency of Social Democratic voters. Until recently, Ericsson was an exception and the politicians, particularly the socialists, have had great difficulties to understand the change that has taken place during the late 1990s. Ericsson's own manufacturing base is almost gone today – for several reasons. The new technologies have led to that Ericsson is a software company today, to a large extent growing outside Sweden while the manufacturing input needed have been outsourced to external suppliers. The restructuring required to accommodate these changes necessitated certain layoffs, which at one point in 1998 led the executive secretary of the Social democratic party to suggest a boycott of Ericsson's mobile phones. At the same time Ericsson's size and success, together with that of Nokia, has made it a concern of Europe and EU as a whole. When a new standard for mobile telephony was to be decided a couple of years ago, Tony Blair, the British Prime minister, and his government took the initiative to unite EU behind Ericsson's and Nokia's standard, the only technology in Europe that could compete on a global basis. The Swedish government was small fry in this context. Recently, even the socialist politicians have started to realise what a tremendous growth engine Ericsson has become in the Swedish economy. Not only in terms of its own growth, but as the main force behind Sweden being perceived as the global hotspot of the new mobile and Internet-related technologies. This is happening at the same time as Ericsson is moving its corporate headquarters to London, not least because of Sweden's punitive taxation of individuals.

Thus, from a clear plus-sum-game relation between the socialist government and the Wallenberg sphere, it is now much more of a mixed game – or worse. The socialist government today even threatens to change the taxation of foundations, which could seriously weaken the controlling power of the Wallenberg sphere.

However, Marcus Wallenberg, CEO of Investor still emphasises the importance of Sweden as the home base of the sphere:

> beside our shareholders and companies, our most important principal is the Swedish academic research community, since the purpose of the Wallenberg Foundations is to provide financial support for advanced research in Sweden.[19]

Safeguarding its Swedish resource base

However, the sphere's Swedish interests are still so dominant and its competence still so closely linked to its resource base in Sweden that the safeguarding of that must still be a core value. A clear indication of that is Investor's investments in new businesses through Novare Kapital (a venture capital outfit) and EQT (a LBO/private equity company) are dominated by Swedish/Nordic projects. However, even if the Swedish base is still of fundamental importance for the sphere it does not preclude the fact that international competence has become so much more important. Thus, Swedish interests need to be seen in a different light. After all, what could better protect Swedish interests in Asea than the merger with BBC to form ABB? That merger had strong support in all quarters while a more recent one, that between Astra and Zeneca, has been much more controversial in this respect. This merger will be further discussed in the next chapter.

Entrepreneurship is all-important

The importance of entrepreneurship is another strong value at the core of the Wallenberg credo. All the figure-heads of the family have embodied and practised entrepreneurship, although it has been expressed somewhat differently. Obviously, Enskilda, the original nucleus of the sphere, was founded thanks to the entrepreneurial drive of AOW. However, the emergence and growth of the Wallenberg sphere are the results of the particular dynamic that was created as a combination of the bank, on the one hand and the entrepreneurship and risk taking of the second (KAW, MW Sr.) and third (JW, MW) generations on the other. The current generations – PW, the former chairman and Marcus, the current CEO of Investor – have demonstrated their belief in the value of entrepreneurship in ways which will be touched upon in the next chapter.

Consolidation and financial prudence

The strong belief in entrepreneurship and risk taking has been balanced by an equally strong policy urging for consolidation and financial prudence. This dates back to the critical developments experienced by Enskilda in the business downturn of the late 1870s when the bank was near bankruptcy (see the appendix!). This policy was first of all applied in conducting the affairs of the bank, in particular embodied by KAW and MW Sr. who jointly managed to rebuild the strength of the bank, but as much by JW. However, it has also been a policy that the Wallenberg sphere has practised vis-à-vis its main holdings during long periods of turn-around phases or early development. As owner, the bank or the investment company has refrained from dividends as well as from ambitions to quickly regain earlier losses until the company has achieved satisfactory and sustainable levels of profitability.

Committed for the long term

One very prominent feature in the whole development of the Wallenberg sphere has been its long term view and staying power. Its commitment has been governed not by the quarterly perspective but by the idea that one also has a long term responsibility for the business that one is involved in, that acute crises should be weathered etc. There are many examples of this from the earlier stages of the group's development, but no shortage of them in more recent times either. A lack of financial resources has forced sell-offs, for example where Alfa-Laval was concerned, but the view taken there seems to have been that Tetra Pak was an owner better placed to make the most of Alfa-Laval's potential. Saab Automobile is perhaps an even more obvious example and one where there is also reason to ask why it took so long to involve a partner with expertise in the industry and plan for the exit of the sphere. Why was it necessary for an acute crisis to occur before its ownership could be gradually phased out? At the same time SKF, for instance, has remained one of the core companies in the group despite a long period of poor average profits where little seems to have been done about them. SKF will be discussed further when the current situation of the sphere is reviewed (Chapter 11). Electrolux is another example where too little has happened over a long period. The conversion from being a very successful industry restructurer –where the management team under Hans Werthén as CEO and later chairman excelled and created a special culture – to reaping success through organic renewal in a few core areas, progressed very slowly for a long time. Were the owners here proving they had the necessary staying power or was it evidence of their lack of competence in handling the specific risks and success factors regarding Electrolux products and markets? A brief comment on recent developments in Electrolux will be included in the next chapter as well.

International competition and stock market quotation keep companies alert

The Wallenberg sphere realised early on that the long term approach of a principal owner may lull the company management into a false sense of security leading to complacency, thus reducing their ambitions for efficiency and growth. This realisation has constituted an important motive for making one of their main goals the internationalisation of the companies they have been involved in. By being forced to grow internationally and hold their own in international competition, the companies would always remain efficient. For the companies in the group which were mainly concerned with the domestic market – something which was more in evidence previously than it is now – a quotation on the stock exchange became important. This would expose them to the demands of other owners as well as force their accounting to be more open as expected of a public company etc. The internationally oriented companies were also quoted on the stock exchange, but in their case a more decisive factor was the supply of risk capital.

Combinations generate synergies

An important part of the Wallenberg credo has been the idea of and search for 'combinations'. Maybe this came naturally considering the type of banking perspective AOW had when he started running the bank originally. When financing an emerging industrialisation – exploiting natural resources etc – it was easy to see the bottlenecks and missing links when making investments profitable. By initiating investments and companies to do something about such voids, the bank could also get new customers. The idea of looking for possible 'combinations' became an integral part of the philosophy of the sphere and was further enhanced by MW. His early experience with ASEA (now ABB) seems to have been a driving force in this respect. The formation of investment companies (Skandinaviska Elverk for the Nordic market and Electro-Invest for international markets), focused on hydropower plants and similar projects, facilitated ASEA's progress in power generation, transformation and transmission projects.

Top quality executives are top priority

The importance of enterprising, creative and decisive leaders and managers, who make things happen, has always been underlined. This was expressed in the words 'no company is in such a bad state that an able managing director cannot turn it around, no company is so good that it cannot be destroyed by a poor MD'.[20] Identifying these good leaders, managing directors and managers is one of the most demanding tasks for owners, because such manager material is a scarce commodity. There are plenty of people who can think, said MW, but there are far fewer who can turn a good analysis and creative ideas into concrete decisions and get them carried out. That does not mean that the importance of analysis and know-how is underestimated either. On the contrary, the leaders in the Wallenberg sphere seem to have surrounded themselves with very able advisors, placed great emphasis on the quality of their data collection and set aside considerable resources for the qualified analysis of major challenges and decision issues. This applies not least to Investor, which in recent years has built up a powerful staff of analysts, employed qualified staff both centrally and in the field and is an assiduous and demanding purchaser of consultancy services. In this way and through the business teams mentioned earlier, the sphere is able to support the people who actually exercise ownership in the associated companies and supplement the information which the managers supply to the board in the respective companies.

One of the important leadership qualities which MW and his brother Jacob Wallenberg are known to have promoted was that people who had been given responsibility should themselves believe in and be committed to the proposals which they put before the board and the owners for a decision and the requisite capital investment – in other words people who took responsibility themselves and did not just delegate it upwards to the board and the owners.

Competitive edge through technological leadership

A salient feature of MW's success imperatives was his belief in the blessings of new technology and the competitive clout technological leadership brings. This belief was a common thread in the whole career of MW as an active owner as Appendix 3 shows. However, it is fair to conclude that his belief in this respect became an institutionalised part of the present overriding value system of the sphere. The strategic holdings of the sphere still include the heaviest R&D spenders in Swedish industry, e.g. ABB, Ericsson, AstraZeneca, SAAB. Investments in venture capital projects are also, to a large extent, high-technology oriented. One should add that MW was not the first Wallenberg to believe in new technology, but he carried on and amplified a core value that the generations before him had adopted, in particular his father, MW Sr., was a key force in introducing and developing new technologies, e.g. for chemical pulping, nitrogene (in Norsk Hydro in Norway) production, and the diesel engine.

'... the only tradition worth caring about'

Finally, renewal wasn't only about new technology, it was also a more general belief. Business success demands all kinds of renewal efforts to stay competitive and make growth possible. The continuity and hence respect for what has been established by previous generations, which characterises the attitude of the Wallenberg sphere on the one hand, should not be confused with the importance the Wallenbergs attributed to incessant renewal on the other. Quite the contrary, on one occasion MW said that the best way to show respect for previous generations was to live up to the principles they admired, namely '... to move on ... from the old to what is to come ... that is the only tradition worth caring about.'[21]

Dynamics of double command

One observation that can be highlighted in this context, and which is of importance as regards the renewal ability, is that the Wallenberg sphere was led by two dominant personalities for long periods of time. They often had differing views on how the business should be run, what its priorities should be and how the role of owner should be played. This happened in the second generation, with the half-brothers K.A. Wallenberg and Marcus

Wallenberg Sr. In the third generation the antagonism between the two brothers Jacob and Marcus was revealed in the merger between Enskilda and Skandinaviska Banken, and when they divided the Wallenberg companies into two parts, one for each of them. One wonders whether this division was made according to what they thought would reflect the brothers' different expertise and way of exercising ownership or whether it was based on other things. On both sides one can point to successes as well as failures, which seem to have a plausible connection to the respective brother's qualities and way of exercising ownership. The final result of the value of variation represented by the two brothers, however, has meant major successes and value creation with further great potential for the future. Appropriate and successful as Marcus Wallenberg's approach to ownership and his concrete intervention in Ericsson was, his approach to ownership in Incentive seems to have been unsuccessful, at least as far as the realisation of Incentive's original aims is concerned – namely to become a company promoting innovations. In Jacob's case his approach in the research-oriented Astra was successful, whilst his revitalisation of the then Swedish Match, came too late and when it did occur it became a far too disparate diversification and conglomerate strategy.

Summing up the overriding values constituting the ownership idea of the sphere

To summarise, the ownership idea of the Wallenberg sphere is built upon a system of dominating values including:

- Responsibility for the sphere as a whole and its holdings as well as the good name of Wallenberg.
- 'Esse non videri' – to focus on achieving results and growth instead of seeking superficial fame or just personal pleasure.
- Taking a wider responsibility – for Sweden but also for development and maintenance of good international institutions.
- The importance of entrepreneurship as a key driving force of the sphere but also as generally applicable to other companies and the economy at large.
- The necessity of financial prudence and consolidation for long term survival and success.
- Achieving sustainable value added requires a long term view and an owner with staying power.
- Internationalisation is a must, in particular for a company originating in a small home market such as Sweden. Therefore, it is crucial to aim for international competitiveness from the very beginning of a new business.
- Active ownership with a long term commitment does not require fully

owned companies (except for certain transitional periods). The advantage of bringing in other owners is not only to leverage the sphere's own equity base but also to get additional pressure on the executive management of a holding.

- A common thread throughout the history of the sphere has been a belief in the benefits of combining industrial and financial competence to create value added.
- 'First the captain, then the ship' was one motto, coined by MW Sr. denoting the importance of having enterprising and 'constructively acquisitive', creative and decisive managers. The significance of this belief is not only demonstrated in the careful selection of chief executives but also in the concern devoted to the development of a cadre of such candidates.
- A strong belief that technological leadership is a key to business success is still reflected in several of the strategic holdings, e.g. in ABB, AstraZeneca, Atlas Copco, Ericsson as well as in new investments. It can be traced back at least to MW Sr. but became a centrepiece value in particular when MW dominated the industrial holdings of the sphere.
- Maybe the most impressive of all the various value elements – apart from the achievement of having combined all of them into one consistent ownership idea – is the emphasis given to the necessity of renewal all through the generations of Wallenbergs – '… the only tradition worth caring about'.

DISTINCTIVE OWNER COMPETENCE – THE WALLENBERG EXAMPLE

Figure 10.1 also indicates the systemic links between the four main components of the fundamental value-creating skills and prerequisites of the successful ownership of the Wallenberg sphere. These four components complement and support one another to make up the core of the specific Wallenberg sphere's of success of active ownership.

Specific infrastructure

However, the picture of the *distinctive ownership competence* would be incomplete without the mention of a further element of owner competence, or rather the *specific infrastructure* of the Wallenberg sphere, as illustrated in Figure 10.5. A key element of this is a cadre of top executive people and *board professionals*. In this study contact networks have also been highlighted and – not least – financial expertise and contacts which the Wallenberg sphere has at its disposal or is able to mobilise. The contact network, culti-

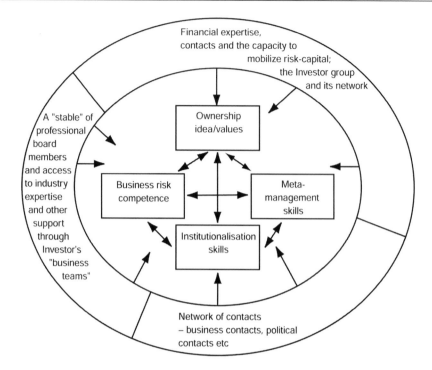

Figure 10.5   The Wallenberg sphere of core holdings.[8] The distinctive ownership competence in the Wallenburg sphere = the combination of the owner-specific fundamental value-creating system and the owner specific infrastructure.

vated and renewed over a long period and passed on from generation to generation, is considered quite unique in its scope and breadth and not just in Sweden – its scope is global and it is admired and envied throughout the world.

Another element in this infrastructure, of decisive significance to the fundamental value creation, is the financial expertise, and contacts regarding, the global capital market. The historical roots, development and significance of this with Enskilda at the hub have been shown.

Furthermore, especially since the 1980s, the financial expertise has developed, into increasingly sophisticated skills within Investor – and enhanced its role as the Wallenberg sphere's most prominent instrument for active ownership.

General applicability?

Do the interdependent components which constitute the ownership competence of the Wallenberg sphere and which have been proven decisive in the sphere's success, have a more general application? Is it reasonable to argue that the unique aspect of each ownership situation must be reflected in the main elements of the competence and in the infrastructure? To be successful, must owners both develop specific expertise for the fundamental value creation and legitimisation, comprising the four elements in the centre of the figure, *and* develop, and be able to mobilise, an appropriate infrastructure of resources, contacts, financial expertise etc. for the specific ownership situation?

Why these components?

If the success formula of the Wallenberg sphere can be generalised, why does the fundamental value-creating owner competence consist of these components and skills? In Part III, Chapter 12, the processes which create value and success in companies will be analysed. It will also be shown how the role of ownership fits into these processes and how each of the components which have been illustrated with the help of examples from the Wallenberg sphere are of central significance in this context.

THE REAL LEARNING

The success formula that has been outlined is one way of interpreting and conceptualising what constitutes the specific owner idea and distinctive competence of the Wallenberg sphere. This can of course be debated, refined further or falsified by others. Such a formula does have its limits when it comes to capturing the dynamics of the achievements of the Wallenberg sphere. Many business success stories can be explained as the results of efforts of extraordinarily gifted individuals or circumstantially – being at the right place at the right time. These factors can be identified in the success story of the Wallenberg sphere too. AOW had the luck to introduce his banking innovation just when the industrialisation of the Swedish economy started to gain momentum. Swedish natural resources had an enormous value potential in booming British and continental markets. MW was unique in his capacity to exercise active ownership and promote growth and value creation in so many companies. But there is something more: the Wallenberg sphere exists today because it succeeded in handing over the leadership and responsibility of the sphere from one generation to the next until its fifth generation today! This sphere and dynasty lived on and expanded while other dynasties have deteriorated at much earlier stages.

Dynamics of lasting success

In trying to learn from the dynamics of what explains the sustainable success of the Wallenberg sphere it is crucial to remember:

- How the sphere managed to balance the strengths of earlier experience with the need and opportunity for renewal.
- That the success of the Wallenberg sphere is something more than the achievement of an outstanding individual in each generation, and that the competence and driving forces behind such individual achievements lived on from one generation to the next.
- That although the education and preparation of new generations of Wallenberg figure-heads have been meticulously planned, the actual succession at the top has not been an untouchable prerogative for the candidate in line. Says Marcus Wallenberg of the fifth generation, CEO of Investor: 'My grandfather MW, as well as my grand uncle JW, kept repeating, that if anyone from the coming generation planned to involve themselves in the business and leadership of the sphere, it must be based on two things: their own burning interest for it *and*, most importantly, competence. If we did not fulfil both criteria, we should step aside. The request for competence is all the more important since our private owner-ship of the sphere is rather limited.'
- On the other hand, after due preparations, Marcus Wallenberg felt comfortable taking over executive responsibilities at Investor. Says he: 'I had the opportunity of spending ten years working for banks in Germany, the UK, Hong Kong, and the US. In addition, I worked within the forest products industry as a marketing executive for four years in Sweden and Germany. That was extremely valuable for my personal development and for my decision to take on the challenging assignments in Investor (first deputy as CEO and then as CEO)'.
- That, although the family figure-heads have had different personal quali-ties, they have all one common denominator: they have surrounded them-selves with strong and capable individuals. MW Sr. established a tradition in always preferring outstanding individuals who, not only fulfilled his tough criteria for a successful CEO, but who also had the quality of chal-lenging him as their chairman and head of the sphere. MW Sr. was simply bored by people who did not have the capacity to do that.
- It is also essential to emphasise that the Wallenberg sphere has not been led and managed as a monolith. Its landmark quality of successful renewal has been a function of the variety allowed at its top as well as its organisational principles have supported variety. During long periods there has been two brothers – AOW and his brother Agathon, KAW and MW Sr., JW and MW – and now two cousins – Jacob W and Marcus W – at the top. This *double commando* has generated constructive variety of

opinions and practices of running the affairs of the sphere. Furthermore, non-family associates have been recruited among the best, and have been allowed to play important roles. Organisationally, decentralisation has been the operational mode giving competent CEOs wide responsibilities and action space.

These lessons are highly relevant when analysing the general challenges that ownership and value creation face today. These points are discussed in Part III, Chapters 12 and 13, of this book.

The Wallenberg Sphere and the Future   11

Renewal – the ability to renew to maintain the validity of its active ownership and value creation formula – has been a hallmark of the Wallenberg sphere historically. What renewal work is being done now and will it suffice to meet future challenges?

ACHIEVEMENTS AND SHORTCOMINGS OF THE FOURTH GENERATION

Before addressing these issues let us recall the dramatic changes that took place and the renewal efforts that were implemented in the fifteen year period from 1982 to 1997 during which time PW was chairman and Claes Dahlbäck CEO of Investor. It should also be mentioned that – in addition to the proactive initiatives listed below – a lot of effort and investment capacity had to be allocated to defend the owner position of the sphere in several cases. Dissolving the alliance his father had formed with PG Gyllenhammar of Volvo was a first priority of PW's that involved a buy back of 25 percent holdings of Atlas Copco and Stora. In the end, it turned out to be a very profitable investment. Raiders were also taking corner positions of strategic holdings, e.g. in Saab–Scania, which threatened the buyout strategy which was later implemented. Buying out raiders, in addition to sizeable restructuring costs took a heavy toll on the resources of the sphere and during the early 1990's Investor was financially squeezed. Therefore, it is probably not surprising to find that an assessment of the active ownership and value creation achievements as a whole during this period provides a mixed picture. Although many constructive and value creating initiatives were taken – some were costly financially and left limited energy to address some remaining weak areas in the sphere.

Several impressive achievements

- Stora became the restructuring vehicle of the forest-based industries of the sphere and made further acquisitions to become a leading European player.
- The ABB merger was instigated and completed, and the company developed further through additional acquisitions, internal growth and massive restructuring (from 'north and west to south and east' – produc-

tion was moved from the developed markets in Western Europe and North America to the emerging ones of Eastern Europe and South Asia).

- OM was started as the first private stock exchange in the world, and later acquired the Stockholm Stock Exchange. OM has successfully pioneered new technologies for computerised trading.
- Ericsson went from one breakthrough (AXE) to the next (mobile telephony systems), to yet another (mobile handsets) and beyond, supported in most initiatives by the leading owners, one of which was the Wallenberg sphere.
- Saab–Scania was bought out from the stock exchange, restructured, and broken-up. Scania was once again listed on the stock exchange in 1996.
- A major restructuring and refocusing of Incentive, later renamed Gambro, was initiated and much progress in the intended direction was achieved.
- Other renewal efforts also included the start-up of Novare Kapital (venture capital) and EQT (LBO projects).
- Investor itself became the core active owner instrument by absorbing other investment companies of the sphere (Providentia, Export-Invest).
- PW was himself succeeded as chairman of Investor by Percy Barnevik in 1997. Two years later, Marcus Wallenberg, representing the fifth generation of the dynasty, became CEO of Investor.

But also shortcomings

However, the shining image that this list radiates is tarnished to some extent by shortcomings, neglecting to cope with some issues or being too slow in taking action in some cases:

- In the case of Saab Automobiles it took too long for the sphere to realise its lack of competence in dealing with the business logic of this type of consumer products and markets. Although the deal with GM was a good move, its delay has cost Investor billions in bridging a long period of loss making and investments in the development of the company before GM took full control (early 2000).
- Ericsson, on the whole, has no doubt been a long-term success story and much of the credit must be given to the two dominating owners. But this success has its flaws as regards these owners. On one occasion in the 1980s Ericsson had to turn to a Swedish state investment bank to finance its market investments in the United States. However, more severe criticism could be directed at these owners for the setbacks Ericsson experienced quite recently but which originate several years ago. Ericsson more or less missed the Internet-led datacom revolution, in particular on the wireline side, where circuit switching technologies were largely replaced by packet switching technologies using IP (Internet protocols) and routers. This

seems to have been attributable to three mistakes: (1) The emergence of the Internet and its implications were acknowledged much too late by Ericsson's management. (2) Once acknowledged it took too long before anything substantial was done about it. Some blame the CEO, Lars Ramqvist for this. He delayed his decision to retire for too long and in the meantime he didn't want to initiate any major new initiatives. A contributing factor in this context was probably that Mr. Ramqvist's own knowledge was in traditional mobile telephony systems, not Internet. (3) The third mistake was the appointment of his successor, who had to be replaced shortly after taking office. Ericsson had to go back to where it started, by reinstalling Mr. Ramqvist as CEO in combination with being chairman. (Mr. Ramqvist has announced his retirement as CEO/executive chairman by the end of 2000 when he will become non-executive chairman). However, Lars Ramqvist is not the only one who is to blame. It is also a matter of poor governance, of active owners not being active enough, and especially not pro-active enough in the turbulently dynamic, telecoms/IT business. The board should have anticipated the technological changes much earlier and acted upon the information that seems to have been available within Ericsson. Obviously the board lacks the kind of technological visionary that MW once was and contributed to making Ericsson the leader in digital switching. The board should have demanded faster and more decisive action once the company started to see the implications of the Internet instead of relying on Mr. Ramqvist to take initiatives, which he did not do. Finally, the succession issue seems to have been neglected or treated rather haphazardly by the board. This criticism of the shortcomings of the board and the dominating owners of Ericsson should not be misinterpreted when it comes to assessing other key aspects of Ericsson's strategic position. Ericsson is still, by far, the world leader in mobile telephony *systems*, accounting for some forty percent of global market share. This is worth mentioning since many analysts seem to make too superficial comparisons between Nokia and Ericsson. Nokia is the global leader in mobile handsets and Ericsson *only* number three globally. Making this comparison analysts tend to underestimate Ericsson's superior position in mobile systems. Furthermore, Ericsson's large technology base, and – not least – its extensive global network of resources, unrivalled to any competitor, will provide a strong platform for it to play a leading role also in the emerging datacom investment wave – unquestionably, in mobile systems but possibly also in wireline systems and the integration of these with wireless systems.

- Electrolux has suffered from similar shortcomings to those of Saab Automobiles – lack of competence in consumer products and markets on the part of the owner. After the acquisition-based expansion phase was over, the company needed a new top management culture and board.

- Even if the Saab–Scania restructuring as a whole was necessary and created added value in the end, it seems initially have been driven by Investor's need for additional cash flow. Making Saab–Scania a fully owned subsidiary was probably necessary to make the radical restructuring that later took place possible – as a temporary arrangement. Instead, Investor integrated the company fully and the traditional strategy of being an 'owner specialist' went astray. For several years, Investor tried to play a dual role of being both owner and management of the Saab–Scania Group.
- SKF is another example where the sphere was unable to manage to come to grips with the fundamental problems of that company. Although the biggest company in its industry world-wide, its market position was rather weak in many local and regional markets. The internal culture was characterised by *resting on one's laurels* rather than being an agile renewer.
- Stora made impressive restructuring moves in the pulp and paper industry both domestically and in the European context but was criticised for being slow in achieving synergies and operational benefits from the new structure. A couple of strategic decisions are also questionable. The first one, probably initiated by Investor, was the acquisition of Swedish Match which at that time (1987) was a widely diversified conglomerate – building materials, consumer packaging and chemicals in addition to matches and disposable lighters. Successively everything was divested – so Stora was performing the active owner role that Investor should have done – thus taking away its focus from its core business. Once again Investor mixed the roles of being owner and group management, by delegating the owner role to Stora. The second decision that is difficult to understand for an outsider is Stora's involvement in a huge greenfield short fibre pulp mill in Brazil but a discussion of this would take us too deeply into an analysis of its position in the pulp & paper industry to be included here.

The mistakes and shortcomings of the Wallenberg sphere during this period became evident when its two supercharged value creating engines – Astra and Ericsson – started to run out of some of their steam in recent years.

PERCY BARNEVIK AT THE HELM – IDEAS AND ACTIONS[1]

A few months after taking the chair of Investor, Percy Barnevik (PB) outlined his ideas about active ownership and governance ('Owner role under change – Development of active ownership; 19980115'). This memo, a summary of which was featured in the 1997 annual report, expressed some general principles and guidelines that should apply within Investor in matters of active ownership, various aspects of governance, board issues etc vis-à-vis its strategic holdings. Other memos and statements have complemented this. Thus, the salient points of his philosophy can be summed up as follows:

- He strongly believes in the role of *Investor as an active owner* both from a principle point of view in that owners have an important value creating role to play and by vigorously endorsing Investor's traditions in this respect. He wants to build on the best practices of Investor and the Wallenberg sphere rather than proposing something entirely and radically new.
- Being an active owner also seems to fit well with the activist character and personality of PB. Or as one of his board colleagues at General Motors, Dennis Weatherstone,[2] expressed it: 'he is a true activist. I think many boards could benefit from an activist such as Percy'.
- PB is a strong believer in the *benefits of measurement* – his early career was that of controller – and therefore he wants clear goals and quantified objectives. Rather than contemplating about the ideal goals and exact objectives he seems to prefer provisional ones that guide the action in the desired direction and get it up to speed without delay. If there should be any raison d'être for Investor as an active owner it is that it must outperform the stock market – that is the goal. The objective that presently prevails is a sustainable outperformance of 3 percent annually.
- One of PB's statements shortly after he had taken the chair in Investor – 'we will have *less patience with slow performers*' – attracted a lot of attention, especially among financial analysts and journalists. This statement was – according to PB – misinterpreted to imply that all holdings presently performing under par were going to be divested. Indeed, PB's own model of active ownership instead includes three steps: (1) Tough demands on all holdings to achieve outstanding performance. Patience regarding shortcomings or delays in this respect will be limited. (2) Only when excellence is impossible within the existing structure and strategic posture will the next step be taken – to improve the prerequisites of the company by a major acquisition, merger or similar giant leap. (3) Eventually, if the first two steps do not yield satisfactory results or they cannot be expected to do so, the only remaining step is a divestment or maybe even closure. Not only has all patience run out by then but it has also been realised that the Wallenberg sphere and Investor is not a competent owner of such a holding, one could say.
- However, applying this active owner model requires some very *important prerequisites*, according to PB. The channelling of performance demands on a certain holding has to be done through the board. The board must also be competent enough to understand what is necessary and possible to achieve within step one and what additional steps are required. Since PB became chairman, some 40 directorships in the core holdings have been renewed in order to increase competence. Three criteria seem to have been applied in this context: (1) industry competence to better fit the business logic of the company concerned; (2) active people with drive, probably with very little patience for slow performance; (3) increasing the

number of competent foreigners in the boards of the multinational holdings. Most of the Swedish based companies in this category have more than 90 percent of their sales outside Sweden but usually very few, if any, have had foreign board members.

- An example of the action taken concerning boards is Electrolux, with probably one of the most *radically renewed boards*. Three foreigners are new – all with an in-depth understanding of consumer products and markets, namely the chief executives of Sony, Heinecken and GM Europe, respectively. In addition, PB was unconventional in bringing in a new chairman from outside the sphere, Mr. Rune Andersson. PB's move was met by a lot of resistance. 'But so what – with such a board and a dynamic and innovative chairman as Rune there will be quite another level of discussion and drive in developing the company', PB remarked.
- Another crucial prerequisite and the first duty of the board is to make sure that *the CEO* is the right person. Quite a lot of changes have been done in this respect since PB became chairman of Investor: in Electrolux, Atlas Copco, SKF, Stora and SEB.
- In all the companies where the CEO had been replaced massive *performance improvement programmes* have been launched to match the demands of the first step of PB's governance model. This also includes other holdings, e.g. ABB and Gambro. These programmes have generated quite satisfactory results, both in the fundamental performance of these companies and their stock market valuation, especially in 1999.
- As regards the *second step* of PB's active ownership model, quite some action has taken place. In the autumn of 1997, SEB acquired one of Sweden's leading insurance companies, *Trygg–Hansa*. Its financial services (life insurance and savings products) business was integrated with that of the bank while its property and casualty business was divested. The first spectacular merger was that of *Stora and Finnish Enso* – also the first Swedish-Finnish merger of any size in the pulp and paper industry – creating the largest, measured by production tonnage, and the second largest by revenues, pulp and paper company in the world. Generally this merger has got positive feedback. Structurally the two companies fitted very well together and the merger advanced the strategic positions in most product lines of the new company. Some concerns were voiced about expected difficulties in accommodating the rather different cultures of the two companies (Enso being state-owned and having a typical Finnish, rather autocratic management style; Stora being private, a Wallenberg company with the idiosyncracies of a softer *democratic* Swedish management culture). However, so far – with a few exceptions – very little is heard externally about such problems. As mentioned earlier, Stora Enso is taking further steps to enhance its global leadership position by

acquiring Consolidated Paper, a leading US corporation in its field of paper products.

- The second big merger, between *Astra and Zeneca* was much more controversial. In the case of Stora Enso the merger was supported because it clearly enhanced the strategic position of both companies and Stora had had difficulties in improving its operational efficiency. As regards Astra the strategic issue was its future growth when its global blockbuster, Losec, would lose its patent protection. Astra's own research portfolio wasn't promising enough in this respect. Therefore, one line of criticism against the deal was that Zeneca did not fill these gaps either, and that the opposite was true – that Zeneca was perceived to suffer from the same shortcomings as Astra. Another argument was that Astra was undervalued in the deal and vice versa concerning Zeneca. In addition, Zeneca was diversified into agro chemicals, a business that would reduce the valuation of the new company. There were also concerns that the British side would come to dominate the management culture and would be more hierarchical and control-oriented than the Swedish with detrimental effects on the creative research climate in Astra (see the story about Losec and Astra Hässle in the previous chapter!). 'I fear that the researchers at Hässle won't take this. They might just walk away' is the kind of statements that could be heard from external commentators. In addition to different opinions about the deal itself and the benefits for Astra there has also been criticism about its expected effects on the Swedish economy and employment. However, the deal went through and Investor has continued to be bullish about the merger. Reports from Investor emphasise the smoothness of the merger process. PB, who was asked to become chairman of the merged company based on his experience of merger processes in ABB, states that this merger is much easier than that of ABB. 'AstraZeneca is in an expanding market while in the case of ABB we had to take out a lot of overcapacity, close down plants, and get rid of people when we merged'.

- A third big merger was agreed upon between *Volvo and Scania*. However, the deal was not approved by the EU – for dubious reasons, it seems.[3] The EU ruling was not only a disappointment for the owners of Volvo and Scania. It seriously damaged the Swedish public confidence in EU in general. Investor had intended to become the largest owner of Volvo, making it one of the core holdings of the sphere. After the EU ruling the owner situation of Scania, in particular, has become quite complicated. Volvo remains the largest owner while Investor sold the main part of its holding in Scania to Volkswagen. With this rather locked owner situation, the liquidity of the Scania share is low. Thus, the small shareholders of Scania are the ones being hurt.

- Finally, if we look at the *third step* in PB's active ownership model there are also examples of divestments and even closures. The latter refers to the closures of Saab's commuter aircraft business, which was losing big money in recent years. This decision had been pending for some time. For several years the company had very successfully supplied what was considered the best propeller-driven plane on the market to the leading carriers in the world. However in recent years the market preference has turned totally in favour of jet planes. Shortly after becoming chairman PB seems to have cut short this decision trauma. In the space of a few months the closure of this business was accomplished. Divestments have included media companies, which resulted in the Wallenberg sphere leaving the media sector completely. Investor sold out its holdings in one TV channel and one Swedish newspaper.

- Of key concern is Investor's so called *investment company discount*,[4] sometimes also called *power discount*.[5] This has been a lingering problem for a long time, but since summer 1998 it has increased by some 50 percent and is now oscillating around 35 percent. This is the case despite of all improvements achieved in fundamental performance in the holdings and impressive increases in the net asset value of Investor. Furthermore, Investor has tried to address the actual *power* aspect by reducing the spread of voting power between A and B shares in some companies. In Electrolux and SKF it has been reduced from 1/1000 to 1/10. In ABB the differentiation has been eliminated completely. It can be assumed that the Wallenberg sphere would like to reduce the 1/1000 differentiation in Ericsson to 1/10 as well, but at the same time there are indications that the other large owner, the Handelsbanken/Industrivärden sphere is resisting such attempts. This difference in views possibly reveals a deeper conflict between the two main owners. It is striking that the Ericsson board has remained unchanged basically since PB became chairman of Investor while the boards of Investor's most other strategic holdings have been the subject of major change. The analysis of the shortcomings of the active ownership of Ericsson above clearly indicated a need for quite some change.
- Another issue, related to the discount problem, is that of *free riders*. People or institutions looking for investment opportunities might have strong confidence in Investor's capability to create value in its holdings – or at least in one or several of them. So, rather than placing their money in the whole portfolio of Investor, they pick the ones that look most promising at that particular point in time. Investor's strategy to cope with this issue is to offer advantages, which are accessible only to Investor shareholders. This is achieved through *New investments*– investments which, initially, are made in non-listed companies (or buy-outs of listed companies). The *New investments* strategy was implemented successively during the 1990s but has gained momentum after 1995. These new investments have already started to generate substantial net gains. In the first 9 months of 1999 alone, the total net gain from divestments was SEK 2135 million

(USD 260 million). These new investments are carried out in three different programmes – related to three different phases in the development of
a business.

- For the *start-up phases* Investor has a fully owned *venture capital* company,
  Novare Kapital, that currently has minority holdings in some thirty
  companies with minority investments of around SEK 5–30 million (USD
  0.7–4 million) each. The total equity base is SEK 500 million (some USD 70
  million). However, there are also plans to broaden the capital base of
  Novare by inviting external investors. Novare is currently expanding,
  with some 15–20 new investments annually, focusing on companies in
  future growth sectors, especially IT, communications, and health care.
  Novare provides active owner assistance to the fledgling companies it
  is investing in, drawing upon its own resources and competence as well
  as the whole network of Investor and the Wallenberg sphere. The investment horizon is three to seven years and a couple of exits have already
  realised value.

- The second new investment programme is focusing on companies in their
  international expansion phase. Here, each investment is in the USD 20–60
  million range. The Investor offices of New York and Hong Kong, in particular, are handling this investment programme. The first major divestment was achieved in 1999 generating a net gain of some SEK 1.5 billion
  (USD 200 million).

- The third focus is on the mature phases of businesses and companies
  where Investor is the main owner of EQT, a *private equity/LBO* firm that
  can draw upon buy-out funds currently with commitments of SEK 11
  billion (USD 1.4 billion). Investor is one of several institutional investors
  in these funds. While the two other programmes of new investments
  focus on IT, communications and health care, EQT is open to projects in
  a variety of industries. Several investments and exits have already been
  successfully completed generating net gains far beyond expectations.
  EQT is expanding internationally by setting up offices in London and
  Munich and by mobilising a large European buy out fund.

OPEN ISSUES FOR THE FUTURE

Time for its own medicine?

Despite a number of decisive measures being taken the discount to net asset
value lingers on, actually even increasing recently (early 2000). Does this
mean that Investor has reached the end of the road? For what is the point
of continuing something that the market doesn't appreciate – and this even
includes the Wallenberg Foundations since they also seem to play the free
rider game. Should Investor apply step three of PB's model to itself? Should
it change the ownership of its own active ownership business?

Or will more patience pay off?

Maybe some additional patience (!) is required. Possibly the market will gain more confidence in the value creation capability of Investor if and when the recent big mergers start to prove themselves. It should also be expected that some of the strategic holdings will reach step two and three in PB's active ownership programme. SAS was mentioned as a possible candidate for divestment above. It is also questionable, according to the analysis of key strengths above, if Investor is the best long-term owner of Electrolux, to take another example. External security analysts and investment managers abound in recommendations to Investor to divest several of its strategic holdings. Another advice is to increase Investor's holding in Ericsson, not only as a good investment per se, but also to achieve a better portfolio balance in relation to the general index of the Stockholm Stock Exchange. Since Investor has set as a goal to beat that index by three percentage points annually, it is already handicapped by the fact that Ericsson's weight in Investor's portfolio is lower than Ericsson's weight in that index.

Marcus Wallenberg is launching 'The Bridge'

In April 1999, Marcus Wallenberg – representing the fifth generation of the dynasty – took over as CEO of Investor. Expectations have been high on him to come out with his ideas of how he intends to shape the future of Investor and the Wallenberg sphere. Several times since becoming CEO, Marcus Wallenberg has expressed his belief in the ownership idea of Investor and the Wallenberg sphere. In particular, he has emphasised the importance of renewal. In that context he has also referred to one of his grandfather's, MW, famous phrases ending: '… the only tradition worth caring about'. However, his statements about the renewal strategy have been quite general, namely 'Transformation of Core Holdings' and 'New Investments'[6] – until recently. The new strategy launched by Marcus Wallenberg at the AGM in March 2000 is named 'The Bridge'. A month earlier he explained what was to come:

> I think we are in a unique and advantageous position in Investor where we can be the bridge between the old and the new economy. We have decided to invest up to 15 percent of our total assets in start-ups and rapidly growing companies in the new technologies of the new economy. We have already invested some 30 percent of that amount and engaged ourselves in more than 100 new ventures. At the same time, our core holdings within the old economy have excellent positions, not only in the traditional markets but also concerning growth opportunities in the new economy. They also collaborate with one another. As you know, Ericsson and Electrolux are now co-operating to develop the 'intelligent home'. At Investor we can do a lot of additional 'bridging' by venturing into businesses using the emerging new technologies and apply them to existing businesses as you will soon be informed about. Furthermore,

I think, we are blessed with having a young generation, which fears nothing and is very entrepreneurial. Sweden remains important for the Wallenberg sphere, for our future business prosperity and for the reason I mentioned earlier.

Marcus Wallenberg, CEO of Investor[7]

One goal of Investor and the sphere in recent years has been to achieve fundamental renewal by riding the wave of *the new economy*, i.e. by investing in promising start-ups. At the end of 1999, the total portfolio of the Investor Group included investments in some sixty companies of this type. In this context, one should not forget that several of Investor's core holdings are already at the forefront of the new economy: Ericsson, of course, is not only well positioned. It is one of the key drivers of the whole global wave. ABB is in the process of transforming itself from a heavy equipment producer to a software and knowledge based company. OM is another example, being the first private stock exchange (1984), an innovator of computerised trading technology, and through its most recent initiative, the first to start an online, cross-border stock exchange – Jiway – in a joint venture with Morgan Stanley. A third example, finally, is SEB leading the Nordic pack in Internet banking and has acquired a foothold in Germany for further international expansion.

The launching of *The Bridge* is a further and innovative step in the renewal of the Wallenberg sphere. Several joint ventures between Investor on the one hand and one or several of the core holding corporations in each case on the other have already been announced as part of this new strategy. These joint ventures aim to exploit the opportunities of the new economy, e.g. in e-commerce, particularly the so-called B2B markets. Examples include:

- ABB and Investor as main owners have formed a European risk capital company focusing on e-B2B commerce, called **b-business partners**, with an equity base of more than one billion Euro. Other owners include Astra-Zeneca, Atlas Copco, Electrolux Saab(Aerospace), Sandvik, SEB, Stora Enso, and WM-data. The new company announced its first investment, Surplex.com a German company based in Düsseldorf, at the end of March 2000. Surplex.com is an Internet-based market place for excess production capacity and stocks of input materials.
- Investor, Ericsson, and Hutchison Whampoa, a Hong Kong based multi-national corporation, have set up a jointly owned risk capital company focused on investments in mobile Internet-related companies in Asia (announced end of March 2000).

Drawing upon the networks – internal as well as external – and competence of the Wallenberg sphere, the new *Bridge* strategy is supposed to speed up the renewal processes of Investor's core holdings as well as increase the proportion of new economy companies in the total portfolio of Investor.

A package too complex?

It is of course much too early to assess if the new *Bridge* strategy will be successful, if it will result in fundamental value creation as well as raise new market confidence enough to reduce or eliminate Investor's investment company discount.

However, it is also possible that there is a new competitive logic in the market for ownership and investments where Investor's disadvantage is that its operations are too complex. Although Investor – as the Wallenberg sphere has done in the past – continues to govern its holdings and new investments so that superior added value is created it is too difficult to communicate this to the market. In that case it should have to stop offering the same 'package', the present Investor share, to all and sundry. Instead, Investor would need to differentiate its offerings, e.g. a blue chip portfolio consisting of a set of its core holdings, another of more risky new ventures etc. Investor itself with its active owner competence and formidable network of contacts could take on lucrative contracts to exercise governance and create added value for various investors and become attractive and highly valued on the stock exchange.

Lessons of history

Looking back to history might provide useful food for thought. One could be justified in concluding that Investor represents a very ambitious attempt to integrate and institutionalise all the value creating competence, resources and infrastructure of the sphere into one entity. Through the early phases of development and until Enskilda was swallowed by S E-Banken, the Wallenberg sphere operated through a very flexible and versatile set of instruments – the bank itself, several investment companies and outfits for stock and bond issues (e.g. Emissionsinstitutet AB). Furthermore, of no less importance, and in the centre of it all, the Wallenberg individuals acted as private capitalists taking risks and mobilising other partners as well as their whole infrastructure of resources.

Liberating the real substance from the formal constraints of Investor?

So, a break-up of Investor – away from the constraints of being listed as one complex entity measured against impossible expectations – might be a better way of using its active ownership competence, and a viable option to do justice to all the inherent value creation capabilities of the Wallenberg sphere.

PART III

Conceptualisation and Professionalisation

Ownership and Value Creation – Towards a Conceptual Framework   12

The purpose of this chapter is to outline a conceptual framework for ownership and value creation. Ownership, its function and role, will be viewed from the perspective of value creation. Thus, the analysis to follow will try to discuss 'why', 'what', and 'how' in this perspective:

- **Why** are ownership and the role of the owner crucial?
- **What** is ownership all about, and what distinguishes ownership from other roles in the process of value creation?
- **What** competence is required to be a value-creating owner?
- **How** are value creation contributions made, and how is ownership exercised to be successful?

In carrying out this analysis, references will be made to the in-depth case study of the Wallenberg sphere in chapter in Part II. In addition, examples from other companies and owner specialists will also be used.

POINTS OF DEPARTURE – THREE FUNDAMENTAL PROPOSITIONS

The conceptual analysis of ownership and value creation consists of three basic assumptions. The first encompasses the overall nature of the open market, and the second the fundamental rationale of the individual company. The third assumption, which we will come back to later, is about ownership and risk. Figure 12.1 attempts to summarise the first two propositions/assumptions.

The process of creative destruction

Schumpeter's brilliant concept, *the process of creative destruction* [1] is a powerful tool to understand the fundamental nature of market capitalism, and, thus, the crucial, external prerequisites for value creation. Schumpeter highlights the evolutionary character of market capitalism rendering it a superior quality: incessant self-renewal. This inherent dynamic makes market capitalism a superior provider of wealth compared to all other economic systems. The forces driving this evolution dynamic are innovations of all kinds: new

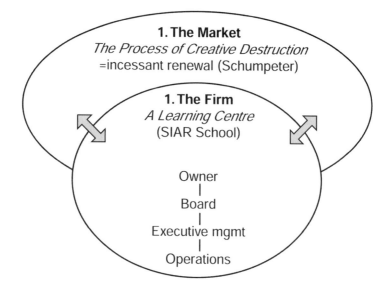

Figure 12.1   Two fundamental propositions about the market and the firm.

products, new process technologies, new service concepts, new forms of organisation etc.

These innovation processes are like mutations in biological systems, meaning, 'that (this process) incessantly revolutionises the economic structure from *within* , incessantly destroying the old one, incessantly creating a new one.' (Schumpeter, p. 83)

In a competitive market, the entrepreneur or the firm tries to come up with a superior product, or process etc that eliminates competition (in a perfect market nobody makes money). However, this is only a temporary blessing. By introducing a superior product or service, the innovator *destroys* the existing offering on the market. Similarly, a new innovation is to be expected that – sooner or later – will repeat the act of destruction. Thus, the pattern of creation and destruction keeps repeating itself. Ultimately, as a result of the incessant renewal, consumers are to benefit by wider choice and more value for money. Examples are legion and easy to identify, not least in the high-tech sector of the new economy. We will bring up a few further on in this chapter to illustrate some of the concepts.

Thus, the essence of an open market is *incessant renewal* . However, the fundamental prerequisite for such a market is well-functioning competition:

- in the end markets for products and services; as well as
- in the resource markets for production factors, including capital.

- The prerequisites about a well-functioning competition also include the market for ownership. Owners act on a market where they compete by allocating their funds differently, by means of different ways to organise ideas and resources, and by how they exercise their ownership.

The firm as a learning centre

The blessings of the market economy, as a superior provider of prosperity through *the process of creative destruction* , do not guarantee the sustainability and success of the individual company. Schumpeter's concept just says that a superior offering introduced by one actor will destroy an existing offering. One company could be established based on the new offering and another, based on the old offering, could go bankrupt.

Thus the sustainable success of a company depends on its ability to deal with the processes of creative destruction, the challenges of incessant renewal, generated by its market environment.

A basic concept in the *SIAR School* [2] is the view of the individual company as a *learning centre* . This view is different from what macroeconomic theory usually proposes as the rationale of the individual company. Leading scholars, such as Oliver E. Williamson,[3] refer to *transaction costs* as the determining factor explaining why certain activities are organised within a company or whether they take place between companies in the open market. Thus, the rationale of the individual company is lower transaction costs for a set of activities that constitute a certain value creation process, compared to the alternative of making the corresponding activities in the open market.

The *SIAR School* recognises the transaction cost view as a necessary prerequisite for the survival of a company, but not a sufficient one. The critical capability of a company is to cope with the incessant demands for renewal, posed by the market environment. Thus, the prerequisites for transaction costs are changing incessantly, and the capability to change, and to adapt, as well as to renew, and to innovate become the core aspects of a company's prospects for sustainable success. This is a matter of learning how to cope with new prerequisites. Thus, viewing a company as a learning centre is more to the point than the transaction cost view. As a consequence, a concept of *organisational learning* is an important element of the theory to be applied here.

However, Figure 12.1 tries to illustrate that the relation between the individual company and its environment is systemic. Thus, the company is part of and is contributing to the formation of its environment while, at the same time, being forced internally to cope with the demands of the external environment. This mutual relationship is a key aspect, which we will come back to later.

In the corporate governance world today the target of governance is usually a rather complex organisation – a corporation of individual businesses and entities, business areas and sub-groups etc. Our conceptual framework addresses that complexity by analysing *the renewal hierarchy* of such a corporation.

Ownership and its two parameters of risk

Our third assumption is about ownership and risk, more exactly, about ownership and two aspects of risk.

General agreement on one of these aspects

There is probably general agreement on one fundamental aspect of ownership. It has to do with supply of risk capital. Owners provide risk capital, equity, to make the start and expansion of a company possible. The special quality of equity is not only its function of financing or being part of the financing of a business operation – however necessary and important. The particular quality of equity capital is its function of absorbing uncertainty. The future prospects of a business operation are uncertain. Investments have to be made, and costs are incurred before revenues can and hopefully will start being generated. Furthermore, there is no guarantee that revenues will be enough to cover all costs incurred and yield a return. Thus, by providing equity capital, the owner is willing to put his equity contribution at risk. Doing this, the owner absorbs the uncertainty due to the time lag between costs and revenues, a time lag that can turn out to be eternal. Since equity capital also bolsters the risks taken by other providers of funds (bonds, bank loans etc), it has a dynamic effect, boosting growth and the development speed of a company by making larger investments possible.

Ownership is more than risking one's own capital

Putting its equity capital at risk is not the only uncertainty-absorbing contribution of ownership. Owners do not make their equity investments as a gambler does by slotting his coin into an one-armed bandit and hoping for sheer luck. Owners try to cope with the risks their investments are being exposed to. There are fundamentally different ways of coping with risks, which will be discussed later. However, as a whole, the ownership function, comprising all types of owners in the market for risk capital, must be concerned with the *reduction/elimination of fundamental risks of the business operations* invested in. Otherwise, future return on investment will be at the mercy of whatever forces are at play.

Thus, by seeing to it that inherent, fundamental risks of a business operation are being reduced, and hopefully eliminated, the uncertainty absorbing function of ownership is further enhanced.

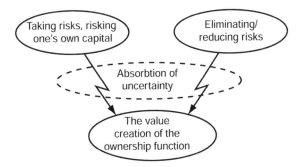

Figure 12.2 Risk and the value creating role of ownership.

Ownership requires competence

Certainly, it takes competence and careful analysis to select an investment opportunity. However, *the real competence test is the capability to reduce and eliminate fundamental risks* . Thus, it should be wise to consider the following imperative: Invest in businesses where you have the competence to take responsibility for the reduction/elimination of fundamental risks, or be aware that you need to acquire that competence! The management of risks as well as the content and composition of ownership competence required to do that will be discussed at length later in this chapter.

Summing up: the dual risk aspects of ownership

Figure 12.2 attempts to sum up and illustrate the proposition about the value-creating role of ownership through its dual relation to risk: taking risks and reducing/eliminating risks.

IMPLICATIONS OF THESE PROPOSITIONS FOR FURTHER CONCEPTUALISATION

So, what are the implications of these propositions for the conceptualisation of ownership and value creation? Let us review the implications of each proposition and then see how they all fit together.

Implications of creative destruction – the renewal imperative

The most important implication of Schumpeter's brilliant concept, *the process of creative destruction* , is that prosperity – for the economy as a whole as well as for the individual business entity – is a function of *incessant renewal* . This means, that however successful a certain business has been, to be sustained it requires incessant renewal to adapt to the external forces of renewal.

The forces driving *the process of creative destruction* are working at two levels, basically. The first one is to be found at the individual level, an entrepreneur or a single company. By exploiting new technologies, new regulations, new life styles etc, an entrepreneur or innovative company can launch a new business concept on the market. This poses a threat to some of the existing businesses on the market. Some degree of renewal will be necessary for the incumbents.

Since the market is an interdependent system, changes at one point will generate a chain reaction of changes. Thus, one could say, *the process of creative destruction* is also a function of the competitive dynamics of a market. The renewal implications are not limited to the immediate and isolated effects of one new entrepreneur entering the market. The scope of the renewal necessary for incumbents has to consider the implications of a new competitive dynamic. When IKEA, the furniture retailer, got its breakthrough, it was not just another retail competitor that entered the market. Large parts of the entire furniture industry were revolutionised.

Is prediction possible?

If *the process of creative destruction* generates such chain reactions, and the competitive dynamics further reinforce the process, how about prediction? Is it possible to predict future competition, market prospects, and demands for renewal? As a consequence, would it be possible to predict future prosperity as well?

Remarkably enough, Schumpeter made a prediction, but a rather gloomy one. At the same time as he emphasised the superiority of the market economy as a provider of prosperity – thanks to *the process of creative destruction* – he foresaw a limit to the forces of innovation and renewal to perpetuate the process. Schumpeter concluded that when renewal processes stop and development of prosperity stagnates, socialism would take over. In his view, a socialistic system would be more efficient at administrating a given level of prosperity.

Fortunately, it could be argued, Schumpeter's concept was greater than his own ability to apply it.[4] Not only because the world turned out better, fortunately. Totalitarian regimes have been defeated and replaced, and successively, trade restrictions have been dismantled, and so forth. The inherent dynamics of individual initiative and creativity, and of the competitive dynamics of the market economy – captured so elegantly by the concept of *the process of creative destruction* – are so powerful that all impediments are likely to be overcome eventually. It is rather a matter of the pace of development and prosperity improvement that will vary depending on our success at tearing down remaining trade barriers, and substituting open societies for obsolete dictatorships etc.

When interpreting the concept of *the process of creative destruction* , one should be aware that *destruction* refers to a certain way of doing business, of applying a technology etc, not to the final destruction of that technology. We are still using the horse and cart, the steam engine and so forth, after the introduction of railways, the combustion engine, and the automobile. However, the applications of the old technologies have changed. The old ones still have relative advantages in certain, more limited applications. At the same time, in certain applications, prosperity is also enhanced by combinations of new and old technologies. Maybe you enjoy horse riding in the wilderness but to get there you prefer to use a combination of airline transport and a rental car. In certain types of logging operations you can still benefit from the flexibility of horses (of a certain breed) in parallel with large scale harvesting processors.

Thus, *the process of creative destruction* , for the market system as a whole, opens up a myriad of opportunities: new combinations, new innovations, supplementary products and services etc. Henry Ford's innovations – the T-Ford and the assembly line – created a mass market for automobiles, revolutionised production technologies, and destroyed some existing approaches in that industry. But these innovations also generated legions of new business opportunities – car dealerships, road construction, petrol stations, new suburbs, and more. Similarly, the pioneering of modern mobile telephony by Ericsson and Swedish Telecoms some twenty years ago lead to a mobile telecommunications market, currently hosting legions of new businesses.

Limited predictability but certain logic

If we are not struck by pessimism, as Schumpeter, but instead believe in Man's incessant drive to create and innovate, *the process of creative destruction* will never end in a final scenario. (So, instead, prospects for socialism are rather gloomy.) In that sense, we cannot predict the final outcome of this process. However, there are forces at work driving the process in a certain direction, as well as differentiating it from one industry to the next, that we can identify and analyse.

- *The process of creative destruction* successively intensifies competition and drives specialisation in an industry. A typical consequence of that is that vertically integrated companies find it increasingly difficult to stay competitive at all levels of their chain of operations. Outsourcing and divestments of non-core businesses ensue.
- Intensified competition drives companies to benefit from economies of scale by searching for larger markets. Thus, it could be argued, *the process of creative destruction* drives globalisation.
- However, this movement towards globalisation is by no means linear. On the contrary, during the development of an industry it can vary from a

stage of globalisation to something else and then back to global competition again. The T-Ford initially spread to markets around the globe because of its uniqueness. Successively, other mass producers of automobiles started to appear, making competition local and regional, primarily, for a long time. Currently, we are witnessing an intensified restructuring of the regional automobile industry, particularly in Europe, in parallel with intensive efforts by leading actors to build their global structures – almost a century after the T-Fords swept the global market. This pattern of development is even more clear in the pulp and paper industry. Some Swedish producers were the innovators of kraft pulp in the early part of the 20th century. Even, several years after World War II, Swedish producers dominated world markets. Then followed a massive expansion of pulp making capacity in several parts of the world, making competition primarily regional. Recent (early 2000) attempts to acquire major US pulp and paper companies by large Scandinavian companies (Champion by UPM-Kymmene and Consolidated Papers by StoraEnso) mark the beginning of re-globalisation.

- It is possible to differentiate *the process of creative destruction* depending on the fundamental characteristics of a certain industry. This aspect is illustrated later in this chapter when different risk patterns and dynamics are analysed.

The risk perspective

Taking the point of view of owners, we need to apply the risk perspective to the *process of creative destruction* . It is obvious, that this process generates risks when an existing business is being threatened by new innovations. Unless the exposed company succeeds with its adaptation to the new competitive situation and its renewal of its old way of doing business, market capitalisation will deteriorate together with the wealth of the owner, as represented by his/her investment in the company. However, renewal also entails new risks that need to be mastered by the owner. New opportunities entail dual risks as well. Exploiting a new opportunity exposes the owner to new risks. However, refraining from the opportunity might entail the opportunity risk of less attractive investment options. Thus, the *process of creative destruction* incessantly generates new risks for owners.

Issues for further analysis

To study the implications of the *process of creative destruction* and the renewal imperative further, we need to analyse the following three issues:

1. What are the different types of risks and which ones are important?
2. What are the means – generic as well as specific – to cope with these risks?

3. What competence requirements on owners will these entail?

Before we come to this analysis, we will first review the implications of the two other propositions.

Implications of the firm as a learning centre

To become successful, and to sustain a successful position, the individual company needs to cope with the demands for renewal, generated by *the process of creative destruction* . We will call this the company's learning capability and we can view the company as a learning centre.

An important distinction

Demands for renewal go on incessantly as highlighted above. However, for a particular business of a company demands for renewal can be more or less dramatic. The same fundamental innovation can be revolutionary for one company and trivial for another. The introduction of a new process technology could be a matter of future existence for a competitor in that market, while for the potential user of that technology it is rather a matter of optimising an investment to replace the old technology, to take a simple example.

General systems theory makes a distinction between two types of changes corresponding to this example: the *principles of positive* and *negative feedback* , respectively. The trivial type of change corresponds to the *principle of negative feedback* . This type of change/renewal can be accommodated within a given system without changing the system itself. A familiar analogy is the thermostat regulating the temperature of a building. If the outside temperature falls, the heating system will generate more heat to restore and maintain the chosen inside temperature. The *principle of positive feedback* , on the other hand, refers to demands for revolutionary renewal. This means that adaptation requires fundamental change of the system itself. For example, if the fall in outside temperature is caused by the coming of a new glacial period, it is of no avail to turn on the heater. The entire house needs to be rebuilt or the inhabitants have to move to another climatic region.

Value creation and concepts of learning

Applying the principles of negative and positive feedback to business reality, we can make an analogous distinction as follows:

- Renewing an established way of doing business without changing its fundamental structure (*negative feedback*).
- Developing a new way of doing business or fundamentally renew an existing one (*positive feedback*).

To fit this with the concept of the firm as a learning centre, we must analyse how value is created, to begin with, in a single business.

The business idea concept

A single business can be defined as a sequential set of operational activities: R&D, production, marketing, sales and distribution resulting in a product or service consumed by a final customer. But what explains the difference in outcome, what distinguishes success from mediocrity or failure?

Drawing upon the analysis above, with some additions, the following success criteria have to be met:

1. Competition has to be eliminated or adequately reduced. In a market of perfect competition, where all competitors are equal, nobody makes money.
2. Such competitive superiority, or *market dominance* , requires a system of several elements that all fit together and support one another.[5] The fabulous success of Tetra Pak cannot be explained solely by its technical innovations. Its commercial concept of providing the packaging function by leasing its filling machines to the customers, and its way of controlling the flow of packaging material through the entire supply chain from sub-suppliers of basic materials to the dairy customer are other key elements in its *success formula* . Similarly, Ericsson's global market leadership in mobile telephony systems is based on a combination of front end technology, possibly the largest customer base among telecom equipment suppliers, and an unrivalled world-wide sales organisation, to mention some of the critical elements. For every new generation of mobile systems, Ericsson gets a head start through this, further reinforcing its strategic position. Similar mechanisms can be observed as regards Microsoft, for instance. To break such a virtual circle of position reinforcement usually requires radically new innovations.
3. All actors involved – customers, distributors, suppliers, and the company itself – dynamically reinforce each other. There is a plus-sum game of growth, customer satisfaction, and enhanced profits. The T-Ford was based on a giant leap in productivity based on production innovations – that also spread to large parts of the manufacturing industry – making it possible for workers to become car buyers as well, thus boosting market growth and additional economies of scale.
4. To be sustainable, a successful business system must have dynamic resilience to accommodate demands for renewal generated by *the process of creative destruction* . At least including the type of changes referred to above as governed by the principle of negative feedback.

The result of a learning process

The fulfilment of these criteria has not occurred by chance. A business characterised by this kind of *beautiful fit* is the result of a learning process, most often quite time demanding. It took IKEA and Tetra Pak, to mention two successful examples, some twenty years to develop a sustainable business platform from which to start penetrating world markets. Microsoft was quicker, its MS-DOS started piggybacking on IBM already in 1981, six years after Bill Gates and Paul Allen had begun their tinkering in the family garage. The Microsoft IPO came in 1986, but it took until 1994, nineteen years after start-up, before Windows 95 was introduced, the software that reached an unprecedented mass market. How long will it take for some of the hyped-up companies of the new economy to establish a sustainable business, generating returns that match their current market capitalisation?

The *beautiful fit* is on the one hand a successful business system of concrete elements of resources, business activities etc. On the other hand, it has its counterpart in an idea system, the *business idea* .[6] This is the mind and memory of the business, embodied by those that made the learning process as well as by those successors who have managed to assimilate it. However, it should be recognised that such assimilation is facilitated by the many arrangements, procedures, administrative systems etc that successively emerged to support the company's *way of doing business* .

The business idea and the process of creative destruction

The learning that the business idea represents, concerning the *process of creative destruction* , is the capability to cope with the typical renewal processes going in its market environment. This includes all the changes that can be accommodated without changing the fundamental structure of the *business idea* and the beautiful system of fit. Such typical renewal processes will be illustrated in a later section of this chapter where different risk dynamics will be analysed.

If the *process of creative destruction* generates innovations that call for more fundamental renewal measures, the *business idea* itself is at stake. This requires learning at another level.

The renewal hierarchy and learning at different levels

The typical large corporation of today, even after the *purgatory* of the early 1990s to focus on core business, organises many different businesses. The rationale of such a multi-business group is that value-added is created. The value of the whole should be larger than the sum of the parts on a stand-alone basis. There are two ways for corporate management to create such value-added. One way is through synergies between the individual businesses. One example is the alleged synergies between the mobile telephony systems of Ericsson and its mobile handsets business. (Some critics argue, though, particularly when its handsets business experiences difficulties, that Ericsson would be better off divesting this business to a consumer products oriented company.) Synergies are supposed to exist in R&D as well as in the market place, selling both systems and handsets to operators.

Another way value-added is created has to do with fundamental renewal of businesses where the old business idea has become obsolete.

The issue of difficult decisions – or can you pull yourself up by your own bootstraps?

While the people embodying and managing an established *business idea* excel at coping with its traditional competition, they are often the last ones to recognise and admit fundamental change when that is called for. We will discuss this phenomenon in more depth in a later section analysing organisational risks. At this point, suffice it to conclude that fundamental change concerning one's own business or professional existence entails some really *difficult decisions* . Such situations sometimes justify the analogy with pulling yourself up in your own bootstraps. A leverage point outside your own system is necessary to get the required effect. A superior level, e.g. corporate management in relation to a single business that needs fundamental renewal, has a natural role to play in such situations.

The group idea – the concept of creating value-added at group level

If a multibusiness corporation has a proven record of creating value-added – based on synergies between its various businesses as well as through its ability to renew obsolete business ideas and create new ones – it has not occurred by chance. The value-added has been generated by another *beautiful fit* , a *group idea* . Analogous to the *business idea* , the *group idea* has been formed in a learning process spanning a long period of time. A case in point is 3M, the Minnesota Mining & Manufacturing Company. Core elements of its *group idea* include combinations of thin carriers, made of different materials, and a huge variety of surface coatings to perform a plethora of functions, e.g. all kinds of tapes and other products.

In fact, the *group* and *growth idea* of 3M turned out to have such potential and wide applicability that it has been possible to form several subgroups within the corporation, e.g. in products for Consumer and Office Markets, Industrial Markets, and Health Care Markets , to mention a few. In that way, one could say, 3M's *group idea* has made the transition to become an *owner idea* by having the potential to generate several groups of business ideas. We will discuss the concept of owner idea in a following section.

The fascinating story and creative learning process of 3M started through a failed mining project. Instead of finding the mineral they had been looking for, the mining entrepreneurs only found sand. However, that could be used for sandpaper, the first combination of a thin paper carrier and a surface coating that could perform a grinding function. It is a long way from that simple combination to 3M's current sophisticated products (in the sense of being used in advanced medical and high tech applications as well as being extremely practical for daily use, e.g. ordinary tape or *Post-it*), but it is the same basic concept.

A group idea: synergies and new growth

Thus, a *group idea* integrates several *business ideas* and creates value-added by exploitation of synergies between these. Furthermore, a group idea is also a *renewal* and new *growth idea* , a kind of *genetic code* to renew existing *business ideas* and generate new offspring, new business ideas having certain traits in common with earlier and existing businesses.

Owners – the ultimate level of the renewal hierarchy of a company

'The buck stops here', to give owners the voice of Peter Wallenberg, honorary chairman of Investor and head of the Wallenberg family as well as chairman of the family foundations (see Part II!). Thus, the ultimate *difficult decision* , to make sure that necessary renewal takes place, ends up at the ultimate owner level. However, there are also professional owner specialists, e.g. Investor, the investment company of the Wallenberg sphere. Investor is superior to a number of multi-business corporations. In addition to making sure that *difficult renewal decisions* are taken concerning these corporations, Investor should create value-added by exploiting the synergies available at the level of an *owner specialist* . There are many other types of *owner specialists*, apart from investment companies such as Investor: venture capital and LBO/MBO specialists such as 3i of the UK, CD&R and Kleiner Perkins of the US, and IndustriKapital of Sweden as well as institutional investors, such as Hermes of the UK and CalPERS of the US with their entourage of relation investment specialists, to name a few examples. There are also corporations where the roles of an owner specialist and a multibusiness corporation, respectively, have been mixed up. One name for this type of schizophrenic phenomenon is *conglomerate* . When the conglomerate corporations emerged in the 1960s, they were based on *group ideas* (hypothetical) such as financial and general management synergies. ITT under Harold Geneen as chairman/ CEO was seen as the model case at that time. As *owner specialists*, the conglomerates seemed to believe that the main requirement for success was financial competence. Most of these companies failed.

However, there are also very successful companies for which it is difficult to define their character, e.g. General Electric. It is not based on a coherent corporate idea. What are the synergies between gas turbines and NCB, the TV channel, for instance? If it is an owner specialist – why does it own most of its business 100 percent? Its competence as an *owner specialist* could be leveraged by reducing its ownership share while extending its portfolio with additional holdings fitting its competence profile! Maybe, its success is explained by the extraordinary talents of its Chairman and CEO for the last twenty years, Jack Welch? In that case, the owners and board of GE have better reconsider the owner idea and structure of the corporation rather than just replace Mr. Welch when he is due to retire in 2001!

Owner idea

The owner level marks the top of the hierarchy of one or several companies, and one or several multibusiness groups. Of course, the group level is not justified unless there are synergies to be exploited between a subgroup of companies, and the ability to create value-added through a consistent *group idea* .

The value creation rationale of the owner level is to reduce and eliminate risks as stated earlier. Analogous with the *business idea* concept at the individual business level, and the *group idea* concept at the level of the multi-business group, we can also conceptualise an *owner idea* that integrates the risk reduction/elimination activities of the owner and creates value-added. An in depth analysis of this will follow after summing up the discussion of the renewal and value creation hierarchy so far.

Summing up: the renewal hierarchy and the vertical organisation of value creation

The analysis of the concept of the firm as a *learning centre* turned out to necessitate the differentiation of roles in a hierarchy. Generated by the *process of creative destruction* , the demands for renewal, in particular those requiring fundamental change (the principle of positive feedback) and *difficult decisions* benefit from the involvement of a superior level in such an hierarchy, as illustrated in Figure 12.3. Each layer in this hierarchy is justified by its ability to add value to the whole. Such value-added is generated by exploitation of synergies between units at the subordinate level as well as by furthering the renewal processes among these. The *distinctive competence* to achieve this, is the result of a historical learning process, an *organising idea* – business idea, group idea , and *owner idea* , respectively, at each level.

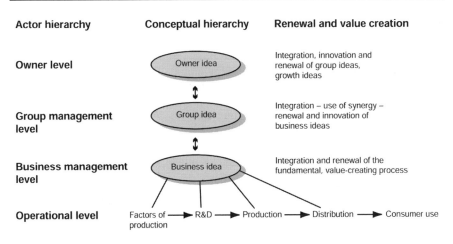

Figure 12.3 The renewal hierarchy and the vertical organisation for value creation.

Implications of ownership and coping with risk

The fundamental role of the ownership function as a whole, in addition to supply of risk capital, is to see to it that fundamental risks of business operations, where risk capital is deployed, are reduced and, if possible, eliminated. However, the ownership function as a whole involves numerous actors with different roles and competencies. Do they all have to be active in reducing and eliminating fundamental risks?

Managing risk – what are the options available?

As concerns coping with fundamental risks, there are basically *two strategic options* to choose: *spreading the risks or reduction/elimination* of such risks.

Table 12.1 (*Two fundamentally different ways of managing risks*) gives an overview of these two options, including two alternative *risk perspectives* that justify each choice. The figure also includes a comparison with the insurance business that might require some additional explanation.

Alternative perspectives of position and risk

The analogy with the insurance field highlighted to the author how important it is to distinguish between these two approaches, also as regards ownership and risk capital investment. It helps also in *positioning* various types of actors in the risk capital market, and to see what kind of owner involvement can be expected.

Table 12.1 Two fundamentally different ways of managing risk

	Portfolio managers	Active owners
Risk perspective	Risks are predetermined, cannot be influenced	Risks can be reduced/eliminated
Risk management strategy	Spreading the risks	Allocation of capital to risks one can handle
	Portfolio optimisation	Active/proactive reduction/elimination of risks
Cf. Insurance business	The actuarial approach	HPR (Highly Protected Risk)/Risk Management Perspective

Excursus: An analogy with insurance actuaries and risk managers

It has to do with this author's own learning process and how earlier experience of the insurance industry inspired this essential distinction as regards risk management strategies within the ownership function. When working as a management consultant with a major Scandinavian insurance company some twenty years ago, a striking feature has been the two different cultures that prevailed within the company. It turned out that one management career ladder originated in the actuarial department. Another set of managers had been recruited among engineers and technical staff that came out of the company's risk prevention programmes, of which the company was famous and took great pride. These two cultures clashed when a former actuary was appointed head of a commercial line of insurance. In one segment of the market, the company suffered heavy losses due to high claim costs. Although, these losses were caused by a few, easily recognisable customers, the new manager did not want to take necessary action. He wanted to wait for statistical evidence as he was used to doing from his mass-market experience as an actuary. Thus, the risk management people of the company saw the problem from a management perspective. They wanted to take action to prevent further losses from the customers involved. The former actuary applied his perspective of optimising a large portfolio of insurance risks. Only if the total structure of that portfolio changed would he take general measures of changing the premium structure.

Thus, what strategy to choose as an investor, depends on what role one wants to play or has the competence to perform. It depends on what perspective one has on one's own position. A strategy of *spreading the risks* is based on the idea that the fundamental risks in an investment, a business, are predetermined and impossible to affect from the actor's own position. One applies a *portfolio strategy* , for example based on a reflection of some type of stock market index. Typical exponents of this type of risk-handling strategy are unit trusts, certain types of pension fund etc. The other option is to see oneself as an *active owner* in the sense that one wants to *manage the risks* one is exposed to by trying to *reduce* , and if possible *eliminate* , the *fundamental risks* of the business in question. Thus, this refers to a different type of owner – certain investment companies, private equity firms, venture capital companies, diversified groups etc.

Mix-up or constructive combination

In reality the application of these two main types of risk management strategies are rarely unmixed. To some extent this is connected with a sub-conscious mixing of these risk management strategies, which has quite often led to more or less catastrophic results. In this respect, the most typical situation is where the owners of a main business diversify on the grounds that the existing business is so risk-filled that they need to spread their risk, without having a clear idea of what else can be done to reduce or eliminate the risks in the business they already have. The financial disasters which were a result of the speculative real estate investments at the end of the 1980s and the beginning of the 1990s can undoubtedly be charged to this error account.

But reality also offers positive examples where the two risk-handling strategies have been combined in a constructive way. One example was given in Chapter 2 in the description of CalPERS, which after Jesse Unruh's outburst of wrath in 1984 ('like hell') began to combine CalPERS' traditional index-based portfolio strategy with active pressure to reduce and eliminate fundamental business risks in the major holdings with below-par returns (*shit-listed* corporations; see Chapter 2!).

The following analysis will focus on the active owner perspective, in other words a discussion of the reduction in, and elimination of, such fundamental risks in different types of business.

Principal possibilities for reducing/eliminating risk

The structuring and analysis of the *different logic* and *dynamics of business risks* in the next section will start from the premise: Business-related risks[7] are generated by changes in consumer preferences, processes of creative destruction etc. Before we begin to differentiate the logic and dynamics of

Table 12.2   Different ways of reducing/eliminating business related risk

Through:	
Dominance	Affecting market developments
	Superior competitive capability
	Market leadership
Organisational	When the competitive situation changes structurally
learning	Developing a whole new business
Planning	Forecasting
	Contingency planning
'Protection' for example	Mobilising power – political, military, mafia
through	Forming cartels

the business risks, we first need to dwell briefly on the principal possibilities, which can be distinguished for reducing and eliminating such risks. Table 12.2 provides an overview of these possibilities.

Market dominance

Three legitimate and basically different ways of reducing or eliminating risks can thus be distinguished. The first possibility is through *dominance* , in other words if one's own business is so strong that it either creates or strongly affects the whole market and/or is superior to the competitors on the same market. It is characteristic of new, successful inventions for example that they create a new market by supplying a need which had previously been met less satisfactorily, or not at all. Microsoft's operating systems need no further arguments to serve as a convincing example of this. Market and competition risks can essentially be got rid of for a long time with this sort of capability to create markets and superiority amongst competitors. In the case of Microsoft, even to the extent that the company is now involved in a lengthy anti-trust lawsuit. In established industries with tough competition, the important thing is to achieve superiority with a *business idea* , characterised by a unique combination of several competitive parameters – quality, cost-effectiveness, service etc. For example Korsnäs, a small Swedish pulp and paper company, has made significantly higher profits – on a sustained basis – with a well-defined product like sack paper thanks to this kind of superiority. Korsnäs and its owners have thus been better than other actors at eliminating/reducing the risks on the sack paper market.

Organisational learning for radical renewal

When the *process of creative destruction* has structurally changed the conditions for a business or when a whole new business is to be developed, radical renewal based on the principle of positive feedback, explained earlier, is required. It is a matter of system reconstruction or the formation of an entirely new business system. In such cases, risk management capability is constituted by *organisational learning* . We shall come to this in the following discussion of different types of risk.

Planning – an instrument for system benign renewal

Insofar as changes to the surrounding world and associated risks are predictable, they can also be eliminated or considerably reduced through planning. Such renewal requirements can be seen as *system benign* . Renewal can be accommodated without fundamental changes of the existing business system. Economic fluctuations and seasonal variations following a repetitive pattern are examples of such changes, which to some extent can be predicted. Risks in the form of surplus stocks in the face of an impending downturn in the economy, or a shortage of raw materials in the face of an upturn can then be avoided or significantly reduced.

Protection

The forms of risk elimination or reduction which occur but which may be more or less legitimate in an open market economy are shown below the dotted line in the figure. Admittedly tariffs can be accepted as legitimate in the market in certain circumstances and for transitional periods, but otherwise this type of risk elimination method belongs to the sphere of *realpolitik* or is directly criminal.

VALUE CREATION AND DIFFERENT TYPES OF RISK

A business and its value creation processes are exposed to many types of risks, e.g.:

- Business (specific to a particular type of business) and industry-related risks.
- Organisational risks.
- Financial risks.
- Discrete risks (specific to a particular investment project, e.g. setting up local production in St Petersburg in Russia).
- Political risks.
- Legal risks.
- (Property and casualty risks – insurance risks.)

The following discussion deals mainly with the first two types of risk, since the ability to handle these may be seen as the most important in value creation, at the same time as this ability must be an integrated part of the owner competence. This does not mean that other types of risk are unimportant. Awareness of these risks (financial, political etc.) is a very important element of owner competence, but the actual analysis of these risks can benefit considerably from expertise in the respective field. The financial risks which companies are increasingly exposed to through increasing international transactions, currency turbulence, the range of different possibilities for handling financial risks etc. require in-depth competence and ability in this specialist field, which only the financial experts possess. The same applies to political risks (in-depth knowledge of the countries involved etc.), legal risks (legal expertise – both with a general overview and specialists in different sub-sectors), insurance risks (risk management experts etc.). These types of experts seldom have the overall view and general competence required to exercising an owner's role in the value creation process as a whole. Therefore the experts' views have to be placed in context by people who have that capacity.

As regards discrete risks, the solution to the problem must be tackled from case to case. Each situation is unique but contains a cross section of different types of risk.

Risk patterns and risk dynamics associated with different business and industry logic

Different types of business have different risk profiles and risk dynamics, which are related to the pattern of factors characterising the conditions for success in a certain type of industry.[8] Our analysis of this is built on the causality displayed in Figure 12.4.

A couple of concrete examples will explain this view. For the sake of simplicity we shall take them both from the pulp and paper industry but the logic in the two examples – the pulp industry and the equipment industry for pulp production – differs radically. The analysis is illustrated and summarised in Tables 12.3 and 12.4.

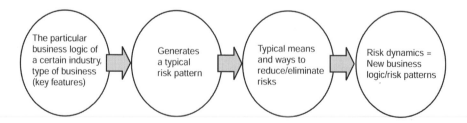

Figure 12.4   The risk dynamics of a particular business logic.

Table 12.3 Risk pattern and risk dynamics in the pulp industry

Characteristic features of the industry's logic	Typical risks/risk patterns	Risk management (-reduction, -elimination)	Risk dynamics
Staple commodity - price determined by world market and industry structure - cost effectiveness a '*must*' for profitability	Capacity utilisation Over-establishment, new actors Timing of investments New, more cost-effective wood baskets New technology Environmental demands	Vertical integration – paper manufacture – paper distribution – paper based products *Terror balance* Customer alliances – development co-operation Quality differentiation Establishment of new 'wood baskets' Development co-operation with equipment suppliers Financial strength	New industry logic, new types of risk, demand for new risk handling competence
Raw-material-based - biggest cost item - control of flow + quality - long term view			
Capital-intensive - high capacity costs - long term commitments			
Cyclical - tied to economic cycle - dependent on all strands of the processing chain - investment cycles - technology cycles			

Table 12.4 Risk pattern and risk dynamics in the pulp equipment industry

Characteristic features of the industry's logic	Typical risks/risk patterns	Risk management (-reduction, -elimination)	Risk dynamics
Stochastic market, projects	Project-related risks	Local partners, local connection and organisation	New industry logic, new types of risk, demand for new risk-handling competence
– large lumps	– dependent on customer and other suppliers	Forward integration →	
– *every 20 years*	– disruptions in progressing project	– after-market service	
Investment cycles	– guarantees, financial risks	– total service commitment	
– profit-driven	Customer-base related risks	– 'own and operate'	
– growth expectations	– long interval between investments	Consortia, financial strength	
Investment waves	– interrupted access	Access to complementary technologies	
– market-led	Technology-related risks	– licensing	
– technology-led	– access to 'best available technology'	– partnership	
– regulation-led	Organisational flexibility, mobilisation capacity for	– R&D together with customers, complementary suppliers	
Complex competition	– stochastic projects	Intermediate role competencies	
– within the same technology	– new investment waves	– project manager is king	
– alternative technology	– adjustment to investment cycles	– only own strategic resources	
– total package contracts	– utilisation of capacity	– Coordination of internal and external resources	
– in-house			
– shared undertakings (consultancies, sub-systems suppliers, component manufacturers)			
– different traditions in different markets			

Differentiated risk logic

In spite of shared points of contact and interdependence, the two industry sectors of the matrix are very different. The pulp market is a *flowing market* (continuous demand for pulp units) even if variations in the expectations and demand for stocks generate an important type of risk. In the equipment industry the fundamental market logic is quite different since the demand arises *stochastically* in the form of investment projects, like bigger or smaller orders lumped together in the form of whole pulp plants, a whole pulp line or new recycling packages (recovery boiler and so on). These also have a *digital character* – nothing or a complete order – with major consequences whatever the outcome.

Risk reduction often generates a new risk logic

Thus the two industry sectors offer different risk patterns and hence present different demands for risk management competence. One basic similarity is that a way of reducing the risk in both cases is some form of forward integration even if the specific driving forces are different. Where pulp production is concerned, the risks are chiefly those generated by the cyclical nature of the business, by the variations in the economic cycle. Vertical integration can raise the average utilisation of capacity and reduce price variations. In the equipment sector vertical integration, for example through *own and operate* is sometimes the only way of getting access to a market/customer base. In both cases, the consequence is that the company is exposed to new types of industry logic and business risks. Pulp and paper companies integrating downstream have experienced considerable difficulties in understanding the quite different business logic of corrugated packaging, for instance. Equipment engineering companies have been faced with entirely different risk patterns in the utility industry as a consequence of *own and operate* engagements.

Similarities span traditionally defined industry sectors

In each type of business a typical risk pattern can be identified and is connected with the industry logic, which operates there. Different manufacturing sectors differ between themselves, as do the various service sectors. The risk profiles and risk dynamics in a financial service sector like leasing are different from those in transport services or health care. The *new new thing* , the industries of the new economy – high tech in IT and bio-technologies, *dot.com* -companies etc – add to this variety by bringing new features to risk patterns and dynamics, e.g. the rapid pace of development, IPO's based on unrealistic, sometimes even a bit desperate expectations. *Time-to-*

market seems to be extremely important for *dot.com* type of companies – a driving force for early IPO's – while in biomedicine, even if this industry is experiencing giant productivity leaps in research methodology, the testing and registration of new drugs remain time consuming. At the same time one can find similarities in the risk-logic and risk-dynamics which span the traditional sector definitions. Raw-materials-based staple commodity industries share common patterns, typical project business industries have their similarities etc. The new risk logic features of the *new economy* certainly require further exploration and analysis, but such an endeavour would easily justify the writing of a whole new book. Still, if a lot would be new, one should not be surprised if not all is new *under the sun* .

Conclusion of the business risk analysis

This analysis of the business and industry-logic-related risk patterns and risk dynamics has emphasised the differences from one type of business to the next. Returning to the previous chapter's study of developments in the Wallenberg sphere, we will recognise this aspect to be a key ingredient of successful ownership. One of the main components in the Wallenberg sphere's *owner competence* was precisely its familiarity with certain types of business and risk logic, whilst its ownership was less successful in dealing with other types of logic.

Ownership and business risk specialisation

This leads us to conclude that different types of business and industry-sector-related risk patterns and dynamics demand different types of competence. Thus ownership too requires specialisation in this respect if it is to be successful.

Hierarchical differentiation of roles

We could also identify a *renewal hierarchy* , the fact that the risk dynamics require renewal on several levels – the operative level, in the integration of a business, in *renewal of the renewal* , in the way businesses are renewed and so on. Thus, this means, that the *organising idea* at each level of the hierarchy must contain a *renewal formula* for the level below.

Renewal at the macro level?

The imperative to renew is not limited to the individual corporation, although outside the direct decision power of corporate owners. As pointed out in the analysis of the situation in France, Germany, and Japan, possibilities to improve corporate governance are dependent upon legal reforms of various kinds. Governments have to adapt economic, industrial, and labour market policies etc to enhance prerequisites for individual companies to prosper. It is essential that the legal and institutional framework reflect the reality of globalised markets in order to safeguard board and executive management accountability to all owners, national as well as international.

Organisational risks

Every time business risks are minimised or eliminated, this is matched by organisational change and renewal. However well one identifies and defines the business' need for renewal, together with how one can eliminate or reduce the business risks generated by the *process of creative destruction* , nothing will happen unless these insights are embraced by incumbent management and implemented in the entire organisation. Organisational renewal requires smooth-running *organisational learning* . Organisational risks therefore mean anything that might block *organisational learning* or lead the renewal process in the wrong direction.

Some of the main organisational risks include:

- *Deficiencies in know-how and competence* : know-how and competence in various respects demand constant renewal. The most serious risk arises when there is no realisation of the need to renew a certain type of competence or develop an entirely new competence and integrate it into the organisation.
- *Myths and misconceptions* : organisations abound with myths. It is part of their cultural fabric of values – true ones as well as imagined and self-deceptive. Emancipating organisational members from such false myths is key to enhance organisational learning.
- *Emotional blocks* : a very common obstacle to renewal is emotional hang-ups – both in individuals and in established relations between individuals and groups. People's need for security is met if they are allowed to run on familiar tracks, whilst the demand for change is seen simply as an external threat.
- *Organisational structure* : an existing organisational structure has originally been designed and/or emerged to support the existing business and its way of achieving success. This structure reflects the specialisation, the skills-development processes etc. which have been important so far. In that way the existing structure constitutes an obstacle to the identification and development of the new skills required. The functional organisation supports specialisation and the economies of scale within each function. When the need to differentiate between different market needs arises, it is

often blocked by the existing set of functions. For example the divisionalisation which may be the solution to the need for differentiation rarely occurs spontaneously in a company which is organised by function.

Another organisational aspect, which may also have a blocking effect, is the company's ownership situation and the way in which ownership is exercised. This relates to the company's vertical organisation, how the Corporate Governance works. The difference between good and bad owners, as mentioned on repeated occasions in this book, is of extraordinary importance. *Ownership makes a difference* !

- *Arrogance* : a not unusual phenomenon and a cause of deep, often catastrophic problems, is when managers and organisational cultures are permeated by arrogance. This can have very different causes, ranging from personal characteristics to a historic success in the company, which has completely blinded its judgement and ability to comprehend changed conditions and new demands. 'This is not a company, it is a country club' is a comment which has been ascribed to the American consultant who was called in to revitalise Swedish Match, the former monopoly company of the once illustrious Kreuger empire (see Part II!), some time in the 1960s.
- *The balance of power* : arrogance, which has obvious consequences, is often an indication and result of misfits in the power structure and thus an expression of abuse of power. Flagrant arrogance and abuse of power can be said to be what finally triggered the Corporate Governance movement in the USA. Changing the power structure is often the very linch-pin of organisational renewal and the handling of organisational risks – a point we shall come back to.
- *Dynamic conservatism* : organisational risks may occur not just in the form of different *static* blocks, which have to be removed to facilitate organisational learning/renewal. Attempts to renew are often also actively opposed by the whole organisation or large parts thereof. The organisational risks thus also have a dynamic character, *dynamic conservatism* .[9]
- *Power struggles and politicising* : the dynamic organisational risks do not just mean active resistance to change, which can in itself be a cause of power struggles – between the forces for change and the forces of active resistance. Power struggles often also mean different competing ideas for change, alternative interpretations of threats and possibilities in the surrounding world, different visions of change. 'Our future lies in maximising exploitation of the new e-commerce opportunities' versus 'We have our future in the further enhancement of our traditional business and by letting others pay for the mistakes before we adopt these new technologies', to take a not altogether unrealistic example.

Meta-management – a key role and core skill in ownership and risk management

The decentralisation principle is a *must* for modern organisation. In actual fact, the productivity development, which is occurring in companies is increasingly dependent on the possibilities for decentralisation as a corollary to the utilisation of the new information and communication technologies. This produces two effects driving the productivity development. One involves specialisation and focus. The other involves shorter feed back loops. Thus, the interval between something requiring a decision – a customer enquiry, a move by a competitor, an offer from a supplier etc. – and the decision itself must be as short as possible. Organisational hierarchies have been massively reduced as a result of this. A new organisational philosophy has emerged which tends towards an organisation without boundaries, where formal hierarchy and decision-making processes mean less and less whilst the relevant competence in each situation, where decisions and action are required, is made available and is the decisive factor. (It should be observed, though, that the principle of decentralisation cannot be applied uniformly. However, elaborating the logic of decentralisation further is outside the scope of this context.)

Decentralisation and meta-management

For decentralisation to work, the right rules of the game as well as the appropriate supporting structure must be created for it. All decentralised decisions and activities must be integrated into something that works as a whole. This also has to work in a dynamically changing environment requiring *incessant renewal* , a new structure for decentralisation and so on.

Creating these conditions can be called *meta-management* . Real decentralisation is not compatible with *super management* , someone constantly monitoring and approving ongoing decisions. Instead, working decentralisation requires *meta-management* , which ensures that the right conditions are always present for the principle of decentralisation to be applicable.

The analysis of *organisational risks* also showed how the old saying that it is difficult to pull yourself up by your own bootlaces is true, and in a more articulated way appropriate to the context. The necessary renewal of an organisation is not guaranteed simply by external competition in end product markets or by the market for corporate control. The adjustment mechanisms are blocked and actively counteracted by various obstacles and forces in the organisation of the company.

Eric Rhenman's[10] definition of *meta-management* was often 'using power or mobilising power in order to change power'. In order to achieve the necessary renewal of an organisation, it is often necessary for the internal balance of power to be shifted by restructuring, for authority to be given to new skills, which have to be made a priority and for the management to be replaced or radically altered. Such changes only occur if they start from a power base outside or above the company, normally from the owner or someone representing the owner(s). As the case study in Part II highlighted, *meta-management* has been a core competence of the Wallenberg sphere.

Conclusions on organisational risks and meta-management

Organisational efficiency and renewal thereof require active management of organisational risks so that the right conditions are created and maintained for *organisational learning* . If this is done a company has a functioning *meta-management* . We can thus draw the conclusion that renewal on one level often requires the exercise of *meta-management* from a higher level.

We can see a parallel between renewal and the management of the business risk dynamic on the one hand and the organisational renewal on the other. The *renewal hierarchy* we might identify in the management of the business risks and the risk dynamic is matched by an *organisational renewal hierarchy* , a need to exercise *meta-management* on several levels. Thereby *meta-management* also becomes an important part of the role of ownership and of *ownership competence* . Thus, even in this respect, we can relate back to an important element in the ownership competence of the Wallenberg sphere.

TWO ADDITIONAL TYPES OF RISK

Before we conclude the definition of the risk reduction/elimination agenda of owners concerned with fundamental risks, we need to review two additional categories of risk not included in the list on page 193. The first one has to do with the risks that can cause value creation and renewal processes to go astray. The second category, sometimes, has a direct bearing on the value creation process, but most of all, it is fundamentally important indirectly, and for providing necessary prerequisites for the business the company concerned wants to perform. These two categories share something in common. They are both about *values* . The first category is inward looking and complements issues of *organisational risks* . The second category is about a company's *external relationships* .

The importance of values

Patricia Pitcher tells the fascinating but sad story about how a company goes down the drain after its founder handed over management of the company to a new CEO, although that person had been a key member of the executive team for a long time.[11] While the founder was a visionary who built his company to realise his vision, his successor turned out to be a typical technocrat. Instead of visionary goals, the new technocratic CEO defined the new goals of the company to be, simply stated, profits. Successively, all key members of the executive team were replaced to conform to this new orientation. As it turned out, this was no orientation at all since the company eventually went out of business.

There are several lessons to be learnt from this story. However, there is one that is particularly significant for our discussion about risks and ownership, namely the importance of values. Before coming to the implications of that, here is some more food for thought...:

- How come that Ivory, the Procter & Gamble soap, has been the leading brand on the US market for such a long time (from the 19th century and until the 1990s)?
- What makes us, as patients, willing to undergo painful and hazardous surgery?
- Why does the Internet exist at all?

The common denominator of all three phenomena has to do with values:

- Ivory dates from the 19th century and its brand position to the quality reputation that the P&G company gained as a supplier of candles and soaps to the US Army during the Civil War. While many other soap makers, because of higher raw materials prices, used substitute oils, the founders of P&G – William Procter and James Gamble – did not compromise with their quality standards despite lower short term profits.
- Who would trust his or her doctor and how come that we accept doctors' high fees if it were not for our belief that the doctors we are consulting honour the ethics of the medical profession?
- Can one imagine that China or the former USSR inventing the communications technology that developed into the Internet, even if they had had the technical prerequisites to do it? Hardly! This technology was developed as a means of defending an open democratic society by making communication between decentralised units possible even if the high command was wiped out. Thus, this technology is anathema to any totalitarian society.

The examples above justify the proposition that *the efficacy of a social system – be it a business, a company or society at large – is highly dependent on the quality of the values permeating that social system* . This proposition is applicable in all types of context as the examples above indicate.

Implications for reduction/elimination of risks

Can a company be governed solely on the basis of the shareholder value criterion? No doubt, shareholder value is important. It is a matter of respecting shareholders – the providers of risk capital as well as the valuers of the company, by deciding at what share price they will keep their shares. At the same time, shareholder value as such is *empty* . It gives no guidance for taking decisions, e.g. concerning long term investments. On the contrary, too strong an emphasis on shareholder value has tended to make boards and executive management short term oriented.

Executive management and exercise of ownership to reduce and eliminate risks can never resort to technocratic tools alone. The really difficult decisions – be it people issues or long term investments – need another type of guidance. You need *values* that give clear guidance about what you as a company or owner want to be, why you want to become that as well as how you want to achieve that. You need an *elaborate system of values* that also tells you when to say no – what opportunities to refrain from, what ways and means not to use etc.

At least, this is the case when your business or active owner involvement starts to mature. An entrepreneur in an early phase of development provides guidance for himself and his organisation by his own obsession with one idea or vision. Jim Clark – the famous Silicon Valley entrepreneur and founder of Silicon Graphics, Netscape, and Healtheon – as portrayed by Michael Lewis (2000), still seems to be obsessed by the idea of inventing *the new new thing* , over and over again.

Looking back at a longer period of successful development, the emergence of an *elaborated system of values* becomes apparent. Ingvar Kamprad – the founder of IKEA, the world's largest furniture retailer – started his company guided by his vision to 'offer good quality furniture at such low prices that many people can afford to buy them'. (Björk, 1998).[12] As the business developed and the organisation grew, IKEA's *set of values* became more and more elaborate. (A *set of values* , by the way, which is strikingly similar to that of Wal-Mart's. Mr. Björk, in his book, pinpoints the similarities between Sam Walton, the founder of Wal-Mart and Ingvar Kamprad, as regards their origin, visions, *business ideas* and *set of values*).

In the case of the Wallenberg sphere (Part II) we could see how the original visions of founding a Scottish type of bank in Sweden, and playing a key role in Swedish industrialisation, successively necessitated the support of a more elaborate system of strong values.

Reinforcement of existing business, eliminating the risks of opportunism and special interests

Thus, it should be clear, that a *system of strong values* serves as a reinforcement of the vision and *business idea* of a company. However, there is also a specific risk elimination aspect of such a system of values. It is a means of making sure that a company is not going astray by becoming *opportunistic* . One example may suffice: instead of taking necessary, but demanding and often controversial measures to renew an existing business, boards and executive management are sometimes tempted to explore *greener pastures* , a new but distracting business opportunity. A consistent *set of values* , infused by an active owner, will keep them on track.

Similarly, this is also a means to keeping *special interests* at bay. In fact, the *beautiful fit* between a concern for sustainable value creation, growth of net asset value, and a consistent *set of values* supporting the *owner idea* , is the best guarantee against domination of *special interests* .

Values and the role of the owner

Values are not created out of the blue, particularly, not the type of good values required to build a business with sustainable value creation potential. Furthermore, values need maintenance as well as renewal. Original creation of such values as well as fundamental renewal cannot be left to bureaucratic systems and bureaucrats. Creation and renewal of values require personal involvement by someone with ideas, strong visions and beliefs. Thus, ownership cannot function in the long run without such personal involvement. There will always be a role for personal ownership.

Licence to do business

It is obvious that companies in their business must satisfy a series of external stakeholders in addition to their owners and business partners. Taxes and charges have to be paid to the authorities, rules must be followed where there is an obligation to provide information etc. But such demands can be converted into direct financial consequences, which are summed up in the net results and the value to the owners. This is about something else, which is both more abstract than this but at the same time to the highest degree concrete and tangible, namely the *legitimacy* of a company. The company has to be accepted by those around it, it has to be legitimate for it to exercise its business. It must acquire *a licence to* do business, to travesty a famous fictional figure. The *legitimacy risks* may be highly evident and have serious financial consequences. A current case in point is Microsoft. The company seems to have been too eager to achieve a dominant market position, even to the extent that it neglected the legitimisation risks that follow with being perceived as a monopolist. On the other hand, a high degree of legitimacy represents considerable value because it creates favourable conditions for direct value creation. Well-known trademarks are an example of this. IKEA and Volvo, to take just two examples, enjoy a legitimacy which extends far beyond their respective core businesses, at the same time as their trademarks are very powerful competitive tools precisely in their core business markets.

Environmental abuse hits back on legitimacy

Environmental issues in the widest sense have become a stumbling block to the legitimacy of many companies in recent years. German and other foreign customers require environmental certificates if they are to buy pulp and paper from Swedish forestry companies. It is not enough for the manufacturing processes to be closed and have virtually zero effluents in the pulp and paper factories. Forestry itself, and the environmental compatibility of forest and timber production, has also been highlighted. It is also easy to find examples from other industries and companies. Shell hit problems in dumping redundant oil rigs, Nestlé is still boycotted in some circles because of its marketing of milk substitutes in the third world etc.

Socially acceptable rewards

One aspect of legitimacy, and thus not an ownership issue alone, is the remuneration of boards, their chairmen, and chief executives. Remuneration issues often become controversial, deriving partly from the fact that the value-creating efforts of the owner specialists and of the board are poorly communicated to the public. In many cases this is also caused by the fact that there is non-existent value creation, sloppiness and an abuse of power. A number of so-called 'bail-out contracts', actually rewarding mismanagement and abuse of power, have been particularly damaging. But executive pay in general have gone far beyond reasonable levels and lost sensible correlation to value created in many cases. Corporate America sets the trend, also internationally, in this respect. Thus, a strong indication of who are in control of the US corporations. However, it is not chief executives who are to be blamed but owners and boards! They must take responsibility, not only for the shareholder value aspect in a narrow sense, but for the legitimacy aspect as well.

Values, legitimacy and institutionalisation

What does legitimacy mean? What is it that determines whether a company or some other actor has legitimacy?

Legitimacy is a question of values, or rather of matching values. The values directing the actions of a company must match the values applied by the outside world, particularly by those who have the opportunity and the interest to assert their values. This match is a kind of minimum requirement for the company to be accepted at all. In those cases where the company's values are respected by the outside world to such an extent that they set a standard, for example in the way that Volvo is associated with car safety, an institution has been formed. In this way, not only has the value of Volvo increased, giving Volvo enhanced competitiveness, but it has also made a significant contribution to what economists call external economies The value of the whole industry and its contribution to the economy as a whole and to traffic safety has increased.

Renewal of external value relations

It is obvious that the legitimisation and institutionalisation processes, the creating of matching values and uniquely respected values, have similarities with the directly value-creating renewal and integration processes. Values also have to be renewed if they are to match the new institutional conditions. Here too there are significant risks, which one has to be able to manage. Organisational blockages offer challenges similar to those encountered when adjusting to new competitive conditions. Meta-management and the exercise of ownership also have to take account of this dimension in handling risk and in the work of renewal, and so on.

The institutional status of the Wallenberg sphere

Once again we may refer to the analysis of the ownership competence in the Wallenberg sphere. The values permeating the group and the renewal thereof have formed an important part of the ownership competence. Thus, these values, implemented by means of an elaborate legitimisation policy and skilful relations-building with important centres of power, nationally as well as internationally, have rendered the Wallenberg sphere institutional status. Thus, the specific values of the Wallenberg sphere have not only contributed to making it a successful owner and value creator, but have also made their mark on large parts of the values of Swedish industry, in particular the internationally-oriented companies. This has markedly contributed to the Swedish business culture being much more internationally oriented and more aware of the conditions of international competition than, for example, the French.

SUMMING UP THE CONCEPTUAL ANALYSIS

This chapter's attempt to conceptualise ownership and value creation has shown that owners have a very central, value-creating role in individual companies, as well as in the economy at large. This role, not only entails providing capital but also reducing the uncertainty, which characterises economic activity in general and competitive companies in particular, and actively contributing to renewal, which is fundamental to all value creation.

Three different types of renewal can be summarised as follows:

- ongoing renewal of established business;
- restructuring and reconstruction, where the ongoing renewal has not worked or when sudden structural changes have occurred in the surrounding world;
- development of entirely new businesses, new growth (the development process and its renewal).

Incessant renewal at all levels

The need for renewal is incessant and constantly present – in primary processes like production, product development, marketing etc. as well as in the overriding integration processes, in the development of new ways of integrating these, renewing them and so on. The existence of a *renewal hierarchy* has been emphasised, where the ownership function has a critical role in creating the conditions for the requisite renewal on underlying levels as well as the renewal of the ownership idea.

In addition to the renewal of direct value creation, the importance of creating the right institutional conditions, creating legitimacy for one's own ownership and the company it involves, is pointed out. Such legitimacy and a strong institutional position facilitate and strengthen direct value creation.

Thus, the function and contribution of ownership – apart from providing risk capital – is to manage risks in an *incessant renewal* process: reducing and eliminating the risks which directly (business risks, organisational risks as well as risks of opportunism and of going astray), and indirectly (institutional risks) are associated with renewal and the creation of added value in companies in a market economy.

The *ownership competence* required to fulfil this multi-dimensional ownership function in the market economy comprises four main elements, which have been illustrated by the Wallenberg sphere.

1. *Business risk competence* : knowledge of business and risk logic, as well as of the risk dynamics in the businesses affected. In addition, knowledge of ways to reduce and eliminate these risks. Each type of business has its own risk logic and dynamic. With increasing competition on the *ownership market* the demand for specialisation, for in-depth knowledge of risk management in the respective type of business logic and dynamic

increases! This kind of specialisation can also be linked to different stages in the development or restructuring of a business. Venture capital companies and so-called management-buy-out-funds (MBO funds) are two examples of specialisation in this dimension.

2. *Meta-management competence* : meta-management requires a knowledge of how one creates the right conditions for different types of business, for different types of business logic etc. – supporting the internal and external organisation, managing situations competently, making the right demands and so on. Meta-management requires an in-depth understanding of how to organise, of being able to handle the most central elements in the organisational production factor, namely power and competence. Meta-management means the ability to mobilise power to allocate and re-allocate power to make sure that the right key person fits the challenges of the situation, and so that the right type (=the type that creates added value) of competence and competence development is supported!

3. *The ownership idea, vision and values* : The ownership idea, the vision and the values it comprises have to provide guidance for the direction and conduct of a business. The system of values is a necessary means to eliminate risks of opportunism, opportunists and 'false prophets' of various kinds. Is shareholder value, which has been such a frequent battle cry in recent years, enough to provide guidance? Creating shareholder value, growth in value, is always necessary – but it is not enough. The Wallenberg success story has shown that the ownership idea and its supporting values comprise so much more than simply increasing the net wealth. Long term successful value creation requires a long term vision and wider legitimacy. The owner is the last resort of the value creation hierarchy to make sure that the company concerned is infused with the right kind of values.

4. *A strong institutional position generates added value* : examples which were pointed out in this context included P&G, Volvo and IKEA, and of course the institutional significance of the Wallenberg sphere in Swedish industry.

AN ADDITIONAL COMMENT ABOUT VALUES

What then are the values involved in a successful ownership idea, in achieving real legitimacy? Naturally there has to be a series of specific values and principles which have been carved out to reflect the risk logic and dynamic which characterises the industry, the respective business's historical experience of success and failure etc. 'But ultimately it is a question of the company management's ethics', claimed Gustav von Hertzen in a discussion of ownership issues.[13]

Of course one can make money – in the short term – by abandoning good practice and good ethics, but sooner or later it usually catches up with one. 'It comes home to roost' as they say.

DISTINCTIVE OWNERSHIP COMPETENCE

In addition to these four main elements in ownership competence, there is one decisive, overall dimension, namely the fact that when all four main elements are in unison and support one another, there is unique and success-ful – *distinctive* – ownership competence. Such unison has emerged as a result of an often long learning process with successful and unsuccessful investments, restructuring, new ventures and other critical decisions, in the way that the Wallenberg example helped us to understand. Such *distinctive ownership competence* indicates the presence of a consistent and unique ownership idea, a *Theory of Ownership* .

TWO OBSTRUCTUVE MISCONCEPTIONS ABOUT OWNERSHIP COMPETENCE

In Part I of this book we showed how the *ownership function* was neglected in large parts of industry for a long time, which means that *ownership compe-tence* was inadequate in large areas and that views and concepts of owner-ship were underdeveloped. Increasing globalisation of markets and corporations, resulting in the intensifying competition for ownership, gener-ates a growing desire and pressure to study various types of successful owner – some examples of which have been given here – and to sharpen ones own ability. This necessary learning process is however obstructed in large parts of our society and industry by certain misconceptions about ownership, which we need to *unlearn* .

In this context two important misconceptions will be discussed. The first false notion involves the adversaries – conscious and subconscious – of the market economy and comprises the Marxist doctrine and its derived ideol-ogies. Although the Berlin wall came down more than a decade ago and the Communist system crumbled, *the mental Berlin wall* seems to be more long-lived, not least in Europe, including the country of this author. State mono-polies, *dirigisme* and central control of various kinds linger on unnecessarily.

The second is to be found among many people who are otherwise suppor-ters of the market economy. It is the misconception that the so-called *stake-holder model* is based on, and in which owners are simply seen as one category of stakeholder of many others in a company.

The Marxist-inspired misconceptions

A basic view in Marxist doctrine is that all value-added is created by the production factor labour. In Marx' view of the world, this meant the work carried out by the employees in a company. The owners, i.e. capitalists, constituted the adversaries, who were using their position of power – control of the requisite financial capital – to exploit the workers, who had no share in the added value created. Economic activity was considered a zero sum game, one party's profit was the other party's loss. An owner does not do any work, does not contribute in any way to the creation of the added value. Capital income is unearned income, even for an active owner.

As a consequence of this view, one was supposed to organise the economy on the planned economy model in Marxist society. That requires all goals to be formulated and all decisions to be taken centrally. Also all needs for renewal had to be predictable and the right adaptation measures had to be adopted using centrally controlled mechanisms. Variety and alternative solutions become disruptive elements in the Marxist world, not to say dangerous to society and even criminal. The practical consequence of this view has been demonstrated to us as clearly as one could wish in the Soviet Union and its satellite states. In conceptual terms, cyberneticists demonstrated the logical impossibility of the planned economy as early as the 1950s in the formulation of The Law of Requisite Variety[14] for anyone who disregarded the economist Hayek[15] for example. Cyberneticists were able to demonstrate that the controlling system had to have a superior wealth of variation in relation to the system controlled, if control was to succeed and be constructive. What would happen otherwise? Precisely! The controlling system has to impose its rigidity on the controlled system by force – like Procrustes, like the Soviet system, like Ford with the Model-T. The difference in the latter example was of course that in open competition Ford was not able to force customers to refrain from buying General Motors' products.

The planned economy system tries to avoid the transaction costs, which are built into the market economy because of all the buying and selling transactions necessary in the latter. They reduce uncertainty in the planned economy in comparison with the market economy, but they drastically restrict the ability to deal with the inevitable external uncertainty. They miss the whole point of the superiority of the market economy system, namely *the learning ability of the many independent actors in which the ownership function plays such an important role* .

Marx and the new economy

It has been argued by some *nouveau Marxists* , that the focus on human capital and the competition for talented people of the new economy finally proves that Marx was right. All value-added is supposed to be produced by human capital. Thus, this line of reasoning maintains the traditional flaws of Marxist theory. Value is not decided by factor cost input – except for temporary periods of a seller's market – but by the value a product or service creates for the consumer. Secondly, production factors do not produce value unless they are co-ordinated by an *organising idea* , a *business idea* as explained earlier. A business idea needs for its renewal the support of superior levels of the value creation hierarchy, a *group idea* and an *owner idea* .

The stakeholder model and related misconceptions

In political life we generally welcome a strong government, we are on our guard against corporativism. Quite simply we want the interests of the whole to be allowed to dominate the special interests, we want to avoid bad compromises and so on. At least that is what we see as some kind of ideal state. Often, reality looks somewhat different and who would want a strong government if the policies it operates are way off the beam?

The capitalist market economy is based on several brilliant social innovations, including the right of ownership, division of labour, freedom of transactions, competition and – not least – the monetary economy instead of barter. With the help of money we release ourselves from the restrictions of time and space for transactions. Thus, we also have a measure with which to value the opportunities for future value-creating transactions. By refraining from the immediate consumption of ongoing value-creating transactions, we can increase resources for future value-creation – after we have set aside a certain quantity of the ongoing value-creating transactions to replace the consumption of the resources, which have made the present value-creation possible. In a world where these resources are scarce, it is of course very important not to use up these resources but instead to increase them so that our future value-creation can grow. The financial measure of all resources is capital. However when it comes to the question of increasing that capital, increasing our resources for future value-creation, we are faced with a dilemma. We have to handle uncertainty, we don't know whether the resources we are creating by refraining from consuming ongoing value-creation will increase the actual future production of value. The clever solution to this dilemma is the invention of risk capital and all the institutions (the stock company, stock exchanges and so on) which have made it possible to use it effectively.

The *stakeholder model* equates capital interest with all the other interests in the business of a company. People supporting this model think that rational decision-making is finding a compromise between different special interests. But then one is ignoring the fact that capital is the measure of all our resources and that risk capital is the limited resource for increasing the possible future value-creation. Thus, capital, especially risk capital, must be given a special position in the organisation and the control of the company because it is that which best safeguards the interests of the whole – the best use and increase of our scarce resources!

OK say some former supporters of the stakeholder model, capital is the most important, but we cannot ignore the claims of other stakeholders on the company! We need to use an optimisation model à la linear programming. We maximise the capital interest by viewing the demands of the other stakeholders as some kind of restrictions!

A plus sum game

Apart from the technical difficulties of such a model, the author believes that this procedure is misconceived and only constitutes a variant of the misrepresentation, which is the stakeholder model. As shown earlier in this chapter, direct value creation in companies is indirectly supported by a good institutional position. Sustained successful value-creation is not possible in a functioning competitive economy unless all the stake-holders involved in the value creation – customers, employees, suppliers of various kinds etc. – get a positive return and feel that they are participating in a *plus sum game* . The same thing applies to the actors who are only indirectly affected – potential customers, employees, suppliers or authorities, media and the public and others. The successful company and the successful owner must find its own creative solution in the way of running the business so that the total optimum plus-sum-game is established. Issues are sometimes brought up whether to be ethical or not, or whether to pursue environmentally compatible policies or not. Such issues might be significantly simplified, maybe even superfluous, if a company/owner is viewing itself as a participant in as well as a constructive contributor to a plus sum game. Thus, one could represent the optimum concept for an owner as in Figure 12.5.

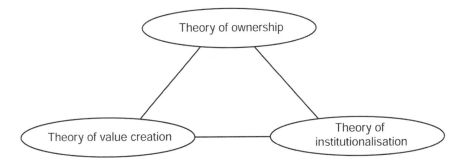

Figure 12.5 Two fundamental propositions about the market and the firm.

The uniquely successful ownership is based on total integration of mastery in direct value creation and the capability for institutional positioning!

But one important prerequisite

However, there is one very important snag in this line of argument. Owners must take their responsibility as owners seriously – to care for sustainable value creation. Unfortunately, the cries for shareholder value, on the part of many shareholders, are rather signs of stakeholder behaviour – maximising their own special interests.

IS CAPITAL STILL AS IMPORTANT?

As a final comment it may be appropriate to deal with the discussion of the significance of capital – financial capital versus other types of capital, for example human capital, intellectual capital, structural capital and similar terms, which have become very popular in recent times. Particularly Skandia's, a Swedish financial services company, pioneering efforts to try and assess and account for the hidden values which are always present on Skandia's 'actual' balance sheet but not expressed by the traditional financial measures, have caught the attention of both financial and academic circles. The chief architect behind Skandia's system for this (called Skandia Navigator[16]), Leif Edvinsson, has been named European 'brain of the year' (1998) for this achievement.

In the author's view there is no contradiction between the importance of financial risk capital and, for example, the concept of human capital. In all types of economic activity financial risk capital seems to be important. On the other hand the following should be borne in mind:

1. Different types of business have different types of logic. In this author's own sector for instance, business management consulting, which is know-how-intensive, great emphasis has to be placed on human capital and how one can handle the ensuing risks and risk dynamics. But at the same time risk capital is needed to run the business and renew the consulting competence. The solution to this dilemma is often for the consultants themselves to become major owners in the consulting firm and be responsible for the requisite risk capital. To some extent this risk capital can be mobilised through contributions in kind, in other words through variable salaries/bonuses, but this is seldom sufficient if there is a need to make constant investments for the future.

   The example illustrates that ownership, in addition to making risk capital available, requires competence specific to each situation to deal

with the risks which arise in the context, not least those which entail human capital becoming dispersed (consultants leaving and setting up as competitors) or not being renewed and further developed.
2. What value creation will finally result in is something we only know when it is to hand, from accounts of what has already happened. It is therefore very important to try and find methods, which allow us a greater understanding of future value creation than the traditional balance sheets. It is particularly important to develop methods adapted to the situation, which reflect the specific business logic in each type of business and in the company in question. In this way one can obtain better management and control tools and also more accurate measures for the current real value of a company, a business.

Conclusion about the value of a company

The real net asset value of a company/business, its actual capital, is its future value creation capacity (discounted net present value). Applying the analytical framework presented in this book leads to the conclusion that it is a function of two main elements, namely:

- The particular risks a certain business/company will be exposed to, generated by the *process of creative destruction.*
- The capability of the company to reduce and possibly eliminate these risks. In other words, the *organisational learning* capability where the owner is the *last resort* at the top of the *renewal hierarchy* of the company.

Strategic Corporate Governance – How to Make it Work?   13

The Hampel report was quoted at the beginning of the book: 'The importance of corporate governance lies in its contribution both to business prosperity and to accountability'. Both aspects are equally essential as well as inseparable. However, the Hampel committee observed that the corporate governance discussion so far had had too much focus on formalistic aspects of accountability. Hence, the committee set out to correct the balance by putting heavier emphasis on prosperity.

Business prosperity and sustained value creation have been the main focus of this book as well, and also the reason why the expression found in the title of this book – *Strategic Corporate Governance* – has been chosen instead of merely *corporate governance*. *Strategic* refers to the importance of the following aspects of ownership and corporate governance:

- That sustainable value creation is the overriding goal of all economic activity as well as the primary goal of all companies.
- That ownership – the individual owner, be it a physical person or a legal entity of some kind as well as the ownership function as a whole – has a key role to play in the process of sustainable value creation.
- That playing such a critical role requires adequate competence.

THE PURPOSE AND STRUCTURE OF THIS CHAPTER

Against this background, the purpose of this chapter is to outline some ideas of how ownership can be professionalised and the ownership function as a whole can be improved based on the analysis in earlier chapters. The ideas presented are primarily addressed to actors in the ownership function – what investors and owners of various kinds can do. This does not imply that one particularly important actor is forgotten – the government. The analysis in Part I emphasised the need for reform in most countries reviewed in order to create appropriate legal and institutional prerequisites for making good corporate governance possible, reforms only the political system of a country can achieve. Although being of fundamental importance, these exhortations should not need to be repeated further here. However, one important implication of the suggestions in this chapter is of course for the actors of the ownership function to put continued pressure on governments to carry out necessary reforms.

We will begin this concluding chapter by summing up the highlights of corporate governance development and the implications for ownership based on the analysis in the first chapter. To generate normative ideas for the professionalisation of ownership, we will draw upon the lessons to be learnt from experienced and successful owners such as the Wallenberg sphere (Part II and its appendix), as well as building on the implications of the conceptual analysis in Chapter 12.

The initial analysis of the corporate governance situation in five countries showed a varied picture. The agenda for improvement measures has to be adapted to the specific situation in each country, and to each corporation as well. Therefore, by necessity, the ideas presented in this chapter will have to be kept at a rather general level.

SUMMARY OF THE CORPORATE GOVERNANCE ANALYSIS

The analysis of the corporate governance situation in the five largest economies in the world, a handful of cross-border mergers, and a comparison of different board concepts can be summarised as follows:

- Corporate governance is considered to be a key issue and area for improvement in all the countries studied, as well as in most other parts of the world as indicated by records of corporate governance policy documents etc. Corporate governance is also on the agenda of international organisations such as the World Bank and the OECD.
- The prerequisites as well as the development stage of corporate governance development vary a lot, making the agenda of corporate governance issues and reforms very different from one country to the next. However, one big divide is whether companies are expected to be run for the benefit of their shareholders primarily or if the so-called stakeholder model is applied. Of the five countries studied, only the USA and the UK are in the first category while the three other belong to the latter.
- Global competition in product markets as well as in capital markets have generated increasing pressure on corporations to comply with some overall requirements, particularly concerning accounting standards and transparency.
- International convergence of corporate governance standards and requirements is still at an early stage where the country of registration dictates what corporate governance arrangements should apply. So, an international 'Combined Code' seems to be far away.
- The good news is, though, that there seems to be at least one shared focus, internationally: the importance of the board for corporate governance.

Actual board concepts vary, and there is also confusion about perceptions of different board concepts – of what is meant by unitary and two-tier boards in reality. There is little progress, beyond mere lip service, to improve the situation in some countries. Still, the quality of the board, its independence and its competence, is high on the corporate governance agenda everywhere.

Current driving forces for change

Booming stock markets and radically improved financial performance by many corporations have eased the pressure for corporate governance reform. Incumbent boards and executive management have tended to become less sensitive to demands from activist institutional investors. However, this is likely to be temporary. The *process of creative destruction* is at work – if ever before – fuelled by uniquely strong driving forces:

- Current and future demographics will change the economic and social prerequisites in many developed countries, including Japan and several European countries. The early consequences of this phenomenon are already seen in the form of rapidly increasing pension savings and a mounting flow of funds into stock markets seeking higher returns than traditional savings products.
- New technologies and an unprecedented speed of technological innovation generate seemingly unlimited opportunities for new business in start-ups as well as in renewal of existing companies.
- Globalisation of markets and competition, accelerated by the fall of Communism in the early 1990s, continues and is further enhanced by changing demographics and by the new technologies in particular.

As a result of these driving forces, the new economy is here already. It is thriving on the ample supply of risk capital and the wave of expectations, hopes and wild dreams about future returns, discounted by some imaginary factor into hyped NPVs (net present value).

Implications for ownership

Demands for competent ownership is rising.

- Mushrooming new ventures of the new economy give multiple proofs of the importance of ownership. It has been witnessed how crucial *competent capital* , e.g. as represented by *business angels* , venture capitalists who can bring a combination of financial risk capital and personal experience into a new venture – is for the emergence, viability and success of start-ups.
- This phenomenon will continue and accelerate to unprecedented propor-

tions in this era of a new *Gründerzeit* , which is still only at the beginning. One new aspect of the business reality of start-ups, as well as of business development in general, is the speed by which market positioning and penetration have to take place. One must aim for the global market much earlier than before. IPOs, at a much earlier stage than before, and while still unprofitable, have turned out to be a way of not only increasing the speed of developing resources, products etc, but also of getting early market recognition.

- Furthermore, when these start-ups and new companies will approach the *moment of truth* , when fundamental performance is expected to match initial expectations, some very tough, constructive, and competent ownership will be called for.
- The new economy will also generate huge opportunities as well as pressure for restructuring of companies of the old economy. This massive renewal wave will place the ownership function and competence at centre stage as well. Maybe this part of the economy is underestimated as regards its potential for new growth as well as its needs for competent ownership since, so far, all the light has been on the new companies.

DEVELOPING THE OWNERSHIP FUNCTION

In outlining normative ideas and suggestions of how to professionalise ownership and improve the ownership function, we will apply four different perspectives:

1. **Value creation perspective** – how can basic ownership competence be developed to support the value creation role of ownership?
2. **Industry development perspective** – how can ownership, seen as an industry of many and different actors, be developed in order to increase the overall efficiency of the ownership function in the economy?
3. **Organisational perspective** – how should the chain (of command) of owner – board of directors – executive management be organised so that we can achieve a rational and constructive differentiation of tasks, roles, and responsibilities?
4. **Governance perspective** – how should ownership be exercised so that renewal, sustainable value creation and accountability be guaranteed?

VALUE CREATION PERSPECTIVE

Incessant renewal and meta-management, to manage the process of taking as well as reducing/eliminating risks, are the cornerstones of strategic corporate governance, of sustainable value creation, according to the analysis presented in this book.

However, to bridge the gulf between current realities and some ideal situation where owners are practising the implications of these two cornerstones fully, at least two important prerequisites have to be established:

- There has to be a **demand** for competent owners. The shareholding public at large as well as a plethora of institutional investors – mutual trusts, pension funds, and insurance companies, to mention some of the typical ones in this context – must recognise the importance and crucial role of active, competent owners in the process of sustainable value creation. To do this, they have to embrace the key elements of the frame of reference presented here, at least as a first step.
- The second prerequisite is that there must be a **supply** of owners who not only embraces this frame of reference, but who are also competent in all the dimensions of value creating competence.

Against this background, let us begin by summing up the key ingredients of the frame of reference outlined in this book. After that we can proceed to a review of the implications and challenges of the key elements of owner competence.

Frame of reference

Our frame of reference can be summed up as answers to three questions:

Why is owner competence required at all?

Sustainable value creation is dependent upon the dynamic interplay between a market and institutional environment, characterised by the *process of creative destruction* on the one hand, and the individual company as a *learning centre* on the other. Figure 13.1. The *process of creative destruction* and the *learning centre* , gives an overview of this interplay and the value creation logic of the individual firm:

The demand for owner competence is generated by the learning process of the individual firm comprising *incessant renewal* /risk taking as well as reduction/elimination of fundamental risks. This leads us to the next question.

What types of competence are required?

The conceptual analysis in Chapter 12 concluded, and as illustrated by the case study of the Wallenberg sphere in Part II, that four types of competence are required. Furthermore, these four types of competence have to fit together and support one another – constitute what we have called a 'beautiful fit' – as Figure 13.2 illustrates:

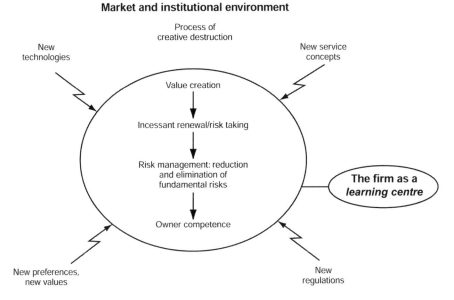

Figure 13.1   The process of creative destruction and the *learning centre.*

These four types of competence correspond to different types of risk, of which three are generated by the business environment, the institutional environment, and the internal organisation itself. In addition, there is one type of risk that has to do with values. A company is always exposed to influences which may represent values alien to its way of sustainable value

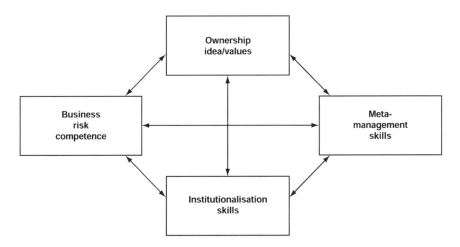

Figure 13.2   A *beautiful fit* of four competence elements.

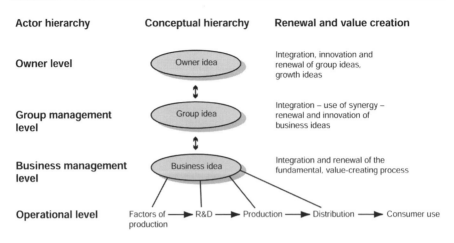

| Actor hierarchy | Conceptual hierarchy | Renewal and value creation |

Figure 13.3   The renewal hierarchy and the vertical organisation for value creation.

creation. This can make the company become opportunistic and be led astray. Another risk is that special interests take precedence over the interest of the company as a whole. The elimination of these types of risk will require competence of another kind than the three first mentioned. We will come to this when we discuss the implications of different types of owner competence in the last section of this chapter.

What distinguishes the owner from other value creators?

The role of the owner is defined by the concept of the hierarchy of value creation. The process of renewal has to comprise several levels – operational level, single business level etc. as Figure 13.3 illustrates.

Furthermore, a superior level has to make sure, by exercising meta-management, that the renewal process is not blocked at the level below. Thus, the owner level is the ultimate resort for the functioning of the individual company or corporation as a learning centre.

Summing up: why the two cornerstones – incessant renewal and meta-management?

The content of the competence required to pursue strategic corporate governance is generated by the *process of creative destruction* , and thus by the necessity of *incessant renewal* , it can be argued. For the individual company, the incessant renewal concerns a specific business environment characterised by its specific risk logic and dynamic. The institutional environment is specific to the individual company as well, and so are the organisational risks of the company. Finally, the renewal processes in the company have to be kept on track by a specific owner idea and its supporting system of values.

Meta-management , on the other hand, is about the way ownership and strategic corporate governance can be exercised. As a corollary to decentralisation, *meta-management* is increasingly gaining ground in modern organisation. However, to play its role at the top of the value creation hierarchy, it is particularly important for the owner specialist to apply the principle of *meta-management* . The purpose of *meta-management* is to create the appropriate prerequisites for a company and for an organisation to function well. Thus, the *meta-management* agenda of an active owner typically includes making sure that the company has:

- The right kind of CEO and leadership to fit its current and expected challenges.
- The right external structure, e.g. regarding ownership and the structure of its industry as well as its own position in that industry.
- The appropriate internal organisation to fit the leadership as well as the situational challenges of the company.
- Always the ability to manage *difficult decisions* of any kind. The owner is the *last resort* to make sure such decisions are adequately dealt with.

KEY ELEMENTS OF OWNER COMPETENCE – IMPLICATIONS AND CHALLENGES

Each of the key elements is discussed in turn.

Business risk management capability

What are the difficulties in value added creation, in the renewal of business operations? What kind of competence should those who are to exercise ownership have and how can this competence be acquired?

One can say that the difficulty with value added creation is to understand each specific situation as well as to find a solution, i.e. a way of reducing or eliminating business related risks, that will safeguard the necessary renewal and thereby value added creation. This competence has two separate yet complementary dimensions, which can consequently be acquired in different yet complementary ways.

The first type of competence is actual *experience* . Nothing can replace the competence that is acquired through confronting numerous situations where the need for renewal is varied and where different ways of handling business risks as they occur are tried. Successes and failures create an individual range of experience that cannot be acquired in any other way. Naturally one must have concrete knowledge of various industries, of market relations, contact networks, competitors etc. Such experience cannot be acquired without having lived through situations where relevant issues, challenges and decisions are generated regularly and where the person concerned is responsible for his involvement. Thus we are also referring to what the basis is for recruiting people who are to exercise ownership. Apart from those who already have had the possibility of exercising ownership, people with qualified corporate management experience can be included in this category: CEOs of large corporations of course, as well as those of medium and certain smaller ones; heads of business areas and other top executives with experience of business responsibility. Finally, certain advisers whose line of business is primarily analysis and recommendations concerning top management issues could qualify as well.

This, however, is not enough. 'Learning without thinking is of no value'.[1] One must also be able to *conceptualise* one's knowledge so that one can not only distinguish the uniqueness of each situation but also develop a situation-specific business idea and an ownership idea. Concrete knowledge about industries and companies can sometimes be misleading, lead to false analogies and uncritically copied solutions if this conceptualisation ability is not fully developed.

Some important points, which were highlighted in Chapter 12, that should be part of conceptualisation include the following:

- The ability to distinguish different types of changes generating different demands on renewal:
  - variations and turbulence in the business environment, which can be handled through renewal within existing business systems, and within the framework of existing business and group ideas;
  - structural changes which mean that existing business systems must be fundamentally renewed and new business ideas/group ideas must be created;
  - paradigmatic changes which are so fundamental that the ownership idea must be renewed.

- An insight into the importance of differentiating industry logic and hence the subsequent dissimilarities of risk logic and risk dynamics as well as the available fundamental possibilities for risk elimination and reduction. The ability to systematically analyse risk is a fundamental part of the ownership competence.
- Awareness of the company's different development phases and time frames in relation to one's own risk management capability. It is not enough to distinguish risk logic by its type of industry or the company's

own competence. The latter must also be related to the development phases in a business where one has this specific ownership competence. Is it in the early development phase where one's own competence is linked to seed money, venture capital etc, or in the mature phase where drastic restructuring measures are called for?

- The competence to evaluate value creation, the connection between ownership contribution in the value creation process, risk management capability – active risk reduction, risk elimination – and growth of value. One can analyse past performance and thus keep track of the type of risk logic one is best at dealing with. When evaluating *future* value creation ability the questions become trickier. As referred earlier, Skandia developed a model called the Navigator – which reflects the future value creating logic that is relevant to Skandia. Every owner in every company must create his own model that reflects the industry logic, development situation and specific competence that is suitable for that particular situation.

How can such a competence be acquired then? Can it best be acquired through abstract exercises and education at business schools or through seminars run by consultants? This can be possible to a certain extent – certain fundamental tools for conceptual analysis could be communicated in this way. Case studies of other successful owners and demanding decisive situations for the owner can be of great help and put one's own experience into perspective. Part of every practising owner's general education should consist of being very familiar with a number of successful owners' success stories and experiences. However, the important and decisive thing is that conceptualisation focuses on the reality that the practising owner is faced with and that it is situational. In actual fact conceptualisation is a constantly moving process in the exercise of situational ownership. It is often valuable in this process to obtain the external points of view from an unbiased consulting study or from an experienced speaking partner or such like.

Meta-management skills

One's own direct experience, if possible, is even more important as regards meta-management skills. This is connected with the fact that the acquired experience is multi-dimensional and above all includes:

- Familiarity with different types of situations, different driving forces and conditions needed to make *meta-management* decisions.
- Experience of bringing about change and those insights into organisational qualities and characteristics that only come to light when trying to or actually bringing about change – the talkers are exposed, the instigators of change can step forward, the real power relations and unholy

alliances are revealed, the new demand for competence is clarified, and so on.

- The ability as a practising owner to use oneself and one's personality as an instrument of change and the possibilities of developing this competence, as well as to use one's role as a basis for practising *meta-management* . We are born with different management talents. Upbringing, education and various cultural environments provide these talents with different contents. In the practical application of these talents in varying *meta-management* situations one can see how this talent can be utilised to bring about the necessary changes. One gets to know one's own strengths and weaknesses as well as getting the opportunity of refining oneself as an instrument of change. In addition to being able to utilise one's own personal talent and personality one must also be in control of the instrument one has at one's disposal – the formal and informal role one can play. This can be as chairman of the board, board member, representative of an institutional owner etc. The conditions for exercising *meta-management* vary – not only between different formal roles. There are also many significant informal differences between different companies in being the board chairman.

Meta-management experience is refined to *meta-management competence* using a well-developed frame of reference and concept for *meta-management* questions, problem solving and implementation. This conceptualisation and intellectual awareness of the different *meta-management* components is extraordinarily important if ownership skills are to be made professional and replace general opinion.

In Chapter 12 we developed the concept of *meta-management* which thus need not be repeated in this discussion. However, some main points of *meta-management* , which is a very demanding area of ownership competence, are summarised below.

Meta-management is defined as the 'mobilisation and use of power to redistribute power'. This is a shortened version of the complex phenomenon that is *meta-management* . However, this shortened version has the advantage of pinpointing the most fundamental and most difficult areas in *meta-management* . The first difficult area is the taboos that surround power – both as a phenomenon and as a term. Paraphrases are often used – influence, responsibility, mandate etc. – to avoid the word power. This is of course quite correct as long as it does not lead to self-deceit nor to hindering the necessary *meta-management* measures. It is very important to speak plainly when conceptualising and communicating the central theme of *meta-management* . The shortened version contains two different aspects of power – the meta-manager's power i.e. the use of power as an instrument of change, and power relations that exist in the organisation which is undergoing *meta-*

management , i.e. that is what must be changed. Obviously, this shortened version of *meta-management* assumes a tacit understanding. In itself, power is of no significance in a company's value creation. Value creation is in fact about competence. The management revolution as it is known, was about separating ownership and power from corporate management because management skills were needed that were obviously lacking in the owners. However, power and competence do belong together because the competence that is promoted is dependent on power relations within a company. *Meta-management* measures to create the right power relations in a company's organisation thus need a deep insight into the necessary skills as well as into the company's organisational learning ability, its own self-renewal competence. *Meta-management* is about changing and developing this renewal ability further, at improving and refocusing the company's *organisational learning* !

How can *meta-management* be developed conceptually and supplement practical experience, so that the effective *meta-management* competence is professionalised? Naturally, familiarity with organisational philosophical terms, with organisational analysis methods can be reinforced through traditional educational means, such as discussions on case studies – provided that they are based on well-developed frames of reference. Such frames of reference should contain both instrumental aspects (the organisation as a tool) and institutional aspects (the organisation as a value system and social construction). Efficient professionalisation will first come about when conceptualisation is applied to one's own situation where one is constantly interpreting how the *organisational learning* ability develops. In nine cases out of ten, this process is impeded – according to the author's experience – because a historical analysis of the development of the company concerned had not been deep enough. Few managers, boards and other practising owners have done enough homework in order to clarify and define a company's distinctive area of competence, its origin, as well as how the *organisational learning* ability has developed. This absence is often a fundamental issue in problem companies – one is unable to see the distinctive *in* competence that is the cause of inefficiency and inability to change.

Legitimisation and institutionalisation competence

The logic of original sin applies in this context. If an owner specialist has a poor reputation its *offspring* , the companies, will also suffer. Conversely, if the owner specialist has institutional status, this will render legitimacy to its holdings as well. Being a company of the Wallenberg sphere automatically opens certain doors. Having CD&R as owner gives credibility to a company.

However, the relationship is mutual, in particular on the negative side. An abuse of important stakeholder values by a company in the portfolio of an owner specialist will tarnish the reputation of the latter as well.

Thus, if an owner specialist has managed its own legitimisation process diligently enough, it has a considerable competence platform to manage the legitimisation risks of its holdings as well.

The Wallenberg sphere is an exemplary case for any owner specialist to learn from. As the analysis in Part II outlined, the legitimisation policy of that sphere highlights all the key aspects of it, in particular:

- The basis for all successful legitimisation efforts is to manage one's business well. All other initiatives will only have short-term effects unless this basic criterion is met. Even hyped-up companies of the new economy will experience this, sooner rather than later. Some observers may argue that Investor, the instrumental owner specialist company of the Wallenberg sphere is a poor example because of its heavy investment company discount. However, this is to a large extent outside the control of Investor itself. So, instead of trying to reduce this discount by *cosmetic* measures, Investor is focusing its energy where it can make a difference – the fundamental value creation of its holdings. As a consequence, the net asset value of Investor continues to grow. Several insightful investors see the discount as an attractive opportunity to acquire assets cheaply by putting their money in Investor while the market at large, possibly, falls into the category of *the majority is always wrong* .

- The second key aspect is to have one's values in order. Legitimisation is about making sure that there is consonance between the value environment of the company and the values at work internally. Good conduct is good business. This is applicable in all social contexts. Furthermore, the market economy rests on trust, and sustainable economic growth is the result of a gigantic plus-sum game. If one party would gain and another lose, it would be a zero-sum game, zero growth. Real cheaters only create minus-sum games in the end because the whole basis of trust had been damaged. This is the logic for the market as a whole, but this applies to the individual company and owner as well. Everybody but opportunists and crooks should realise this. Sometimes, however, judgement is blurred by opportunities of making a quick buck, compromising some basic values along the way. It is a key task, not only of a conscientious owner, but also one concerned with sustainable value creation, to eliminate such risks.

- Legitimisation can be seen as some kind of hygiene factor, a minimum for every company and owner to pass. Without legitimacy there is no licence to do business. However, some companies succeed beyond that in their effort to develop their relations to external stakeholders and centres of power. They become institutions by managing to impose their values on the environment to the extent that external centres of power and groups of people defend the existence of the company in question, or its products and initiatives. Sometimes, this even constrains the freedom of action of the company itself. A case in point occurred some years ago when the Coca-Cola Company changed the formula of its standard Coke. The general public of Coke consumers defended what had become an institution and the Coca-Cola Company had to reintroduce *Classic Coke* . Good examples of institution builders can be found among the American tycoons of the late 19th and early 20th century who managed to transform their notorious character as *Robber Barons* to being the great benefactors of American education and culture as well as being perceived as pillars of society. They became the model for the custom, prevalent since then among American business people, that the person who succeeds in creating a fortune should also give something back to the society that had made this possible. One hopes that the contemporary Russian *Robber Barons* learn that lesson too, and, at least, make their contribution by keeping and investing more of their *robber* gains in Russia.

Owner vision/idea and the specific value system

Can this critical part of the whole area of ownership competence be professionalised at all? Is the logic of this aspect of *ownership competence* so dominated by soft issues that the whole thing is a question of personal involvement, of inner driving forces that cannot be artificially created?

At least, the phenomenon can be analysed and communicated. Visions, fundamental owner ideas and the necessary supportive values can be discussed. The importance of internal and external ties can be accepted – at least intellectually, but can one ensure that it is espoused and embodied by those who are expected to exercise the ownership function? The continued success of the Wallenberg sphere has been due to the family's ability to hand down ownership competence from generation to generation. Everyone is eagerly watching to see how the fifth generation will succeed at the helm of the sphere. The younger generation's leadership skills are being discussed and analysed – do they understand banking and business, can they exercise meta-management and surround themselves with the right corporate leaders, professional board members and advisers? However, the crucial aspect to be concerned about is how they will manage to embrace the owner idea and value system they inherit as well as how they manage to adapt these to current and future challenges. If they succeed with this, it will be decidedly easier to supplement the remaining elements of ownership competence with external talent.

But what about the employee-controlled owner-actors – the big pension funds, mutual trusts, and other institutional investors without major personal owner involvement? Can they develop their active ownership role and contribute to the fundamental value creation in a more sustained and consistent way than what has hitherto been the case? Can their ownership skills be also professionalised and developed as regards their owner idea, visions and the supporting values? Will they have the courage to act forcefully without strong ownership ideas and clear values in conflicts with chairmen/CEOs of large corporations?

An awareness of these important aspects of *ownership competence* is a critical first step towards professionalising ownership as well as developing the soft issues such as values, visions and the value-creating idea of ownership.

At the same time, it should be recognised that nothing can replace private ownership and involvement at the personal level - with risk capital, of course – but, even more important, with ideas, visions, strong values, and commitment to succeed in building a business. There is plenty of empirical evidence to prove the importance of *competent capital* for the success of new ventures. Furthermore, all the big success stories – the Wal-Marts, the IKEAs, the Standard Oils, the Microsofts, and many more – are the result of visionary, unstoppable entrepreneurs, of private and very personal ownership.

Thus, it is very encouraging to notice how the young generations, particularly since the middle of the 1990s, increasingly see their future in new ventures. A kind of virtuous circle seems to be at work as well, further accelerating the emergence of the new economy. Early successful entrepreneurs of the new era become risk capitalists deploying their fortunes, together with their experience, in new start-ups. Since the same phenomenon seems to be happening in Europe, and not only in the USA, hopefully it will turn out to be an effective remedy against *Eurosclerosis.*

However, private ownership, visionary thinking, and personal commitment should not be reserved for new ventures, solely. This is also necessary for successful renewal, restructuring, and re-invention of the corporations of the old economy. Investor of the Wallenberg sphere will try to be 'the bridge' between the old and the new economies. Other owner specialists should try other strategies. Sir Richard Branson of the Virgin Group (British) and Mr. Stenbeck of The Kinnevik Group (Swedish-American), who boldly challenge monopolies and established complacency, are possibly additional examples to serve as inspiration. How can we get more owners who would take on such challenges? Let us discuss this further in the next section.

INDUSTRY DEVELOPMENT PERSPECTIVE

In the earlier chapters of the book ownership was seen as an industry containing actors who have in common that they are involved in mobilising and channelling/ reallocating risk capital as well as in exercising some form of ownership function in the creation of value-added in companies – or have the opportunity of doing so. In an ownership market there is competition to use risk capital and to organise resources for creating value added. An analysis of current development trends showed increased competition and globalisation in the ownership industry which leads to actors having to review their own competitive ability and to assess what kind of renewal and specialisation/focusing is needed in their particular case. These dynamics mean that the industry is heading towards a higher level of sophistication, of specialisation, and of division of labour and of complexity. At least three dimensions can be distinguished in this development:

- Vertical specialisation and layering within the industry, in other words the actors can be differentiated in the risk capital flow: trust funds/pension funds – investment companies/venture capital companies – multi-business corporations – single businesses.
- Horizontal specialisation, in other words actors on the same level of the risk capital flow specialise in different industries, in owning companies with a similar industry logic, for example cyclical companies, high technology companies, pharmaceutical companies, service companies etc.
- Development stage specialisation, in other words one can specialise in being a long-term owner or choose to play a shorter-term role at a certain development stage: for example in the early stages of a company or business (seed money phase, venture capital phase) or in a restructuring phase in a company in a mature or over-mature industry. It is a challenge for Europe to see how well developed the American risk capital market is in this respect.

The individual actor's positioning in the ownership industry does not only mean that his own specialisation is defined more clearly, and that his position is determined in relation to competing owners on the same level or on other levels. Each actor, moreover, plays a meta-management role, i.e. influences the structure and specialisation on an underlying level. This goes without saying for some owner-actors. An investment company, for example, decides on the contents of its investment portfolio and more or less actively influences how the individual companies in its portfolio develop. For other owner-actors, particularly those further upstream the flow of risk capital, this is a tough challenge if the ownership industry is to be developed in a satisfactory manner.

The different owner-actor positions are described later on where two important parameters – the strategy of managing risks and the actual meta-management role – will be discussed.

Owner-actors' positioning

For an actor in the ownership industry the initial positioning occurs when he has to decide where he should aim in the vertical chain of risk capital flow. What expectations do the principals/the higher-ranking owners have as regards the actor? What skills and ownership ideas form the basis for continued operations? These and similar questions form the starting-point for positioning.

Spreading or eliminating risks?

The first parameter that should be analysed as regards positioning is thus *the strategy of managing risks* . Which of the two essential roles that were discussed in Chapter 12 on conceptualisation does one most closely resemble? The risk spreading role or the risk eliminating role? As shown in the CalPERS case study these two types of roles do not preclude one another. They can constructively complement each other. However, the main focus must be either one or the other since the chosen strategy of managing risks forms the basis for the whole ownership strategy. Examples of the disasters that resulted after various owner-actors unconsciously mixed the two roles together are not difficult to find as mentioned earlier. A wrongly applied risk spreading strategy has resulted in clay-footed monsters of diversified businesses without the competence or financial strength to reduce the fundamental risks of that particular business. To prevent General Electric ending up in such a mess, Jack Welch, CEO and Chairman of that corporation, set out his famous rule: *No. 1 or 2 – or fix, close or sell* . To qualify in GE's portfolio, a business had to be number one or two in the global market. If not, the chief executive in charge had to *fix* that within a limited period of time. The remaining options were to divest the business to another owner or, in the worst case, close down the operation.

The GE/Jack Welch example applies to an active risk eliminator. As regards institutional investors/owners such as trust funds and pension funds, there is a natural focus on risk spreading due to several reasons:

- The parties concerned – pension and trust fund savers – must have their pensions paid out at a given time, and trust fund savers must be able to cash in their shares and so on. This means that these funds must readily be accessible in the form of cash. This limits the possibility for concentrated long-term ownership. Investments need not be short term, however freedom of action – to be able to dismantle a stockholding with immediate effect – must always be present there.
- The required return – for example, guaranteed high and regular returns – can have similar consequences.
- Size can also be a deciding factor in choosing the risk management strategy. The large pension funds, for example CalPERS, TIAA-CREF or Hermes would become so dominating as owners if they concentrated

their holdings that it would be more difficult to combine this with demands for liquidity from their stakeholders.

What meta-management role?

However, giving priority to a risk spreading strategy does not imply that the owner can choose to play a passive ownership role in an efficient market economy. We can disregard the small, that is to say seen from a macro point of view, marginal investors whose own actions do not have any influence at all on the risk capital market as a whole. The demand for deliberate positioning and for playing the ownership role has markedly increased in the development stage the market economy countries and their companies find themselves in today. Many institutional investors have become so large that their buying or selling decisions influence the risk capital market where they are active. Thus, they influence their own investment prerequisites. It should be in their own interest to create as favourable an environment as possible for their own investments and their own investment competence. It therefore follows that one is responsible not only for one's own investments as isolated occurrences but also for how efficient the risk capital market and the ownership industry are.

Thus, it is not sufficient for an institutional owner to have a conscious risk management strategy only. They must also clarify the *meta-management role* they can and should play. What underlying influence is needed in the ownership industry to facilitate a more efficient value creation and how can each institutional investor make a distinctive contribution?

Another encouraging trend?

Given the current size and growth rate of pension funds, trust funds and similar institutional investors, channelling enormous volumes of savings to risk capital markets, their *meta-management* role becomes more and more crucial. Against this background, it is interesting to see how some institutional investors are allocating increasing amounts to, what is called, *relations investments* , i.e. to *owner specialists* / private equity firms taking positions in companies where this owner specialist applies an active risk management role. CalPERS of the USA and Hermes of the UK were mentioned in Part I as examples of such institutional investors but there are several others. Many LBO funds get the lion's share of their money from institutional investors, for instance.

This seems to be an encouraging trend that deserves further encouragement. It supports the development and further sophistication of the market for ownership. However, this is largely an Anglo-American phenomenon since pension savings and mutual trust funds are still in their infancy stages in many European countries, and in Japan as well.

So, we return to our conclusion in Part I. Another impediment to dynamic and sustainable growth has to be removed at the macro level. It is high time European and Japanese governments put their acts together.

Institutionalise by building good institutions

There is an increasing awareness of the importance of good and stable institutions for the smooth functioning of an economy, as well as for its growth dynamics.[2] Good corporate governance is part of a good institutional framework. Accountable boards and bosses, transparent accounting, disclosure of insider trading, and other key aspects of *Codes of conduct* enhance trust, and thus reduce transaction costs in the economy.

Thus, the corporate governance arena offers ample opportunities for corporations to legitimise themselves and possibly gain institutional status by taking initiatives to improve corporate governance in general. They can set examples on their own part, as did General Motors when they outlined their corporate governance principles. Another pioneer was Campbell Soup with their policy document, 'Accountable bosses are better bosses' some years ago. More recent examples are The Sony Corporation (by reforming their board and becoming a model for other Japanese corporations to follow) as well as Aventis, the French-German merger of Rhône-Poulenc and Hoescht, when they appointed Mr. Vienot as chairman to mark the commitment of the merged company to good corporate governance. Mr. Vienot chaired the most famous French committees on corporate governance.

Another way, of course, is to be a good citizen by contributing in joint efforts to develop a *Combined Code* and then comply with it. The UK achievement is the example that comes to mind.

CORPORATE GOVERNANCE PRINCIPLES TO SUPPORT COMPETENT COMMITTED OWNERSHIP

It was stated in the beginning of this chapter that accountability and prosperity aspects are equally important and are inseparable. They support one another.

One common principle, to be found in most corporate governance policies, e.g. in those of CalPERS as well as in those of many other activists, is the principle of one share, one vote. This is rooted in the fundamental principle that all shareholders should be treated equally. Thus, differentiated voting rights are regarded to be anathema.

However, given that different owners apply different risk management strategies, and, as a consequence, differ in willingness to absorb risk, it is questionable whether this principle should apply in all contexts.

It takes time to make significant value creation contributions. Therefore, it is essential for the active owner involved to have enough time on his hands to realise his/her visions. Mass psychology and other uncontrollable forces result in that *the market is always wrong* . The fundamental value creation processes cannot adapt to the whims of the stock markets.

Differentiated voting rights – within reasonable limits – could provide the committed owner with the stability needed to function as value creator.

The risks of abusing other shareholders' rights by such arrangements should be fewer with increasing competition in global markets.

THE ORGANISATIONAL PERSPECTIVE

Following the discussion in the two previous sections on the fundamental need for professionalisation, on how ownership's contribution to renewal and value creation could be developed as well as how plurality and specialisation could be strengthened further in the ownership industry, we will end by focusing on the efficiency of the individual renewal or value creating system. In other words, ideas for how the vertical organisation of owner – board - management can be made as effective and efficient as possible in each company.

The problem is divided here into two sections or two differing views, even if they are linked closely together. Firstly, the organisational view will be discussed and its importance in the division of roles between the three levels: owner – board - management. In the following section the governance view will be put forward, in other words how ownership is practised and how its fundamental renewal and value creating processes could be enhanced.

The earlier analysis has shown the possibilities for a natural division of labour in the value creating and renewal hierarchy between owners/different owner levels on the one hand and the different management levels in multi-business groups and individual businesses/companies etc. on the other. When focusing on the individual business's or the individual company's vertical organisation yet another level can be seen – the board. Its role is both the most demanding and the most problematic, as Figure 13.4, *The Board 's dual role* , illustrates.

The board is part of both the *ownership function* – it practices the day to day, direct kind of ownership on the executive management – and of the management function by being responsible to the owners for how the company is run.

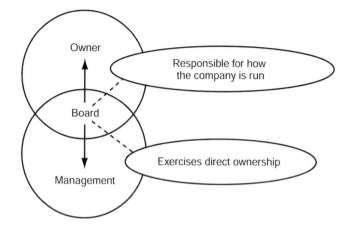

Figure 13.4   The Board's dual role.

The board and the owners

The board is supposed to represent all shareholders and to meet the demands of the collective interests of the owners. In the most common cases, the large listed corporations have a very heterogeneous ownership where the individual owner, institutions or owner groups often have differing interests and time frames as far as the company is concerned. In some companies there is one dominating owner whereas the other owners are generally very fragmented and heterogeneous. In other companies there can be a couple of large owner groups of equal weight as in the case of Ericsson. As shown in the study of the Wallenberg sphere, the two large owners of Ericsson have managed to co-operate constructively on most critical issues. This is, of course, not always the case in similar owner constellations, rather the opposite. Typical conflicts of interest that can arise relate to both corporate aims, strategy etc. – for example, how far should they diversify, how should long-term investments be prioritised, and so on – and to the demands on returns, dividend policy etc. Behind these conflicts there are often other driving forces – the aim of a particular owner group to keep ownership control by avoiding new investments and expansion which would require new and large injections of capital that could alter the power structure and so on. When looking at the Corporate Governance phenomenon in the USA one could see that one of its triggers was just this favouritism of certain owners as well as a management that wanted to defend its own position against the majority of the diverse owners.

In the USA and the UK, the development and acceptance of a Corporate Governance policy has become an important instrument for safeguarding the collective interests of the owners. Thus, in the USA, company boards have taken the lead sometimes – for example the boards of General Motors and Campbell Soup were early movers in this respect. However, as recounted in Part I, the driving force behind these and other initiatives has been the American pension funds with CalPERS in the lead. American corporate boards, most of which are involved in sub-committees of various kinds, have Corporate Governance committees which maintain an on-going surveillance to make sure that owners' interests are being respected and who report on their work to the annual general meeting.

Many companies in other countries have successively adopted Corporate Governance principles to their own way of working. It should be in each board's interests to set out the rules and communicate them to the stock market and to the general public who represent the collective interests of the owners. Thus a good principle to begin with is that the collective interests are best served if the company's total long-term potential is safeguarded and if long-term, sustained shareholder value is maximised. The earlier analysis showed that it was something more than what financial whiz kids can define using a few simple formulas. Boards must possess the whole range of ownership skills – renewal capability and risk management competence depending on the company's line of business, organisation, credibility and institutional position – called for by that company.

Ownership can mean important differences for the board in another respect. If there is a dominating owner or owner group with long-term interests in the company then there should also be an owner idea that can provide guidance in the company's development and an owner who can be the board's speaking partner in matters of grave consequence. Dialogue between the owners would thus be more than a formal procedure during the annual general meeting. If the issue relates to an *ownerless* company, i.e. when ownership is so fragmented that no one can or will assume direct ownership, can the board take upon itself to try to act as owner? Historically this has not appeared to be the feasible path to take. Without some form of demands from the owners, the board clearly loses its bite and becomes at the mercy of the management. The board's power and skills are no match for the management in such a situation. The *meta-management* relations between owners, boards, and executive management are always needed.

The relationship clearly illustrates how crucially important it is for even relatively small owners – for example institutional investors, each with a holding of a few percent of votes or capital – to carry out their responsibility as regards the board's quality and accountability. Even a limited ownership can make a big difference in this respect, as the previous examples have shown.

Alignment of the interests of owners and directors of the board

Since even a limited ownership stake can make a difference, the issue of directors owning shares in the company comes in focus. Increasingly, remuneration packages for directors include share options or shares. Wisely designed such incentive systems possibly fulfil a constructive function. Usually, however, the directors benefiting from it do not take too much of a risk. We know from studies of start-ups how important *competent capital* is for the success of such young companies. *Business angels,* risk capitalists who combine significant equity stakes with relevant competence, play a crucial value-creating role in start-ups. Would not the same logic apply for established companies and large corporations? In that case, institutional investors and other owners ought to consider to putting demands on people to make a sizeable investment in corporations where they would like to candidate for board directorship.

The board and the management

If we assume, for the case of simplicity, that we are dealing with a unitary board and an actual two-tier structure of responsibilities between the board and the executive management – then how can the board define its role in relation to the executive management? In some cases it has appeared fruitful to emphasise and discuss the following three criteria of the *3D formula: Distance, Dialogue* and *Differentiation.*

- *Distance* : an important aspect of the relationship is the importance of the board safeguarding its ability to maintain an overview and global picture of the company. The board must preserve its integrity when evaluating management proposals, investment decisions etc. as well as when reviewing management salaries. Without such a detached view the board will be co-opted by the company's executive management and will risk becoming involved in various types of sub-optimal decision-making.
- *Dialogue* : maintaining this distance and integrity must however be combined with an on-going dialogue with the company's executive management. Whilst the board acts as the owners' instrument for the direct and on-going exercise of ownership and owner control, it is also responsible for how the company is run. The executive responsibility should be delegated to the company's executive management, but, preferably, the delegating should be in the form of a continuous dialogue where the implication of important decisions is interpreted jointly by the board and the executive management.
- *Differentiation* : in the dialogue and interaction between the board and management it becomes important to clarify the different roles. Table 13.1 shows some aspects of such differentiation.

Table 13.1 Division of roles between the board and management

Function	Style	Focus
Board		
Meta-management	Restrained, optimising the renewal balance	Risk oriented
Corporate management		
Executive leadership	Forceful, acquisitive	Growth/expansion oriented

The fundamental function of exercising management differs in that the board applies *meta-management* in its relations with the executive management. This is both for reasons of practicality and of principle. The board has limited time at its disposal. In the first instance it must concentrate on creating the right prerequisites to enable the day-to-day running of the company to function. In that respect it is most adamant that there is a competent executive management.

An important quality in executive management – and a condition for the board not to get involved in detailed decisions – is that the executive management acts as the driving force and has high goals as regards growth and expansion. The board's task is thereby to be the restraining force. As one of the most professional board members put it, 'my most important task is to say no'. This naturally does not mean that the board should be against expansion or thwart innovation. On the contrary the most important task of the ownership function, repeated earlier on numerous occasions, is to ensure that the renewal of businesses and companies is functioning. Thus this is also the main function of the board. However, it is important for the board to maintain the balance between old and new – that what currently exists is not neglected because the company's executive management has discovered new and exciting business opportunities. It is not unusual for new business opportunities to cause continued risk elimination in existing operations to be neglected whilst underestimating the risks in the new operations. This happens particularly when the different risk logic and dynamics as well as their repercussions, which characterise the new businesses, have not yet been understood. Capital is eroded from two directions and the result is total disaster. Thus in role differentiation it should be emphasised that the board must have a greater risk awareness, risk orientation and – of course – risk evaluation/risk management competence. The executive management should first and foremost be keen on expansion. If the board makes sure that the executive management does have such a profile then an important organisational risk has also been eliminated – of executive management being inactive!

This analysis of role differentiation between the board and the executive management can be summarised by the following:

- management should be young, ambitious, have drive, be expansive, energetic – besides possessing the necessary technical skills, of course; whilst
- the board should be wise, experienced, able to assess and manage risk, have a detached but holistic perspective whilst being both supportive and questioning.

An ideal picture that perhaps most would agree with. How does one get there? Let us discuss this in the final section of this chapter that sets out the governance perspective.

An additional D

Let us add a fourth D to the formula above making it $3D + D$. The added D stands for *Decisions*. What decisions should be taken by the board, and what should be delegated to the executive management? A general guideline for defining the decision agenda of the board would include decisions, which are essential for the *meta-management* role of the board. Thus, all decisions required to creating and changing the fundamental prerequisites of the company, e.g. concerning:

- Top management: CEO appointments and dismissals. In addition, it is usually a good idea to apply the so-called *grandfather principle*. The board approves appointments and dismissals proposed by the CEO of the next layer of executives reporting directly to the CEO.
- Organisational and other major policy formation issues.
- Strategy formation and major implementation steps.
- M & A and strategic partnering issues.
- Resource allocation and major investment projects.
- Major financing issues.

Complications with mixed board concepts

A unitary board with a clear two-tier structure concerning the division of roles between the board and the executive management makes life, if not simple, at least straightforward.

This stands out in comparison with situations of mixed board concepts where complications occur regarding matters of principle as well as of a practical nature.

How should the fundamentally important idea of meta-management, as well as the $3D + D$ formula, be applied?

One consequence is that the board has to be split up in two parts – one comprising independent directors, and one including the executive directors.

Another consequence concerns the committees of the board. One reason for having committees is that it provides the opportunity of deepening the analysis of certain, demanding issues. It is also a way of benefiting from a certain expertise within the board, e.g. in matters of accounting and auditing. Other members may lack the technical knowledge to contribute in the detailed discussions. The second reason for having committees is to deal with matters where executive directors have special interests to defend and promote. In such instances, only independent directors are eligible. If the whole board were independent, the latter type of committee would not be necessary. If the CEO is the only executive director on the board, he/she just has to leave the room when certain matters are discussed. Having several executive directors on the board enlarges the scope of complications since each one usually has executive responsibility for a part of the corporation. All experience shows that it is difficult, if not impossible, for the same person to accommodate his/her special interest with that of the whole.

GOVERNANCE PERSPECTIVE

How does one bring about Corporate Governance, appropriate and efficient owner control? Needless to say, this is a huge issue involving many aspects and some of which we have touched upon in earlier parts of this book. This final section of the book is not the place to present a comprehensive program for corporate governance. We will limit ourselves here to focusing on the board's competence and possibilities of exercising professional corporate governance. We will specifically deal with two of the most important aspects for further improvement, if appropriate and efficient corporate governance is to be safeguarded, namely:

- The recruitment of board members and the board's composition as a whole as well as the role of the chairman.
- The need for day-to-day support for the board in its exercise of ownership.

The board's recruitment and composition

A frequent criticism of the boards of large companies in most countries is that they are recruited – as far as the members chosen at the AGM are concerned – from a limited circle of people, from some kind of board elite.

The reason for this is usually twofold. One reason is that a particular owner group, or sphere of companies are dominating a company, and thus also the nomination of directors. Another reason is that, generally, the supply of good candidates is scarce.

The fact that some dominating owner groups utilise their networks of contacts and personal relationships to recruit board members is not necessarily negative. On the contrary, the Wallenberg sphere/Investor is an example worthy of imitation as regards systematically building up a team of professional board members. This is done by releasing the top people in the sphere from their executive positions, such as those of managing director and chief executive of the operational companies, when they still have 10–15 years' worth of highly productive skills and managerial strength left in them.

However, the Investor example can be developed further not only in other investment companies and owner specialist groups. It also becomes extremely important to institutional investors who have been so passive in the past. If they are to take ownership responsibility it is not enough to vote for those candidates nominated by other owners at the annual general meeting or to be a member of the nominating committee. They must actively participate in the development of a competent recruitment base for board members. This is an important remaining chapter in the institutions' ownership policy – both formulating it as well as carrying it out.

Merely placing one's own top officers on the boards of listed companies is no solution to this challenge. There is even a risk that it is counterproductive:

- One has an extremely limited capacity, which soon risks being used up. The only valid argument for some kind of personal direct participation is that one could thereby gain personal knowledge and experience as regards qualified board work.
- One can get into conflicts of loyalty between one's own institution's main interest, for example pension savings, on the one hand and the company's capital needs on the other.
- But above all one abandons the *meta-management principle* , i.e. to work indirectly by creating the right prerequisites rather than trying to directly control. The large institutions must leverage their own capacity by having a network of skilled resources on hand.

Earlier analyses have shown that different situations place demands on different types of ownership skills. Increased competition within the ownership industry as well, increases these demands and necessitates further specialisation. Each type of industry needs deep insights into the logic and dynamics that characterise the business-related risks that are present there. The company's development situation generates its own specific challenges. Organisational and institutional prerequisites lead to varying demands for a competent *meta-management* as well as for the ability to form the values that lend legitimacy to the company, and provide guidance for the operational management of the company etc.

Recruitment to and composition of the board must reflect these challenges and these competence demands. The institutions still have a long way to go in this respect. There is still a lot to be achieved on a national basis. In addition, rapid globalisation of markets and corporations call for international recruitment of directors to get boards with adequate competence.

A board should not be solely made up of individuals who by simple arithmetic have all the skills that the company concerned actually demands. A board is not merely a group of individuals, it should be a functioning team as well. This does not necessarily happen spontaneously on the board members' election at the annual general meeting. It is thus necessary to have an active leadership, with the chairman of the board as the prime mover, and who participates in board recruitment. Many understand this, yet this important aspect should be particularly emphasised, not least because reality in these cases does not agree with the formalities. Formally, the elected board chooses its chairman from amongst its members, in accordance with the Companies Act.

The crucial role of chairman

The chairman shall not merely be seen as being 'primus inter pares' among directors, neither as some kind of monitor of meetings of the board. The chairman has to play a key leadership role in several respects. Criteria to consider in assessing candidates and recruiting and electing a chairperson should include:

- **Motivation** to make a strong personal commitment to lead the company and the board.
- **Enough time** to carry out the demanding assignment of chairmanship.
- **Multifaceted competence**:
  - team builder (within the board);
  - leader of the board as a whole as well as in relation to each member (assessing individual performance, giving feedback etc);
  - *meta-manager* in relation to executive management and setting an example for the board as a whole;
  - risk management competence reflecting the situation of the company;
  - industry competence.

- **Network** of contacts – business as well as institutional.
- **External status**, credibility.

Owners' infrastructure to support the board in its work

A real factor of strength and an important component in the Wallenberg sphere's/Investor's *distinctive ownership competence* is the supportive infrastructure of a network of contacts, financial expertise, analytical resources, access to different types of skills and the expertise that the owner group has at its disposal. Within Investor, teams have been set up for each core holding to provide support to the director(s) concerned. Thus, the sphere's board members are not merely relying on their own personal expertise and networks. The individual board member or the board as a whole is not one-sidedly dependent on the support of the company – often on the management's terms.

The board's independence and ability to carry out its demands and dual role – of both exercising direct ownership on the management and being responsible to the annual general meeting and the owners for how the company is run – presupposes access to such an infrastructure. However, this is rarely the case today and is not seen to be of utmost necessity either. There is a great difference between large, established owner groups/investment companies in this respect.

Independent board members of American companies became considerably more effective as board members and in exercising ownership when they were provided with information and external analyses from CalPERS and other activist institutional investors in addition to the information they received from the company's management. CalPERS, in their current policy, have stated this to be a task of high priority in the continued practice of Corporate Governance.

Much more could be done by institutional investors to develop an active network of independent directors, as well as candidates for directorships, to draw upon when corporations need *new blood* . To make them effective, top quality support would be needed. This should be built up systematically. Many independent directors do not have a *home base* , an executive position in one company with access to a basic infrastructure and regular interchange of ideas and information in their daily work. More and more independent directors will become professional directors as boards are being professionalised. Institutional investors, particularly the big ones, could provide such systematic support. The network of active independent directors they develop could be organised as a *faculty* . Such a *faculty* should have access to facilities to meet regularly to exchange experience. It should have resources to make their own studies as well as a curriculum of training and director development courses. Investor, the key instrument of active ownership of the Wallenberg sphere, could be one model to start from, but each institutional investor has to find its own way.

It is obvious that institutional investors are still in the initial development stages as far as such ideas are concerned. A representative of a fund that the author spoke to stressed for example that 'we don't even have the time and resources to use lawyers to deal with the formalities during the annual general meetings'. This could be an obvious first step to take – at least if we are to take the CalPERS experience seriously. The first position that CalPERS filled was in fact a Chief Counsel who knew the legal requirements for the exercise of ownership. However, as the CalPERS example has also shown, it was only a necessary but insufficient step to really achieve what one had intended. Much more was needed – strong management with 'fire in the belly',[3] a long learning process, sustainability and, not least, co-operation with a number of other institutional actors.

Still, there is a long way to go

If one should sum up in a few words what the corporate governance movement has achieved so far it would be that it has given *ownership legitimacy* . The distorted balance of power between executive management and owners/ the ownership function is at least less distorted now than ten years ago. It has become legitimate *to make bosses accountable* , even if many institutional owners have to learn to do that for a start.

However, this is far from enough. In fact, this is only 'the end of the beginning', to quote someone who did not shy for huge undertakings. If owners and the ownership function as a whole are going to take on their crucial value-creation roles, *much much* more is needed. Pressing for accountability tends to be reactive. Making a contribution to enhance sustainable value creation, business prosperity, demands a proactive owner. This is a huge challenge – but necessary to take on.

Two categories of actors, in particular, should feel obliged to take on this challenge: institutional investors – pension funds, mutual funds etc. – and the private individual as an investor, small and large:

- The institutional investors should assume this challenge, for several reasons. They are early positioned in the flow of risk capital, and usually, they are large. Thus, they are in a position to play an extremely important *meta-management role* , to influence the whole structure of the market of ownership, corporate control and governance. They can allocate their money directly to business corporations. Since the institutional investor often is very large, its chunk of investment in each target also tends to be large. Thus, the bulk of such direct investment goes to large corporations, primarily. However, they can also operate as a wholesaler – make investments in owner specialists of various sorts: venture capital companies, private equity firms etc. Doing this systematically, they would play an active role in developing the industry structure as well as the renewal dynamics of the economies where they are active. In parallel, they should develop their faculties of independent directors to support their investment allocation strategy.

- Everything starts with the individual, private investor though. First of all as owners/entrepreneurs of new firms. This is an indispensable prerequisite of a dynamic economy. However, we let the big institutions manage our indirect investments and assets to an increasing extent. It is essential that we do not abdicate from our responsibilities as owners in this respect. We get what we deserve. Corporate governance, *institutional investor governance*, should apply to the institutional investors as well. They should be accountable for how they exercise their *franchised* ownership as agents of the private owners, how they contribute to fundamental and sustainable value-creation in their total portfolios of investments. Furthermore, as citizens we can also influence politicians to improve institutional frameworks and make the investment environment more *owner friendly*. In some cultures, associations of small shareholders can provide effective support and leverage individual initiatives. But other means are also needed to take on the huge challenges of ownership.

Hopefully, this book has served as a small contribution to that end.

Appendix 1: Interview List

A1

As part of the work on this book, the following persons have been interviewed by the author once, and in some cases several times, in face to face meetings and/or by telephone during the period of summer 1999–spring 2000. (Abbreviations: Chm = Chairman; vChm = vice Chairman; Dir. = Director of the Board; (ne) = non-executive; CEO = Chief Executive Officer; MD = Managing Director; SEVP = Senior Executive Vice President.)

IN ALPHABETICAL ORDER:

Åström, Håkan, SEVP, Pharmacia Corporation

Auzimour, Jean-Pierre, Directeur, Cap Gemini Ernst & Young; retired Chm, Groupe Bossard

Baldock, Brian, Dir.(ne), Marks & Spencer

Barnevik, Percy, Chm, ABB, AstraZeneca, Investor, Sandvik; Dir.(ne), General Motors

Batchelder, David, CEO, Batchelder & Partners

Berg, Lars, Member of Management Board, and head of Telecoms, Mannesmann

Berggren, Bo. Dr., Chm, SAS Sverige; retired Chm, Astra and Stora

Berglöf, Erik, Professor, Stockholm School of Economics; Director of the Stockholm Institute of Transition Economics and East European Economics

Bergström, Clas, Professor, Stockholm School of Economics

Bertsch, Kenneth A., Director, Corporate Governance, Teachers Insurance and Annuity Association/College Retirement Equities Fund (TIAA-CREF)

Björkman, Johan, Chm, Ljungberggruppen, Shanditek

Boldt, Bob L., CFA, Senior Investment Officer, CalPERS

Brufer, Ramsey, Corporate Governance Executive, SPP

Cadbury, Dominic, Sir, Governor, the Wellcome Foundation; retired Chm, Cadbury Schweppes

Cairncross, Frances, Management Editor, The Economist

Crist, William D., President of the Board of Administration, CalPERS

Cromme, Gerhard, Dr., Chm, Management Board, Thyssen Krupp

Crowell, Nancy M., MD, Health Care Investment Banking, SG Cowen

Cruz, Stephen, head of Baltic Region, Gemini Consulting
de Jounge, Arendt, VP/Investments, First Security Van Kasper
Edkins, Michelle, Corporate Governance Executive, Hermes
Forsgård, Lars-Erik, Chief Executive, Small Shareholders Association of
Sweden
Fourtou, Jean-René, vChm, Management Board, Aventis
Gillan, Kayla, General Counsel, CalPERS
Gogel, Donald, President and CEO, Clayton, Dubilier & Rice (CD & R)
Grabe, Lennart, CEO, Swedish Postal Ofiice
Greener, Anthony, Sir, Chm, Diageo
Grünthal, Raoul, CEO, SBI
Hanson, Dale, CEO, Capital Partners
Hagströmer, Sven, Chm, Custos, Hagströmer & Qviberg
Hedelius, Tom, Chm, Handelsbanken; vChm, Ericsson
Johnsson, Finn, CEO, Mölnlycke Health Care; Chm, MVI; Dir.(ne) Volvo,
Industrivärden, Skanska; former MD, United Distillers
Kopper, Hilmar, Chm, Supervisory Board, Daimler Chrysler, Deutsche Bank
Koppes, Richard, Jones Day Reavis & Pogue and Stanford Law School;
former General Counsel, CalPERS
Larsson, Hans, Chm, NCC, Nobia; Dir. Handelsbanken, Holmen
Lind, Lars, CEO, MVI, Merchant Venture Investments
Lindgren, Håkan, Professor, Stockholm School of Economics
Lorsch, Jay W., Professor, Harvard Business School
Lund, Olof, Chm(ne), Tieto Enator, The SIAR Foundation; Dir.(ne) Pharma-
cia Corporation
Magnusson, Bernt, Chm, AssiDomän, Swedish Match; vChm, AvestaShef-
field; Dir.(ne) Burma Castrol, Merita Nordbanken
Marcus, David E., Senior Vice President, Director of European Investments,
Franklin Mutual Advisers
Marsch-Barner, Reinhard, Dr., Syndikus, Deutsche Bank
Miles, Glenn, International Corporate Governance Manager, CalPERS
Millberg, Lars, International Corporate Governance Executive, Small Share-
holders Association of Sweden
Millstein, Ira, Senior Partner, Weil, Gotshal & Manges
Monks, Robert A.G., Principal, Lens Investment Management
Normann, Richard, Professor; Chm, SMG
Nyberg, Daniel, PhD, assistant professor, Stockholm School of Economics
O'Neill, Brendan R., Dr., Chief Executive, ICI Chemical Industries
Qviberg, Mats, CEO, Öresund
Rhenman, Henrik, Senior Portfolio Manager, Carnegie Asset Management
Ros, Carl-Wilhelm, Chm Atle, Framfab; Dir.(ne), SEB; former First SEVP,
Ericsson
Rydin, Bo, Chm, Industrivärden, SCA

Savén, Björn, CEO, Industri Kapital

Seillère, Ernest Antoine, Président, CGIP

Skog, Rolf, Secretary to the Company Law Committee of Sweden

Spångberg, Kjell, Chm, Emerging Technologies

Spångberg, Per, Investor Relations manager, Investor

Steinberg, David, analyst, Deutsche Bank/Alex Brown

Stymne, Bengt, Professor, Stockholm School of Economics; Chm, Stockholm School of Entrepreneurship

Sutherland, Peter, MD, Goldman Sachs International; Co-chm (ne), BP Amoco; Dir.(ne) Investor, Ericsson, SKF

Thelin, Peter, Partner, Brummer & Partners

Vindevåg, Leif, Manager Strategic Research, OM Stockholm Exchange

Wager, Jeffrey D., MD, Commonwealth Pharmaceutical Partners

Wallenberg, Marcus, CEO, Investor AB

Wheatherstone, Dennis, retired Chm/CEO, J.P. Morgan; Dir.(ne), GM, Merck, Air Liquide

Zetterberg, Christer, Chm, IDI, Turn It, Micro Laser System, Segerström & Svensson; former CEO, Volvo

Appendix 2: Frame of Reference

A2

The purpose of this appendix is to provide the reader with an orientation of my thinking on ownership and related issues, particularly what influences and experiences have formed my perspectives and concepts of these phenomena. A brief comment on how my frame of reference relates to those of other writers on ownership will also be included.

I would like to distinguish between three main elements: (1) theoretical foundations of this book; (2) tapping the experience of practitioners and various experts; (3) my personal experience of ownership and related issues.

THEORETICAL FOUNDATIONS OF THIS BOOK

The theoretical foundations of this book can be split in two major influences. The first one refers to my general views on value creation, organisation and management. The second major influence is related to the particular topic of corporate governance.

The SIAR School

The perspectives applied as well as the conceptualisation of key issues of ownership and of sustainable value creation in this book originate from, what is sometimes referred to as, the *SIAR School of Strategic Management*.I have had the privilege of having spent the main part of my professional career in SIAR, Scandinavian Institutes of Administrative Research.[1] A unique characteristic of SIAR has been its clinical research methodology combining management consulting and research into one integrated process. This resulted not only in a successful management consulting business, but also in a rich body of knowledge, the SIAR School of Strategic Management.[2]

An overall research focus of SIAR has been *The Challenges of Large Organisations in a Structurally Changing Environment* (the name of its first, but still ongoing, research programme). What turned out to be the most demanding issues and challenges of companies and their management were generated by structural or irreversible changes in the business environment of companies. SIAR substituted the *organisational learning paradigm* for the prevailing planning paradigm to develop management philosophies, concepts and tools for companies to cope with structural change. Another important implication was that the *SIAR School* integrated aspects of strategy and organisation in its holistic concepts of value creation. The *SIAR School* of thought is further elaborated in Part III (Chapter 12) of this book where, among other things, it is shown what a crucial role the owner is supposed to play in order to make the organisational learning of a company function properly and efficiently.[3]

Another distinguishing feature of the *SIAR School* should be added – the historical perspective. All kinds of organisations, companies, industries, and other social contexts have been formed by their history. Current features and ways of conduct of an organisation, as well as actions taken by it, can be observed. However, to understand their significance and rationale one has to analyse the history of the organisation concerned (applying an analytical tool based on the concept of *organisational learning*). The historical perspective is a recurrent theme in this book.

The knowledge philosophy of the SIAR School

Business enterprises as well as organisation of all kinds and complexity are human creations. A common feature of successful companies is their uniqueness. Both aspects represent fundamental observations concerning the character of the social world with profound implications for what kind of knowledge is of interest as well as for the methodology to develop it and the ways of validating knowledge.

However, many scholars of the social world suffer from *physics envy* to travesty Freud. They believe that the social world is governed by regularities similar to the *laws of nature.*Thus, to find good solutions to a particular problem they look for what they believe to be universal answers. Such a misconception not only leads to a lot of meaningless research, it can have catastrophic consequences, e.g. the Marxist theories of determinism.

SIAR developed a clinical research methodology based on a theory of knowledge, which recognised the particular features of the social world. Inputs to this came from many philosophers of knowledge (Popper, Kuhn, Schutz, Husserl, Habermas, Weber, to mention some of the important ones). It would be outside the scope of this book to elaborate this further. However, the interested reader can find more about this in Normann (1970/1980) and (1977) as well as in Lind, Rhenman (1989) and Carlsson (2000).[4]

Implications of the SIAR philosophy of knowledge in this book can be seen in the prominence given to in depth case studies, in particular, that of the Wallenberg sphere. The value of the case study is not only created by some kind of *nice to know how they did it.*By analysing what Popper refers to as *the logic of the situation,*the Wallenberg case showed a unique solution to a set of dilemmas facing other owner specialists as well. Thus, the contribution to knowledge my book makes is to highlight what these dilemmas are and provide a *language* that is helpful in discussing issues of value creation and the role of owner specialists. If we want to take our knowledge about these issues one step further we are not helped by formulating hypotheses based on this case study and try to test them on some kind of *statistically significant* sample. In this context such a phenomenon does not exist in my view. Instead, additional in depth case studies of other owner specialists would make it possible to enrich our *language* concerning issues and dilemmas facing owner specialists. Knowledge development about social systems – how to understand as well as how to improve them, e.g. how to create added value – is a matter of *language* development.

Other scholars of corporate governance

I am greatly indebted to a number of scholars and other writers on corporate governance and related issues of ownership. This is evidenced by the numerous references made in the text to other books and sources. In addition, the literature reference list includes several works, which have provided important background orientation.

Some of the most important writers to help me understand issues as well as the concrete corporate governance situation in various countries include Charkham (1994), Drucker (several publications), Hopt et al. (1998), Jensen (several publications), Lorsch (1989, 1995), Monks (1996) and Roe (1994). In addition, the UK Committee Reports on Corporate Governance (particularly, Cadbury and Hampel) and the policy documents issued by CalPERS and TIAA-CREF have been helpful.

How does my frame of reference relate to that of other writers?

The best known writer on corporate governance and ownership – not least from a conceptual point of view – is probably Professor Michael C. Jensen of Harvard Business School. Based on extensive empirical studies as well as a thorough frame of reference as an economist as well as an organisation theorist, he has developed an impressive set of perspectives, theories and analytical tools to address issues of corporate governance and control of corporations. He has highlighted the problems of agency costs and developed models to calculate such costs. This cost occurs as a result of the separation between ownership and the actual control of the company, and is driven by differences in interest between the parties involved. Professor Jensen has also shown how a company is subject to several types of control, of which corporate governance is the internal control. (For an overview of Professor Jensen's ideas and research, see Jensen et al. 1999!).

Professor Jensen's findings and ideas provide important input for my own thinking on matters of ownership, corporate governance, and 'the market for corporate control' (although as regards the latter concept, Chandler's (1990) historical review and ideas made a deep impression on me). Thus, my own thinking on ownership issues partly overlaps with, and partly focuses on aspects beyond those covered by Professor Jensen. Applying somewhat different perspectives, we have reached the same conclusion regarding the so-called stakeholder model (both critical). However, when addressing the *logic, content,* as well as *owner competence of value creation,* I am going beyond what he addresses in his research and writings.

TAPPING THE EXPERIENCE OF OTHERS

As pointed out in the Acknowledgements, I am indebted to many practitioners as well as expert bystanders of ownership and corporate governance, which includes some of the best regarded in the world, for invaluable insights and ideas. The interview list in Appendix 1 includes the people I have met since the summer of 1999 and onwards. However, work on an earlier research programme and several books on ownership and corporate governance issues since 1993 has included numerous additional interviews and discussions with such experts and practitioners. It has had a deep impact on my frame of reference even if it is not always easy to distinguish external influences from my *own* insights.

MY PERSONAL EXPERIENCE OF OWNERSHIP AND CORPORATE GOVERNANCE ISSUES

My personal contact with issues of value creation, ownership and corporate governance has taken place in two different contexts: (1) in my management consulting work; (2) in management positions, director of boards, and as private equity investor.

Consulting experience as formative input of my frame of reference

Some of the most significant consulting experience for the development of my views on ownership includes:

* Transformation of multibusiness companies into mixed investment/ multibusiness corporations, mostly driven by threats of nationalisation of one of the businesses of the client companies in each case. By changing the legal structure of the corporation, the nationalisation threat could be isolated to just one business, leaving the rest of the corporation untouched. However, in the process, the roles of ownership versus executive and operational management had to be clarified.

- From the mid-1970s, the author was responsible for the creation and management of an industry practice to support SIAR's consulting services to international pulp & paper companies. This assignment provided rich opportunities to compare the significantly different corporate governance environments, particularly in North American and Scandinavian corporations, as well as the implications of these, e.g. for capital formation and demands of short term returns on investment.
- Most of my experience of M&A related international industry restructuring assignments have been in the pulp & paper industry or with companies being suppliers to that industry.
- Several assignments to improve governance of co-operatively owned corporations – consumer as well as producer co-operatives – highlighted the disadvantages of not having clear ownership roles as well as how special interests of the various members took precedence over goals aiming at developing the co-operative corporation as a whole.
- Early involvement (from 1989) in the transformation of the command economies, particularly of former USSR republics in the Baltic countries and Russia, has been very educational, not least with regard to the sensitive interdependence between institutional environments, corporate governance, and efficient business operations. In one of the first assignments, which was to set up a joint venture between a Scandinavian company and a local partner for commercial insurance, the partner agreement and charter of the joint venture had to include a detailed set of rules. Later, this formed large parts of the first insurance law in that country. Although, it was often difficult to establish appropriate prerequisites for companies to operate smoothly, when it was possible, it also proved that good corporate governance principles are applicable in all kinds of contexts.
- Privatisation assignments, as well as projects to promote privatisation of government service monopolies have provided ample opportunities to study the dynamic effects of market competition and competent ownership.[5]
- Frequent assignments of strategic due diligence of acquisition targets for LBO/MBO and private equity firms have repeatedly demonstrated the difference a change of ownership can make for the future prosperity of such target companies.
- Several clinical research themes were pursued in parallel with these client assignments, enhancing lessons learnt, e.g. concerning *the viability of conglomerate strategies*, and *the active ownership role of Group management of a multibusiness corporation*.

Some additional personal experience

Observation and involvement as consultant in matters of value creation, ownership, and corporate governance is one thing. Direct, personal involvement, e.g. as private equity investor/ owner of a business, and/or as director of a board, is quite another. Working as investment manager before commencing my consulting career, I sat on the boards of several holdings – mainly comprising manufacturing companies. Functioning as temporary CEO while recruiting new management to a subsidiary, I had many opportunities to learn about the interplay between executive management and the board. I was lucky to have a good teacher. The chairman of the investment company I worked for, and of several of the holdings as well, was a business lawyer who later became a successful owner/entrepreneur and risk capitalist. Thus, formal aspects as well as business and value creation orientation, were parts of that valuable tuition.

As a matter of principle as well as for practical reasons, it is not feasible to combine the directorship of external boards with management consulting. However, being a partner as well as holding management positions in a consulting operation for many years, offered multiple challenges concerning ownership and governance. In the new knowledge economy where human capital is the scarce resource, the partnership format of participating ownership should fit in well in many types of business.

I am currently (since mid 1999) acquiring new perspectives on ownership and governance through my private equity investment in and as director of the board of a start-up company of the new economy (unique technologies for Internet equipment and IT security).

Appendix 3: The Wallenberg Sphere

A3

Facts, critical events, and examples of active ownership: appendix to Part II

THE WALLENBERG SPHERE TODAY: A BRIEF PRESENTATION OF INVESTOR, ITS ACTIVE OWNER INSTRUMENT

The Wallenberg sphere today is constituted by three main elements,[1] namely the Wallenberg Foundations, Investor AB and its core holdings:

The Wallenberg Foundations

These include several beneficiary foundations, which gathers the fortunes of earlier generations of Wallenbergs. The Wallenberg Foundations are the biggest donors to several Swedish universities and research institutes. The assets of these foundations are dominated by a major holding in Investor, making them together the biggest owner of Investor both in terms of voting power (41.4 percent) and share of capital (19.3 percent). In addition, the Wallenberg Foundations have some direct holdings in the core holdings of the sphere, the most significant being in Ericsson, Gambro and SEB (see footnotes of Table A3.2). The boards of the most important foundations are currently (2000) chaired by Peter Wallenberg, retired chairman and now honorary chairman of Investor. Although the ownership of the core holdings are split between the foundations and Investor as active owner it is one entity with the organisation of Investor at the hub of the sphere.

Investor AB

Investor AB is a Swedish investment company listed on the Stockholm Stock Exchange. This investment company has successively become the main owner instrument of the Wallenberg sphere. Figure A3.1 gives a bird's eye view of Investor's current investment strategy and capital allocation. The dominant part of assets are invested in the core holdings (see next subsection) but increasing funds are allocated to three other categories called 'New Investments'.

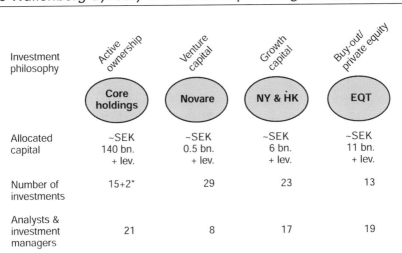

	Active ownership	Venture capital	Growth capital	Buy-out/ private equity
Investment philosophy	Core holdings	Novare	NY & HK	EQT
Allocated capital	~SEK 140 bn. + lev.	~SEK 0.5 bn. + lev.	~SEK 6 bn. + lev.	~SEK 11 bn. + lev.
Number of investments	15+2*	29	23	13
Analysts & investment managers	21	8	17	19

* These numbers refers to 15 core holdings of listed companies, presented in the next section, and two additional, namely SAAB Automobile – until January 2000 owned 50/50 by Investor and GM – and the fully owned Grand Hotel Group in Stockholm.

Source: Published by courtesy of Mr. Marcus Wallenberg, CEO of Investor.

Figure A3.1   Organisation and investment approach.

Figure A3.1 also shows the number of key staff allocated to the four categories of investments. These staff are also key resources in providing support to a cadre of senior executives and directors on the boards of the holdings of Investor. The most senior of these directors and executives are also directors of the board of Investor.

The current (elected by the AGM 1999) board of Investor is shown in Table A3.1.

Core holdings Of Investor

As of December 31, 1999 Investor's portfolio of listed core holdings was presented as shown in Table A3.2 in its Annual Report. Figures for total market capitalisation of each company and the ranking of Financial Times global 500 list have been added.

Table A3.3 gives a brief profile of each of these companies as regards their foundation, origin in the Wallenberg sphere, size, focus and strategic position etc.

THE WALLENBERG DYNASTY AND LEADERSHIP – FIVE GENERATIONS

The simplified family tree in Figure A3.2 highlights the individuals in five

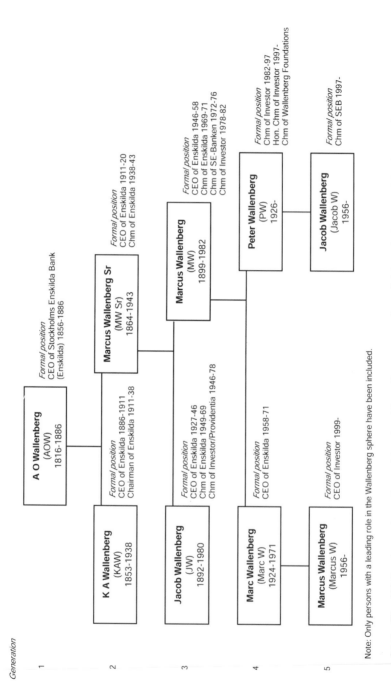

Note: Only persons with a leading role in the Wallenberg sphere have been included.

Figure A3.2   The Wallenberg dynasty and leadership – five generations (abbreviation used in the text).

Table A3.1   The Board of Investor AB

Name (former roles in the sphere)		Other directorships within the sphere (important outside directorships)
Chairman:	Percy Barnevik (ex CEO of ABB)	Chm ABB, AstraZeneca (Outside the sphere: Chm Sandvik, director of GM)
Exec. vice chm:	Claes Dahlbäck (ex CEO of Investor)	Chm StoraEnso, Gambro, EQT; vice chm SEB
Exec. vice chm:	Jacob Wallenberg (ex deputy CEO Investor)	Chm SEB; director Atlas Copco, Electrolux, WM-data, Wallenberg Foundations
Director	Anders Scharp (ex CEO of Electrolux)	Chm Atlas Copco, Scania, SAAB and SKF (outside the sphere: Chm Swedish Employers Confederation)
Director	Håkan Mogren (ex CEO of Astra)	Exec vice chm AstraZeneca, director of Gambro
Director	Mauritz Sahlin (ex CEO of SKF)	Chm Novare Kapital AB, director Scania, SKF (outside the sphere: Sandvik, Statoil, Norway)
Director	Peter D. Sutherland	Director ABB, Ericsson (outside the sphere: co-chm BP Amoco)
Director	Björn Svedberg (ex CEO, Chm Ericsson, ex CEO SEB)	Director ABB, Gambro, SAAB AB (outside the sphere: director of Saga Petroleum, Norway)
Director	Michael Treschow (ex CEO Atlas Copco)	CEO and director of Electrolux, vice chm SAAB Automobile, director Atlas Copco
Director	Marcus Wallenberg (ex-deputy CEO Investor)	CEO Investor, vice chm Ericsson, Saab AB; director Gambro, Scania (Volvo), SEB, StoraEnso, Wallenberg Foundations
Honorary Chm	Peter Wallenberg (retired chm Investor, Atlas Copco)	Honorary chm Atlas Copco

generations of Wallenbergs and their leading positions in the two core companies of the sphere. These companies were:

- Stockholms Enskilda Bank, abbreviated Enskilda, founded in 1856 and merged with Skandinaviska Banken in 1972. The merged bank was called

Table A3.2   Investor's core holdings (at December 31, 1999)

Company	Market value SEKm 12/31 1999	Share of portfolio (%)	Share of capital (%)	Share of voting rights (%)	Total market value SEK billion 991231	FT 500 1998 rank
Pharmaceuticals/ health care		31				
AstraZeneca	32956	21	5	5	659	43[a]
Gambro	5251[b]	3	20	26	26	–
Engineering		34				
Scania	16905	11	28	49	60	–
ABB	14972	10	5	5	299	92
Atlas Copco	7911	5	15	21	53	–
Volvo	4814	3	5	2	96	118
SKF	2931	2	13	27	23	–
Electrolux	2810	2	4	21	70	274
Saab AB	1772	1	20	36	9	–
IT/Telecoms		29				
Ericsson	37992[c]	25	3	22	1266	148
WM-data	5818	4	14	6	42	–
Financial services		4				
SEB	5809[d]	4	10	10	58	–
OM Gruppen	2375	2	15	15	16	–
Forest products		7				
StoraEnso	11558	7	10	24	116	397
Service		1				
SAS Sverige	1000	1	19	19	53	–
Total	154874	100			2846	

[a] Pro forma.
[b] The direct holding of the Wallenberg Foundations add some SEK 1.4 billion to the total sphere holding and 5% of voting power.
[c] Ditto for Ericsson adds some SEK 15.2 billion and 16.5% of voting power.
[d] Ditto for SEB adds some SEK 6.4 billion and 11% of voting power.

Skandinaviska Enskilda Banken, abbreviated S E-Banken. In 1999 this bank was renamed SEB.

- Investor, founded in 1916, the leading holding/investment company of the Wallenberg sphere. During long periods other similar but less important holding/investment companies existed within the sphere. During the early 1990s all these have been acquired by Investor, the last one in 1994.

The abbreviation is also used in the text for each of the Wallenberg dynasty members as marked in Figure A3.2.

Table A3.3 Profile of core holding companies (1998 figures)

Core holding	Year of founda-tion[a]	W sphere since[a]	Turnover SEKm	EBIT SEKm	No of employees	Overall focus and market position	Main business area (s)/market position (turnover, SEKm; % of total)
Pharmaceuticals/ Health care							
AstraZeneca (pro forma)	1913	1924	136269	28299	59588	Global no 5 of the pharmaceutical industry	Pharmaceuticals (100.843; 74%) Losec world's largest pharmaceutical product
Gambro	1963	1994	18734	5374	17332	Original innovator of artificial kidney	Renal care services (9.180; 49%) No 2 globally; Renal care products (7.306; 39%) No 3 globally
Engineering							
Scania	1891	1924 (1911)	45312	3214	23537	Heavy trucks (>16 tons) Sometimes referred to as the 'Rolls Royce' of heavy trucks	Heavy trucks (27.187; 60%) No 5 globally
ABB	1890	1898	245432	16782	199232	Electric power, automation. World leader	Power Generation (67.814; 26%) Global top league

Table A3.3 (continued)

Core holding	Year of found-ation[a]	W sphere since[a]	Turnover SEKm	EBIT SEKm	No of employees	Overall focus and market position	Main business area (s)/market position (turnover, SEKm; % of total)	
							Automation (robotics etc.) (55.936; 22%)	Global leader
							Complete systems and contracting (50.761; 20%)	Global top league
Atlas Copco	1873	1878	33740	4345	23857	Compressors, rock drilling. World leader	Compressors (17.343; 51%)	Global leader
							Power tools and assembly systems (9.960; 30%)	Global leader
							Construction & mining equipment (6.437; 19%)	Global leader
Volvo[b]	1907	1999	214900 111100[c]	11619	79820	Commercial vehicles and construction equipment	Volvo Trucks (63.800; 57%[c])	Global no 3 in heavy trucks
							Volvo Construction (19.500; 18%[c])	Global no 3
							Volvo Buses (14.300; 13%[c])	Global no 2 (large buses)

SKF	1907	1932	37688	– 999	44958	Bearings Global no 1	Bearings (32.453; 82%) Seals (4.129; 10%)	Global no 1 North America leader
Electrolux	1912	1959	117524	5850	99322	Original inventor of vacuum cleaners and refrigerators. General household appliances.	Household appliances (84.581; 72%)	Global no 1 in vacuum cleaners. European leader in white goods.
							Outdoor products (19.295; 16%)	Global leader
SAAB AB	1937	1937	7539	875	7742	Defense material. Sole domestic supplier of military aircraft; high tech products	Military aerospace (4.572; 59%)	First commercially offered 4th generation fighter aircraft (JAS Gripen)
IT/Telecoms								
Ericsson	1876	1932	184438	19273	103667	Telecom equipment. World leader of mobile telephony systems	Network operators (123.200; 67%) Consumer products (45.200; 24%)	World leader in mobile systems Global no 3 in mobile handsets
WM-Data	1969	1994	12380	911	6068	IT consulting No 1 in Sweden		

Table A3.3 (*continued*)

Core holding	Year of found-ation[a]	W sphere since[a]	Turnover SEKm	EBIT SEKm	No of employees	Overall focus and market position	Main business area (s)/market position (turnover, SEKm; % of total)
Financial services							
SEB	1856	1856	19442	4801	12771	Universal banking/financial services. Sweden's largest business-to-business bank, asset management provider and Internet bank	Retail and Financial Services (7.912; 41%); SEB Merchant Banking (5.082; 27%) Sweden's no 1 asset management service provider No 1 in Sweden
OM Group	1984	1984	1567	375	623	First listed stock exchange company in the world Introduced derivatives to Swedish market. Pioneering electrical power exchanges etc.	Transactions (1.133; 72%) OM Technology (434; 28%) Dominating stock exchange in Sweden Global provider

Forestry Industry

StoraEnso	1288	1870s	93302	6353	40679	Pulp & paper and board, forestry products. Global leader by tonnage produced; no 2 by revenue	Packaging board (20.883; 22%) Magazine paper (16.430; 18%)	Global leader in liquid board

Services

SAS Sverige	1946	1946	40946	1990	27071	Aeroline services. Part of Star Alliance	SAS air transport (38.080; 93%) SAS International Hotels (2.866; 7%)

[a] Refers to the original Swedish company as regards ABB (ASEA), AstraZeneca (Astra), StoraEnso (STORA).
[b] Including cars which was sold to Ford in early 1999.
[c] Excluding cars.

THE HISTORY AND CRITICAL EVENTS IN THE DEVELOPMENT OF THE WALLENBERG SHPERE

Stockholms Enskilda Bank – the origin and the long-time centre of the Wallenberg sphere

Stockholms Enskilda (=Private) Bank (in the following called Enskilda) was founded by André Oscar Wallenberg (AOW) in 1856. Until the merger with Skandinaviska Banken in 1972 (called Skandinaviska Enskilda Banken, abbreviated S E-Banken. In 1999 this bank was renamed SEB) it remained the powerful centre of the Wallenberg sphere.

The founding features

The founding features of this bank came to be recurrent characteristics for the future development of the Wallenberg sphere:

- AOW, a son of a southern Swedish clergyman and bishop became a marine officer and acquired international experience through assignments in the merchant navy. Later, at least one representative of each Wallenberg generation went through the Swedish Marine Academy and served as marine officer for at least a short period. An international education and, especially, work experience in a variety of banks and financial firms in several countries have been a common feature of all Wallenberg family members aiming for a business career.
- AOW left the merchant navy with multiple ambitions to take part in the dynamic transformation of the Swedish society that gained momentum in the middle of the 19th century.
- As a politician and member of parliament, lobbyist and industrious writer of parliamentary motions and newspaper articles he became a strong promoter of liberalisation of all strands of society – deregulation of business in general, reformation of banking legislation, the introduction of the metric system as well as the emancipation of women. He established close relations with the liberal minister of finance at that time, Gripenstedt who became the great liberal reformer of Swedish economic legislation. In particular, their collaboration led to the liberalisation of Swedish bank legislation.
- Later generations of Wallenbergs have always been anxious to have good relations with the government, especially with its most important representatives – the prime minister as well as the ministers of finance and foreign affairs. The Wallenbergs have also offered their services to the government on several occasions. K.A. Wallenberg (KAW), then chairman of the bank, became minister of foreign affairs during the Great War. However, far more significant contributions in public service were

achieved by his brother, MW Sr. The latter successfully led the crucial trade negotiations with the British Government during the Great War. He gained British and later international recognition for his capabilities and was later appointed to the Young Commission in negotiating German war reparations. He also became chairman of the Finance Committee of the League of Nations. During World War II, the two brothers, Jacob (JW) and Marcus Wallenberg (MW), served on several government commissions and drawing upon their extensive international networks of contacts on both sides of the war they could pick up valuable information and make informal contacts on behalf of the government. MW followed in his father's footsteps in that he became involved in the Swedish trade negotiations with the British Government during World War II.

- AOW was adamant in his ambition to introduce the Scottish banking concept to Sweden and after some attempts eventually succeeded through the foundation of Enskilda in 1856, the first private and commercial bank in Stockholm. Thus, he became both a banking innovator – Enskilda became the model bank for a number of others – and he broke the banking monopoly of the Riksbank (The Bank of Sweden) in Stockholm. AOW's biographer, Professor Göran B. Nilsson argues that AOW's entrepreneurial idea was not limited merely to Enskilda. He applied his entrepreneurial ambitions to the whole banking sector and capital market of Sweden.[2]

- Thus, AOW's ambitions to reform and develop the banking sector also led to his involvement in setting up Skandinaviska Kreditaktiebolaget in Gothenburg in 1864. This bank was later renamed Skandinaviska Banken and became SEB's merging partner more than a century later. However, AOW didn't limit his ambitions to his home ground. He took part in international discussions about financing issues, which gave him contacts and quite a lot of influence in these matters, especially in France. This pioneering spirit, introducing innovations and extending the frontiers of the sphere can also be traced in the following generations of Wallenbergs. KAW, his son, was involved in setting up banks in France (Banque des Pays du Nord) and in the UK (British Bank of Northern Commerce). The formation of Investor by MW Sr. in 1916 to take care of Enskilda's industrial holdings was also an early initiative – long before the other leading banks in Sweden were forced by law to do this after the Kreuger crisis (see below!).

- The industrial orientation and the entrepreneurial spirit of the Wallenberg sphere also had its origin in the initiatives of AOW. In addition to the banks' early involvement in the financing of infrastructure and industry investments, AOW took equity positions privately and outside the bank, mainly in shipping where he for a period was number one in Sweden. A guiding principle for AOW was to keep the bank away from taking equity positions.

- When Enskilda was set up the equity capital was supplied by 72 share-holders. AOW himself subscribed to only 5 percent of the total shares. However, 'Wallenberg was appointed the bank's Managing Director and... he enjoyed from the outset, great freedom of action in conducting its affairs.'[3] Thus his power base was his competence and contact network rather than his own capital and wealth. This is a feature that probably became a hallmark of the Wallenberg tradition. The drive to realise the full potential of an opportunity was more important than having full owner control. AOW had tried part of his new banking concept on a small scale in Sundsvall, the centre of the forest industry in northern Sweden. When he saw that it worked he wanted to develop it on a full scale in Stockholm. Partners and outside capital were then required. The staggering impact of the Wallenberg sphere cannot be understood unless this aspect is taken into account.

- Finally, the timing of the start of the bank was close to perfect. Swedish industrialisation, based to a large extent on exploitation of vast Swedish virgin forests, iron ore and other natural resources, e.g. hydropower had just started to gain momentum. Great Britain was the booming export market par excellence for these goods and the Crimean War (1853–56) had boosted prices for timber and other Swedish products. In the follow-ing 100 years, the industrialisation of Sweden enjoyed an economic growth rate unparalleled ever since for such a long period. The annual average growth was 4 percent and by the end of the 1960s, when this development phase came to an end, Sweden had been transformed from the poorhouse of Europe to one of the richest countries in the world.

- Enskilda had positioned itself to become one of the leading actors in this development. What Swedish industry needed included import of tech-nology and capital as well as international contacts to sell their products at good prices. Enskilda could supply both -by providing banking services and financial resources – as well as the business experience and international contacts that AOW had built up.

Critical events in the development of Enskilda and the Wallenberg sphere

The conditions at the outset and AOW's way of setting up Enskilda turned out to have a significant impact on the future character of Enskilda and the whole sphere. In addition, in order to understand the further formation of the sphere and its present characteristics, we need to review some of the critical events that Enskilda and its leading figures encountered during the many years that followed. This analysis will cover three such critical events and their implications for the further development of the Wallenberg sphere, namely:

• The crisis of 1878–79.
• The Kreuger crash of 1932 and its aftermath.
• The merger between Enskilda and Skandinaviska Banken in 1972 to form S E-Banken, Skandinaviska Enskilda Banken (now called just SEB).

At the end of this section we will also briefly discuss a recent event, which is still too recent to assess as regards its critical importance for the future development of the Wallenberg sphere. This refers to the AGM in 1997, when Percy Barnevik became chairman of Investor. The event was significant since it has only happened once before, in the 1940s, that the top position of the sphere has been held by a non-Wallenberg person.

The crisis of 1878–79

Enskilda' s pioneering of the Scottish banking concept with the addition of some proprietary innovations led to rapid expansion – both in terms of bulging deposits from the general public and short term lending to finance exports. The success of Enskilda attracted new banking start-ups leading to successively increasing competition. Among the new competitors was a bank established in Stockholm by a group of people that decided to leave the board and management of Enskilda. This had been spurred by a growing discontent with AOW's management style which has been described as both extremely energetic and paternalistic/autocratic. The increasing competition led to a stagnation in the short-term lending market. Although successful in attracting deposits, Enskilda was forced to engage in bonds and other long term investment projects – and increasingly in railway bonds and industry investment loans.

The business recession of 1877 hit many companies and railway construction projects, where Enskilda was financially committed, hard. Deteriorating confidence amongst the general public led to a run on the bank and large amounts of deposits were withdrawn. Enskilda was near bankruptcy in 1879. However, the bank managed to overcome the crisis by a combination of both government support (re-financing in a railway fund set up by the government) and its own measures. Enskilda managed to reduce its outstanding loans and also to raise new equity by attracting some 30 new owners/investors. This crisis had sweeping consequences for the further development of Enskilda and the Wallenberg sphere. In particular, the following deserve to be emphasised.

1. The crisis was a tough lesson in the virtue of financial prudence and rock-

solid solvency. A strong tradition of consolidation emanated from this which was particularly embodied by KAW who started his career in the bank already in 1874 and became managing director following his fathers death in 1886. Later his nephew, JW, became known throughout his life for his financial prudence and conservatism. Since they were leading the bank jointly for a long period – KAW was chairman until his death in 1938, and JW CEO from 1927 and before that deputy CEO from 1920 – they reinforced each other in upholding the values of consolidation.

2. Another crucial lesson from the crisis and events leading up to it was the vulnerability of not having stronger family control of the bank. AOW had had difficulties to get enough support for some of his ideas because of his weak owner position (only 5 percent from the start). The experience of having some of the original founders/directors and bank staff deserting Enskilda to start a competing bank prompted the need to build the board and management on a core team of truly loyal associates. KAW joined the board and executive management at an early age (21 years old) and he persuaded his younger brother, MW Sr. to abandon his career of becoming a judge (for the rest of his life he was always called and referred to as the Judge although he only reached the position of deputy judge at the lower courts) to join the bank in 1890. MW Sr. had expressed serious concern regarding the management of the bank's assets and had become an early speaking partner of KAW after their father's death, particularly since another brother, Gustaf, had been a disappointment in this respect. For the coming generations of Wallenbergs this experience seems to have triggered a very systematic and careful preparation programme for each family member to qualify for leading positions in the sphere.

The experience of deserting associates also further emphasised the importance of building loyalty among other staff. AOW had already introduced a generous bonus programme rewarding extraordinary performance. This tradition was further developed and the Wallenberg sphere became known for its generosity in rewarding extraordinary performance and for how well they catered for their staff. In return they managed to attract extraordinarily talented people who remained loyal to the sphere and the family as well.

As regards the actual owner control, AOW had already managed to increase the family holding of Enskilda to some 20 percent. KAW continued this effort and managed to increase the holding to 40 percent. Later he instigated a foundation in his and his wife's name – Knut and Alice Wallenberg's Foundation – which eventually inherited his entire fortune and which is still – by far the largest of the Wallenberg Foundations – the final key owner of Investor and other companies in the Wallenberg sphere.

3. A third implication of great consequence for the future character of the

Wallenberg sphere was that the crisis initiated an ambition to restructure and turn around these companies hit by the crisis in Enskilda's portfolio of loans. Several of these companies went bankrupt at the end of the 1870s. Enskilda ended up with the shares as collateral while other claims successively were written off following the policy of consolidation that Enskilda decided to apply.

KAW started such restructuring work already during the 1880s with some success. However, it was when his younger brother, The Judge, MW Sr. came into the bank that this type of activity became a major feature of Enskilda and the Wallenberg sphere. The early cases of direct involvement in industry corporations, e.g. the Hofors company (land holding including forests and a steel mill, later to become part of SKF) and Atlas (the origin of today's Atlas Copco) concerned restructuring and turn-around operations. Later MW Sr. and Enskilda became more and more involved in corporate finance activities and active ownership whilst helping companies to grow. MW Sr. also broadened his work in supporting Swedish industrial growth by initiating the founding of the Stockholm School of Economics in 1903 – one of the first business schools in Europe. Typical for the international orientation and ambition to settle for anything less than world class of MW Sr. in connection with this is that he sent a study team to all the best European and American business schools at the time. The setting up of the Stockholm School of Economics was to be based on best available experience. He also instigated the Federation of Swedish industries and became its first chairman. What MW Sr. had started his youngest son, MW, developed even further. In fact, he is widely considered to be the most influential Swedish owner/industrialist of the 20th century. Until 1946 when he became CEO of Enskilda his older brother JW was the leading authority in the bank. MW wanted to find his own territory within the sphere right from the start. His focus on the industry side seemed to fit his talents and personality. The success of several Swedish companies, e.g. Ericsson, Asea (now ABB), Atlas Copco is difficult to imagine without MW's involvement and contributions during their critical moments.

He had enormous energy and working capacity and could draw upon an unmatched network of international contacts developed by other family members and by himself. He became chairman of more than thirty companies and a director of as many more. Thus he, more than anyone else, expanded the Wallenberg sphere enormously during his long and active career spanning almost sixty years.

The pure banking side of Enskilda was not his preferred focus although he took steps to modernise the bank during his CEO-period. However, he was the key driving force in achieving the merger between Enskilda and Skandinaviska Banken. Another thing was his eye for synergies between the industry and financial sectors. He believed in what he called combinations. A typical example is that he set up companies, e.g. Electro-Invest that could invest in power plants where ASEA (now ABB) could supply all power generation, transformation and transmission equipment etc and Enskilda, of course, delivered the necessary external financing.

4. Finally, the weak position that Enskilda suffered for a long period after the crisis of the late 1870s, not only lead to a strong ambition and dedicated efforts to improve its consolidation. Many of the start-up companies and reconstruction projects the bank became involved in actually had private investors taking the risk. KAW was the driving force in this and he mobilised wealthy friends and business partners – what we today would call business angels – to absorb the risks involved. A dynamic symbiosis was established between Enskilda and these private investors. A scholar making an in-depth study of Enskilda and the breakthrough of industrialisation around 1900[4] concludes his analysis:

> Enskilda did not let banking legislation confine its business to the role of cash holder, provider of working capital and mediator of bond loans. It created liquid means for the risky entrepreneurial ventures at that time ... (where) ... the immediate risks were absorbed by the top management of the bank and other wealthy persons. Thus, one could say that the wealth of these individuals became a functional capital in the transformation process. In that way some of the small capital resources of the country were mobilised for this purpose. Thus, Enskilda contributed, not least, to the fact that Swedish industry could be built up – in contrast to the Norwegian industry – largely based on indigenous equity capital.

The crash of the Kreuger empire

Another Swede, Ivar Kreuger enjoyed much larger international fame and significance during the 1920s and early 1930s than the Wallenbergs. A construction engineer by training he made his first fortune by successfully introducing the reinforced concrete construction method to Sweden. Together with a partner he established a construction company, Kreuger & Toll, which exploited the new construction method. This company later became the major holding company of his vast industrial empire.

However, what brought him international fame and the big money was his achievements in a completely different business – and his way of doing business. His family owned a safety match producing company in southern Sweden. This company suffered from financial difficulties – together with many other companies in this industry due to fragmentation and over-capacity – and became the starting point for the creation of a globally leading corporation in its market. At the peak of its development in the early 1930s it controlled 250 manufacturing plants in 43 countries and had gained a mono-poly position – legally or de facto – in 25 countries. Its global market share was 75 percent. Kreuger used his rapidly growing financial capacity to acquire formal monopoly status in a number of countries in exchange for long term loans to governments. Many countries were suffering from the post-war crisis in the 1920s and had low or non-existent credit ratings. Kreuger's capacity to provide loans was further boosted by a financial inno-vation of his – *participating debentures.*[5]

These participating debentures were issued on all leading international stock exchanges where the Match Group was listed. Seemingly the Kreuger Group managed to get through the Wall Street crash of 1929 unharmed. Kreuger was widely praised – among others by president Hoover who invited him to the White House – for his entrepreneurial and financial inge-nuity which seemed to keep him afloat and prospering while many former financial powerhouses were in shambles after 1929. In reality, the Kreuger empire was badly hit by the financial turmoil too. A liquidity crisis started to build up soon after. Kreuger became dependent on short-term loans which was possible to get because the solvency of the group still seemed unshat-tered. Reported profit development was still satisfactory. However, the liquidity crisis worsened and several Swedish banks, especially Kreuger's main Swedish bank, Skandinaviska Banken, became heavily exposed. Even the Riksbank, the Bank of Sweden, had to provide a large portion of what became the final loan after intervention by the Swedish Government.

Finally, Kreuger himself realised that he had ended up in an impossible situation since he had hidden the real problems – from even his closest associates – by creative book keeping and similar illegal measures for a long time. In March 1932, he killed himself and his empire was dissolved.

Enskilda and the Wallenbergs also had substantial claims on the Kreuger empire. However, its conservative line in assessing risks had made it much more cautious than the other Swedish banks. Enskilda and MW Sr. refused to take part in the final rescue operation for the Kreuger Group even after strong pressure from the Swedish Prime Minister. In order to cover all earlier loans granted, Enskilda had required substantial collateral in the form of shares in several of the companies of the Kreuger sphere, e.g. Ericsson, SKF and other less internationally known companies.

Thus, while other Swedish banks were severely weakened, Enskilda came through stronger than before – and the Wallenberg sphere was further enlarged by excellent companies such as Ericsson and SKF.

Once again, the conservative risk assessment and consolidation policy that was triggered by the critical events Enskilda experienced some fifty years earlier had triumphed.

The merger of Enskilda and Skandinaviska Banken

It was MW who was the driving force behind the merger between Enskilda and Skandinaviska Banken. During the 1960s Enskilda started to lose ground in the Swedish banking market and risked being caught in a development trap. Its key lending customers, the big Swedish industry corporations, were in an intensive phase of expansion requiring external financing. At the same time Enskilda's three main sources of funds were diminishing or seriously threatened.

1. Enskilda's ability to attract deposits was hampered by its confinement to the Stockholm area as regards its branch network. Enskilda's total deposits amounted only to 30 percent of those of Skandinaviska Banken. Enskilda had started to set up some branch offices outside Stockholm but it turned out to be quite a costly operation.
2. During the post-war expansion period of the 1940s and 1950s – in addition to rapidly growing deposits – Enskilda had managed to increase its visible equity by selling off assets representing substantial hidden reserves. This had been partly forced by a law forbidding banks to hold shares of external companies (if they could be sold without book losses – a law which had been introduced as a result of the devastating consequences of the Kreuger crash on some of the banks). Thus, this source of funding had successively dried up.
3. During the 1960s the Social Democratic Government introduced increasingly socialistic reforms and Government control of resource allocation in the Swedish economy. The housing construction sector was given priority together with public sector investments in infrastructure. The banking sector became heavily regulated and constrained as a consequence. Thus, Enskilda's traditional character of merchant bank was in jeopardy. There was very limited capital available to be mediated by Enskilda. Its situation was further aggravated by a very strict control of foreign currency. Thus, also international capital markets as a source of funds were practically closed for Enskilda.

Viewed from the other side of the prospective merger, Enskilda would compensate for some of Skandinaviska Banken's weaknesses – its strained liquidity and capital base. The long tradition of concentration and consolidation Enskilda had practised over the years meant that it deviated significantly from the other banks concerning liquid assets and the strengths of its capital base. In addition, a merger would give Skandinaviska Banken access to Enskilda's attractive portfolio of big company clients. There were also considerable cost saving opportunities as regards the rationalisation of branch networks (mainly in the Stockholm region) and shared costs for back office investments.

However, MW's view of Enskilda's strategic situation was not shared by his elder brother, JW. MW managed to replace him as chairman of SEB as a first step, before he started serious negotiations in 1969.

When the merger proposal came up before the AGM it was uncompromisingly resisted by JW who referred to his fathers saying: 'you should have a small but good business'. JW did not believe that volume expansion was necessary for Enskilda's survival. Times would change and Enskilda's old merchant bank formula would be successful again.

The merger was passed nonetheless but it did not develop quite the way MW had planned. He had expected to maintain the old Enskilda core and way of running the Wallenberg sphere within the new company. MW was to be the chairman of the larger bank and his son, Marc W was to become deputy CEO under L-E Thunholm, the CEO of Skandinaviska Banken. It was also understood that MW should retire three years later and be succeeded by Mr. Thunholm while Marc W should become CEO. In the merger negotiations MW had been forced to give up substantial parts of the voting power the Wallenberg sphere potentially would have had in the merged bank (ownership of Skandinaviska Banken was quite fragmented). However, he calculated that the personal influence and power as chairman and leading executive, respectively, that he and his son were to get in the new bank would be enough to look after the interests of the Wallenberg sphere. His expectations were dramatically and tragically ruined. Only weeks before the actual implementation of the merger, Marc W committed suicide. The pressure on him to safeguard the interests and influence of the Wallenberg sphere seems to have become too much. MW managed to prolong his chairmanship for one year until 1976 and then to become honorary chairman.

Although MW personally played a key role as chairman – and still informally as honorary chairman – the Skandinaviska Banken culture and management style, by sheer size, came to dominate the new bank. The merger turned out to be very successful from a financial performance point of view – at least during the 1970s and most of the 1980s. So there was no external pressure on the management of the new bank to reconsider the Skandinaviska Banken formula of rapid volume expansion and a decentralised, rather loosely controlled organisation. The conservative and centralised decision making that characterised the old Wallenberg bank was completely turned upside down in the new bank. Some twenty years later, this seemed to have been a big mistake. The financial crisis that hit the Swedish economy in the early 1990s, brought S E-Banken to the brink of bankruptcy and it had to apply for support by the government agency set up to deal with the banking situation. The new management could turn-around the situation just enough to make it possible for S E-Banken to withdraw its application.

Investor becomes the key owner instrument of the sphere

The development of the bank after the merger made it obvious that the Wallenberg sphere had to establish another centre of gravity, a resourceful instrument to support and exercise its active ownership role in its strategic holdings. Earlier Enskilda had provided all the infrastructure and support, e.g. the so called statistical department of the old bank had been a key resource in this respect. Already before MW's death in 1982 the investment companies, Investor and Providentia, started to become his instrument and centre of gravity. This became even more evident when PW took over as head of the sphere. Furthermore, the Wallenberg sphere reduced its ownership in the bank to a mere 0.5 percent. Peter Wallenberg remained on the board of the new bank although operationally the Wallenberg sphere and the bank distanced themselves from each other. This rift was further enlarged when PW was not elected chairman of the bank on Dr. Thunholm's retirement in 1984. PW was pitched against PG Gyllenhammar – at that time still the strongman of Volvo and one of the few real contestors of Wallenberg power in Swedish industry. This power struggle was resolved by appointing a neutral candidate, an old Skandinaviska Banken incumbent and its CEO at the time, Curt G Olsson.

It should be mentioned that the tug-of-war concerning the chairmanship of S E-Banken was only a limited reflection of a much larger power struggle between PW and PG Gyllenhammar. Originally, MW had quite low expectations regarding his younger son PW. A few years after Marc W, the designated crown prince of the Wallenberg sphere, committed suicide, MW approached and made an alliance with PG Gyllenhammar. The intention was to avoid that Mr. Gyllenhammar managed to take control of the sphere after MW's death. As part of this alliance, ownership positions were exchanged. Volvo acquired a 25 percent holding in Stora and Atlas Copco while the Wallenberg sphere took a position in Volvo.

PW first welcomed this alliance and when MW died, PW even tried to get control of Volvo by acquiring a big enough minority holding. In all, PW managed to get some 20 percent of the Volvo votes but spread among several entities of the Wallenberg sphere. When Mr. Gyllenhammar finally discovered this, he counteracted by building cross-ownership with another Swedish group. The alliance broke up and the Wallenberg sphere acquired Volvo's holdings in Stora and Atlas Copco etc. The many doubts on PW's ability to have the capacity to take on the leadership of the sphere – both on the part of his father and large parts of the Swedish business community as well – may have been a blessing in disguise. Dismantling the alliance with Gyllenhammar/Volvo was only the flying start of what was to become an intensive period of restructuring and active ownership with PW as chairman of Investor and figure-head of the Wallenberg sphere.

As a consequence of the distant relations with S E-Banken, the Wallenberg sphere even considered setting up an investment bank in its ambition to transform the Investor investment company group into a resourceful and versatile instrument for active ownership. However, S E-Banken counteracted and started such a bank itself, which became a frequent service provider to the Wallenberg sphere, i.e. operationally to the Investor Group. Part of the success of this countermeasure could have been that this bank had been named Enskilda – the name by which the old Wallenberg bank was known, both in the Swedish business community and internationally.

However, the separation of the merged bank and the Wallenberg sphere as well as the establishment of Investor as the hub of the sphere, only account for the first act in this drama. After the crisis in S E-Banken in the early 1990s, the Wallenberg sphere once again became the dominant owner. In addition to the holdings of Investor and the Wallenberg Foundation totalling some 20 percent, there are closely related institutions controlling another 10 percent. The Wallenberg sphere further manifests its control of the bank by strong personal ties. Jacob Wallenberg, the son of PW, is now chairman of the board. In addition, Claes Dahlbäck, former CEO of Investor is vice chairman whilst the CEO, Lars Thunell is a former close ally of Percy Barnevik. Mr. Thunell was CFO of first Asea and then ABB for several years. The bank, which was recently renamed just SEB, is strategically important for the Wallenberg sphere since it is one of the largest institutional investors in Sweden. SEB manages large mutual funds as well as pension and life insurance funds further enhanced by having acquired Trygg–Hansa, one of the largest Swedish insurance companies, a couple of years ago.

Percy Barnevik at the helm

The highest executive position of the Wallenberg sphere has been held by a non-family person only once before. This was in 1943 when MW Sr. died and had to be replaced as chairman of SEB. This lasted for two periods until 1949. The first non-family chairman (Mr. Hellner) died in 1946 and was succeeded by a second non-family person (Mr. Ljunglöf).

Can parallels be drawn between the situation at that time and when Percy Barnevik (PB) took the helm as chairman of Investor in 1997?

Interpreting the significance of this, one has to distinguish between substance and formality -to use one of PB's expressions.[6] In 1943, JW and MW were in control of the Wallenberg sphere as CEO and deputy CEO of Enskilda, respectively. The appointment of Mr. Hellner at that time was seen as temporary and more of a honorary gesture, Mr. Hellner was 78 years old and already vice chairman of the board. He was supposed to retire shortly and leave the chair to JW who in turn would be replaced by MW as CEO of Enskilda. However, a complication occurred. When Mr. Hellner died in 1946,

Enskilda with JW as CEO was pressured by the American authorities concerning the so-called Bosch affair.[7] MW forced JW to leave the bank entirely to appease the Americans and facilitate MW's negotiations to eliminate the blacklisting that threatened Enskilda and the whole sphere. That strategy succeeded and three years later JW could officially return to the bank and take the chair. Thus, the arrangement with non-family members was a formality – in substance the Wallenberg brothers were calling the shots the whole time.

Now, for the first time, the Wallenberg sphere is headed by a non-family person who is also a key decision-maker by substance. Of course, PW is still the head of the family and as chairman of the Wallenberg Foundations also has a lot of substance to bring to the table. However there are clear indications that it is now PB who is in command in forming and exercising – together with the board, Marcus W and his executive management at Investor -active ownership of the sphere. One such indication was the Scania-Volvo deal where the CEO of Scania managed to get the support of PW for staying independent. Some confusion in the media triggered a statement by Investor where it was explicitly declared that PW had nothing to do with the decision making in Investor and that he represented only one owner. Whether this was the start of a real power struggle or whether it – as some commentators suggested – was just part of the negotiation tactics – is open to speculation. Anyway -whatever impact it may have had – the final Volvo bid was SEK 13 billion higher than when this row started.

Another reason for PB having an actual role of substance is that he would never have accepted anything else. His career and reputation as a professional executive is unmatched by any other Swede – ever, it could be argued. When he accepted to take the chair of Investor he was already on the board of Du Pont and General Motors. He has been elected European Executive of the Year four times in a row. His achievements in ASEA and ABB have been compared – on a peer basis – with those of Jack Welch at General Electric. PB was probably in a position to set the terms for his assignment in the Wallenberg sphere. He was not lacking alternatives, and furthermore, he has managed his personal wealth so well that he is financially independent.

Finally, and most importantly, the Wallenberg sphere needed a person of PB's talent and experience at the helm to cope with all the new challenges of globalisation, shareholder demands etc. Furthermore, the fifth generation of Wallenbergs was still too young and inexperienced to take the lead.

The choice of PB to lead the Wallenberg sphere and Investor is a demonstration in itself of the best traditions of the Wallenberg sphere. They wanted the best candidate for the task – not a family member or a yes-man to safeguard the family control of the sphere. Thus, the same principles still apply, as they did when Sigfrid Enström once and PB some eighty years later were recruited to head up ASEA (now ABB).

ACTIVE OWNERSHIP AND LONG-TERM COMMITMENT – SOME CONCRETE EXAMPLES OF THE WALLENBERG SPHERE

A look at Investor core holdings at December 31, 1999 (see Table A3.1) and the brief profile of each company (Table A3.2) reveals that out of the fourteen companies listed (in addition to the quite recent holding in Volvo), ten date back to before World War II as key holdings of the sphere. One company has been added in the 1990s (WM-Data), one in the 1980s (OM-Gruppen), one has its origin in the 1960s (Gambro) although it has been completely restructured quite recently, and one dates back to the 1950s (Electrolux). This summary does not give a fair reflection of Investor's and the Wallenberg's sphere renewal ambitions and initiatives to invest in new companies (this aspect is covered further in Chapter 11!). However, it does reflect the long-term commitment of the Wallenberg sphere. This commitment entailed a never ending active ownership. The Wallenberg sphere and those individuals exercising this ownership have been instrumental in renewing the business, organisation and management of these companies – in most cases in a proactive and successful way. To illustrate the type of active ownership that has been exercised within the Wallenberg sphere two cases will be reviewed briefly below – first ABB, followed by the case of Saab and Scania.

ABB

When Swedish Asea and Swiss Brown Boveri merged to form ABB on January 1, 1988, the merger finally succeeded after at least two serious earlier attempts initiated by MW as chairman – first in 1964 and then once more in the early 1970s. MW was chairman of Asea for twenty years between 1956 to 1976 but a member of the board already from 1930, vice chairman 1948–56 and honorary chairman from 1976 up to his death in 1982. Some exploratory contacts had already been made with Brown Boveri in the 1940s. Now, when the merger finally succeeded Asea was chaired by Dr. Curt Nicolin, who had succeeded MW in 1976 and before that had been CEO of Asea from 1961. Dr. Nicolin became one of MW's closest and most trusted associates and is one of the most influential industrialists in post-war Sweden.[8]

Dr. Nicolin snapped up Percy Barnevik from Sandvik and convinced MW that Barnevik was the man they needed to become CEO of Asea in 1980. With Dr. Nicolin as chairman and Percy Barnevik as CEO, a spectacular transformation of Asea took place, which culminated in the ABB merger and the further development of that new corporation. In preparation for this merger a profitability revolution took place in Asea from 1980 onwards which even outpaced Jack Welch's widely admired transformation of General Electric. The next step was to restructure the Nordic power equipment industry. Asea acquired the dominating companies in this industry in the other Nordic countries – Norway, Denmark and Finland. A strong Nordic home base was established before the giant leap of merging with Brown Boveri to make ABB the global leader in its field.

Finding good CEOs have been a common thread of the Wallenberg sphere's active ownership of Asea/ABB. Asea first became one of the largest banking clients of SEB just before the turn of the century a hundred years ago.

When liquidity and solvency was restored in Enskilda after the crisis in the late 1870s one dynamic sector Enskilda targeted was the electrical power industry – particularly the financing of investments in hydropower construction. KAW spotted on Asea which was in desperate need of financing sources for its rapid expansion. Enskilda also took an owner position when another bank client (De Laval/Separator – later to become Alfa Laval) became too financially squeezed to take part in a new issue of shares. It soon became clear to the Wallenberg brothers that Asea needed more than new loans and equity. An urgent need for new management and reorganisation was their diagnosis. MW Sr. now took command and managed to find an experienced electrical engineer, Sigfrid Edström who had worked for Westinghouse and GE in the US, and had been responsible for the electrification of the streetcar (trams) system in Zürich and Gothenburg – and who was still only 32 years old. After tough negotiations and when Mr. Edström's demands including a substantial increase in Asea's equity and a personal guarantee by KAW that his salary would be met, he accepted. He stayed as CEO from 1903 to 1933 subsequently becoming chairman until 1949. A rapid expansion of Asea took place – very much a result of the dynamics between a strong CEO with drive, the unusually capable Mr. Edström and a strong and supportive owner/banker. Enskilda and MW Sr. initiated and financed a number of large electrical power projects, especially in Sweden and Norway. Thus Norsk Hydro is one of MW Sr.'s initiatives where Enskilda was also instrumental in channelling financial resources from French banks. Norsk Hydro and many other projects created a market for Asea equipment. MW Sr. was also involved in contacts with AEG, a German competitor, to get better order in the international competition.

His son, MW became involved in Asea at the late 1920s as the leader of negotiations with General Electric, which had acquired a holding in Asea. GE's plans were to acquire 25 percent and establish an international cartel. MW managed to convince GE to give up these plans concerning Asea and sell their shares to the Wallenberg sphere. In addition to these shares, the Wallenberg sphere had started to increase its holdings in Asea to create a strong negotiation basis with GE. The close relation that existed from then on between Asea and MW until his death in 1982 was driven by a very strong personal preference for the company – a company sometimes described as the apple of his eye.

A reason for his strong feeling for ASEA probably had to do with MW's belief in new, advanced technologies for economic development and growth. ASEA was an El Dorado in this respect: power generation technologies such as gas turbines, nuclear reactors and transmission technologies such as HVDC (High Voltage Direct Current) where ASEA made ground-breaking innovations and is still global leader. One of the ASEA subsidiaries developed a commercially unsuccessful Swedish jet engine in the 1950s as a side line to gas turbines. The Swedish Air Force, the principal customer, chose another make. However, the forceful, ingenious and persistent project manager, Curt Nicolin, had caught the attention of MW. Dr. Nicolin was appointed CEO of this subsidiary and a few years later he became CEO of the entire ASEA Group.

MW's strong belief in advanced technology as a key success factor had a material impact on ASEA's strategic focus. For a long time the company was by far the leading R&D spender in Sweden (until Ericsson took the lead in the 1990s). Another example – with decisive implications both for ASEA and Ericsson – was MW's early recognition of the transistor and the new electronics. As early as 1954, MW gave a public speech where he outlined clear visions of the future implications of this new technology. In practice this meant that ASEA not only got involved in the development and production of semiconductors but also developed a whole range of process control applications as well as became a leader in robotics. MW's visions in the electronics field also had a tremendous impact in other Wallenberg sphere companies, notably in Ericsson, where MW's initiatives must get much of the credit for its success in digital switching.

Thus, in summary, the active ownership exercised by the Wallenberg sphere vis-à-vis ASEA – and later ABB, where the Swedish part remains the most profitable and controls most of the frontier technologies – has included a wide range of value creating initiatives, e.g.:

- Early turn-around and financing at the beginning of the 20th century.
- Key role in identifying and appointing strong and well-suited CEOs from 1903 onwards.
- Instrumental in changing ownership structure: buying out GE in the late 1920s as well as instigating the ABB merger.
- Strategic business development support, e.g. by initiating 'combinations' – financing big electropower projects such as the early development of Norsk Hydro and later, together with ASEA setting up Electro-Invest with the business mission of investing in and financing large industrial and power projects.
- Stimulating and strongly supporting ASEA's and later ABB's high technology and R&D focus.
- Tireless and ceaseless monitoring of the company to balance development

and financial performance objectives through participation in or chairmanship of the board from MW Sr. and MW through the times to Dr. Curt Nicolin and now Percy Bamevik as both chairman of ABB and Investor.

Without this active ownership it is questionable whether ASEA would have survived at all, not to mention the forming of ABB.

Saab and Scania

The Wallenberg sphere is being criticised in Chapter 11 for sometimes having mixed up its traditional role of owner specialist with that of an ordinary multibusiness group management.

One such case happened when Investor delisted and acquired full ownership of the Saab Scania group in 1991. The original motive was to get control of the full cash flow potential of that group, in particular generated by heavy truck maker Scania and defence contracts within the Saab part of the group.

Before unveiling what happened to that idea and what followed later, let us review briefly the historical background of this group including earlier active ownership initiatives by the Wallenberg sphere.

The history of the Saab group and Scania which were separate until a merger of the two in 1969 goes back a long time – as does the involvement of the Wallenberg sphere. The history of this relationship is also the story of several major renewals driven by big technology shifts that these companies have been involved in:

- from railway equipment (roller stock etc) to automobiles and trucks (both Scania and the Saab group);
- from railway equipment to aircraft and space technology (Saab);
- a spin off from aircraft to automobiles (Saab);
- integration of advanced digital systems (Saab, partly in joint ventures with Ericsson).

Early history of Scania and the Wallenberg sphere

Scania dated its start to 1891 although the name of Scania does not appear until 1911. The origin of the company was called Vabis which produced railway stock in a town close to Stockholm, Södertälje, where still the headquarter of Scania is located. The Wallenberg connection was early in an indirect way. Vabis was started by people leaving another railway stock producing company in Södertälje which was acquired by Atlas (now Atlas Copco), another Wallenberg company, to expand its capacity to produce railway stock in the late 1880s.

Towards the end of the 1890s Vabis started to develop a combustion engine and experimented with various applications – one being inspection trolleys for its traditional business. Thanks to good profits from the railway business, the company could also afford to experiment with several models of automobiles and small lorries of their own design. When the railway equipment business started to deteriorate a few years into the 20th century, it became obvious that if the new combustion engine business and its road applications should be continued it had to stand on its own. Many companies producing cars and lorries had started to pop up and imported makes emerged as tough competitors. One domestic company, Scania, had started around the turn of the century and focused from the beginning on making cars and lorries. However, Scania relied to a large extent on external sourcing of major components, not least imported ones from Germany, and became more successful than Vabis in this market. A merger was initiated between the two companies in 1911 where Vabis wanted to benefit from the competence of Scania while the latter needed extended capacity in production and sales. The merger was financed by Emissionsinstitutet AB, a company co-owned by Enskilda and Skandinaviska Banken, and part of Enskilda's arsenal of investment banking outfits at the time.

In the post-war crisis after the Great War, the new company suffered badly and had to be reconstructed. Thus, in 1924 Enskilda entered as formal owner as a consequence of having shares as collateral for earlier loans and financial commitments. After additional new issues of shares Enskilda ended up owning 100 percent of the company. This lasted until the late 1950s when Enskilda started to transfer Scania(-Vabis) shares to the shareholders of Enskilda and in 1964 the remaining holding was sold to Investor/Providentia – the two leading investment companies of the Wallenberg sphere at the time.

The reconstruction of Scania(-Vabis) in the 1920s included a concentration to the market niche that eventually made the company one of the leading and most profitable in its global industry, namely heavy trucks. Although at that time, a heavy truck was defined at a modest 2–3 tons (today, heavy trucks are defined as larger than 16 tons).

The involvement in the company generated accumulated losses on the part of the Wallenberg sphere, in this case Enskilda, of more than SEK 15 million – a big amount in the 1920s and 1930s considering that the annual turnover in 1929 was SEK 5 million and in 1939 SEK 10 million only. At the same time the Scania(-Vabis) case illustrates better than most the long term committed ownership of the Wallenberg sphere, emphasises business historian, Håkan Lindgren.[9] Professor Lindgren also highlights how the Wallenberg sphere in cases like this always prioritise consolidation of the company itself before reclaiming old losses as owner.

After World War II, Scania(-Vabis) started to expand internationally eventually making the company one of three global leaders in heavy trucks (the two others are Mercedes and Volvo). Scania(-Vabis) established early a stronghold in Brazil and other Latin American markets, where it is still the leading company with a market share of almost 40 percent.

A key driving force behind Scania(-Vabis) turnaround and international expansion was MW who became chairman of the board already in the 1930s and remained as long as it stayed as an independent company (after the merger of Saab and Scania in 1969 MW became chairman of the new company and stayed in that position until 1980).

Origin and early history of SAAB

When this is written in late 1999/early 2000 a circle is being closed: the current Saab company is merging with the other main defence material company of Sweden, Celsius of which the Bofors company is a major part. It was Bofors that founded the original SAAB (abbreviation of – in English – Swedish Aeroplane Aktiebolag; Aktiebolag means limited company).

The original SAAB company was merged with the aviation technology department of ASJ, controlled by the Wallenberg sphere, whose main business was railway equipment and maintenance. MW was chairman of that company and he also was elected chairman of the new SAAB in 1939. He remained in that position until 1969 when Saab and Scania merged to form Saab Scania (see above!). The business focus from the start was development and manufacturing of aeroplanes, in particular military aircraft. The formation of this company and its focus on military aircraft was heavily supported by the Government of neutral Sweden at the time. Saab became very successful in this role, eventually it became the sole aircraft supplier to the Swedish airforce. Technologically since the 1940s, it has developed four generations of jet engined military aircraft. Interestingly enough, Saab was the first company in the world to make a fourth generation (digitalised system based) military aircraft operational. This achievement is to a large extent attributable to close collaboration with the defence arm of Ericsson, the global leader in digitalised mobile telephony and microwave technology.

One technological failure, though, has been mentioned in the review of ABB above. A jet engine developed by the sister company of the Wallenberg sphere never achieved commercial acceptance.

After World War II a decision was taken in the company to start development of the Saab car -building on the competence and resources of airplane manufacturing. As some elder readers may recall the design of the first Saab cars were inspired by airplane features. The profile of the car looked like a cross-section of the wing of a propeller driven plane. The car project was strongly supported by MW as chairman of the board while his brother, JW, opposed it and remained a sceptic. Technologically, Saab has nurtured an innovative tradition, introducing several novelties, e.g. the turbo-charged engine in a standard car. Commercially, though, it has not been able to achieve sustainable success.

The Saab Scania merger

A key driving force behind this merger in 1969 was the difficulties of the Saab cars to achieve sustainable profitability. The idea was that the solid competence of Scania (in connection with the merger the old Scania-Vabis was renamed just Scania) should benefit the struggling SAAB automobile division. The defence and other high technology parts of the Saab group had limited, if any, bearing on the Scania business. However, little synergy become realised between Saab automobile and Scania – if not the opposite. Scania defended its independence fiercely within the diversified Saab Scania group. The merger also resulted in direct competition in view of the fact that Scania since long is the general agent for Volkswagen in Sweden. Possibly some synergy was achieved in engine development. Scania had since the 1950s applied turbo charge technology to its truck engines, which may have benefited the car business.

The disappointment on the Wallenberg sphere part became obvious when MW some years later in 1977 announced a merger with Volvo. This had been initiated by PG Gyllenhammar, the CEO of Volvo at the time but was initially supported also by the CEO of Saab Scania, Dr. Mileikowsky. MW responded enthusiastically – an old ambition to become owner of Volvo was going to come true. In addition, this merger could be the cure needed for the ailing Saab automobiles business.

However, the management of both Saab and Scania divisions strongly resisted, successively supported by Dr. Mileikowsky, the CEO of Saab Scania. MW backed off and the merger plans were aborted – for the time being.

From cash flow generator to added value created by active ownership – the break-up of the Saab Scania group in the 1990s

After the abandoning of the Volvo merger plans top management of Saab Scania was replaced. During the late 1970s and the 1980s the company tried to get alliances for Saab automobiles with several partners, among them Mazda, Ford and Fiat – without lasting success. However, a joint venture with Fiat/Lancia was implemented aiming at development of a joint plat-form for a new Saab and Lancia model, respectively.

Some restructuring of the Saab Scania group took place including divest-ment of its computer division, DataSaab, which was acquired by Ericsson.

However, on the whole the Wallenberg sphere seems not to have been a particularly active owner of Saab Scania in the 1980s. One contributing factor to this may have been that PW, the new head of the sphere since his father's death in 1982, kept arms length distance to the company. His relation with its chairman who had been a close associate of MW has been described[10] in rather negative terms.

A radical shift took place at the very end of the 1980s. This was marked by a spin off of Saab Automobiles as a separate company and an agreement with General Motors of co-ownership (50/50). GM was also going to take management responsibility for Saab Automobiles and later it got an option to buy out Investor, which GM also did in January 2000. Saab Automobiles is now a fully owned subsidiary of General Motors.

As mentioned earlier, a next major step of the Wallenberg sphere was to buy out the entire Saab Scania group from the stock exchange in 1991. Internally this project was code named Fighter and had as a primary motive to generate cash flow for Investor.[11]

During the following three years this strategy was applied generating accumulated cash flow for Investor equal to its investment in buying out the Saab Scania group from the stock exchange. In the meantime it had been realised by the Wallenberg sphere that keeping Saab Scania as a fully integrated cash generating source within Investor was not a viable option for the long haul. Each business of the Saab Scania group required its own prerequisites to develop a viable future strategy. A break-up of the group was necessary as well as to establish readiness to form an owner structure that fitted each company on a case to case basis.

- In 1995 the group was split in two separate companies, Saab AB and Scania AB.
- Scania was re-introduced as an independent company and listed on the stock exchanges of Stockholm and New York in 1996. Investor kept a substantial holding, 45 percent, but the remaining divestment generated SEK 18.9 billion – more than the investment to buy out the whole Saab Scania group five years earlier.
- In 1999 Investor agreed to sell its entire holding of Scania to Volvo in connection with an offer from Volvo to acquire the whole company. However this deal was aborted by an antitrust ruling by the EU.
- Saab AB has been restructured and listed on the Stockholm Stock Exchange in 1998. To prepare for that the Regional Aircraft business (SAAB 340 and SAAB 2000 turbo-prop models) was closed down in 1997. Five business areas remained.

  - Military Aerospace (Aircraft and Missiles; Advanced avionics systems are supplied by a company jointly owned by SAAB and Ericsson).
  - Space (Satellite technology; another company jointly owned by Ericsson and Saab is a critical supplier also in this business).

- Training systems (Advanced simulation systems).
- Commercial Aircraft (partner and sub-supplier to Aerospatiale and others).
- Combitech (Several high-tech niche products).

• An earlier established (1995) joint venture with British Aerospace (Bae) to market military aircraft developed into a more permanent relation when Bae acquired 35 percent of SAAB in 1998. In this way Saab will be better positioned to take part in the ongoing restructuring of the European defence industry.
• This platform was further strengthened by the acquisition of Celsius, one of the few remaining, Swedish defence industry companies, was completed in February 2000.

The transformation of the Investor 100 percent holding of Saab Scania during the 1990s is estimated[12] to have yielded some 25 percent return annually calculated on the initial investment in 1991.

Thus, the financial success achieved just confirms the importance of active ownership and is a good illustration of how the Wallenberg sphere has applied its competence and exercised its power as major owner.

Notes

Introduction

1. The frame of reference applied here is commented upon in Appendix 2, Frame of Reference.
2. The body of thought developed in the clinical research/management consulting firm where the author has spent most of his career; see Appendix 2, Frame of Reference for further detail!

Chapter 1

1. *Partial Listing of Corporate Governance Guidelines and Codes of Best Practice'*, appendix to *International Comparison of Board'Best practices' in Developed Markets* by Holly J. Gregory of Weil, Gotshal & Manges, September 1999.
2. In discussions with the author in late August 1999.
3. *Committee on Corporate Governance. Final Report*, London, January 1998. The committee producing the report was chaired by Sir Ronnie Hampel, retired chairman of ICI, hence the name of the report.
4. Richard H. Koppes (see below!) used this epithet when introducing Mr. Monks as the keynote speaker at an IBA (International Bar Association) corporate governance colloquium in Zürich in April 2000 where this author participated.

Chapter 2

1. Greenmail: 'the practice of buying a large amount of stock in a company in order to threaten to take over control of the company if the stock is not bought back from the buyer at an inflated price. (green ('money') + (black) mail)', quoted from Webster's *Encyclopedic Unabridged Dictionary of the English Language*, 1989 edition. Portland House, New York.
2. Figures are taken from the book *Watching the Watchers* by Monks, Robert A.G., and Minow, Nell, p. 205. Blackwell, Cambridge, MA, 1996.
3. For an in-depth analysis of the background of this see Roe, Mark J.: *Strong Managers, Weak Owners. The Political Roots of American Corporate Finance*. Princeton University Press, Princeton, New Jersey, 1994.
4. CEO = Chief Executive Officer.
5. Someone who has identified potential value added opportunities in a company and who aggressively attempts to acquire that company in order to realize such a potential.
6. USA = United Shareholders Association.
7. Senior partner of Weil, Gotshal & Manges LLP, N.Y. Dr. Millstein is a frequent participant on various corporate governance committees, e.g. as chairman of the joint World Bank-OECD sponsored Private sector Advisory Group on corporate governance.
8. Millstein is referring to Berle and Means as the authors of *The Modern Corporation and Private Property* published in 1932. Among other things, the book inspired the setting up of the SEC

(The Securities and Exchange Commission) to monitor the American capital market, and it also inspired legislation aimed at promoting the liquidity of the stock market and counteract market concentration.

9. In an interview with the author, August 1999.

Chapter 3

1. The interested reader can easily access these documents from CalPERS home page: www.calpers.ca.gov.
2. TIAA-CREF is an abbreviation of Teachers Insurance and Annuity Association-College Retirement Equities Fund. It presents itself as '... a leading national financial services organization and the premier pension system for people in education and research.' (TIAA-CREF Snapshot, 1999).
3. *Varför växer företagen i Ohio– men inte i Sverige? Förutsättningar för tillväxten och sysselsättningen– en jämförelse av två industriella kluster i Sverige och Ohio* (Engl. translation of orig. title: *Why do companies grow in Ohio– but not in Sweden? Pre-requisites for growth and employment– a comparison of two industry clusters in Sweden and Ohio*), by P Braunerhielm, IUI, and B. Carlsson, Case Western Reserve University, Ohio. Nutek and SAF, March 1998.
4. Buffett, Warren E.: *The Essays of Warren Buffett: Lessons for Corporate America*. Selected, Arranged, and Introduced by Lawrence A. Cunningham. 1997; 1998. See pages 198–9.
5. In conversations with the author, Autumn 1999.
6. Charan, Ram: *Boards at Work. How Corporate Boards Create Competitive Advantage.* Jossey-Bass Publishers, San Francisco, CA, 1998.
7. Bowen, William G.: *Inside the Boardroom. Governance by Directors and Trustees.* Wiley, New York, 1994.
8. Lorsch, Jay W., *Pawns or Potentates: The Reality of America's Corporate Boards*, Boston, MA: Harvard Business School Press, 1989.
9. In discussions with the author in Sacramento, August 1999.

Chapter 4

1. Page 11, The Setting of the Report, section 1.2 of Report of the Committee on The Financial Aspects of Corporate Governance. 1 December 1992.
2. See note 1.
3. Page 14, Introduction, section 2.2 ibid.
4. The source referred to here is an essay by Mairi Maclean, in Business History, Vol. 41, No 1 (Jan. *1999*). Maclean is referring to a study made by M.J. Canyon, and P. Gregg, *Pay at the Top: A study of the Sensitivity of Top Director Remuneration to Company Specific Shocks*, National Institute Economic Review, No 3 (1994), pp. 82–83.
5. Chairman's Preface *of Directors' Remuneration. Report of a Study Group* chaired by Sir Richard Greenbury, 17 July 1995.
6. Annex, page 66 of Committee On Corporate Governance. Final Report, January 1998.
7. See note 6.
8. Section 1.1, page 7 of Committee On Corporate Governance. Final Report, January 1998.
9. Copyright 1998 The London Stock Exchange Ltd. Gee Publishing Ltd, London.
10. Hermes is wholly owned by the British Telecom Pension Scheme and manages the pension schemes of both BT and the Post Office. It has equity assets of some GBP 23 billlion (summer 1999) under management.

11. See comments about Professor Michael C. Jensen's research in Appendix 2, *Frame of reference*, of this book.
12. Ibid.
13. *Beyond the Information Revolution*. The Atlantic Monthly, October 1999.
14. See Michael Lewis book *The New New Thing. A Silicon Valley Story* (about multiple mega innovator Jim Clark, the entrepreneur behind Silicon Graphics and Netscape)! Norton, New York, 2000.

Chapter 5

1. The eight German stock exchanges are located in Berlin, Bremen, Düsseldorf, Frankfurt, Hannover, Hamburg, Munich, and Stuttgart.
2. This expression has been coined by Alexander Gerschenkron, a Russian economist who succeeded Joseph Schumpeter at Harvard University as professor of Economics. The author's source of reference is a paper, *Understanding Industrial Revolutions*, by Dr. Daniel Nyberg of the Stockholm School of Economics where professor Gerschenkron's ideas and writings are summarised.
3. Drucker, Peter F.,1999: *Management Challenges for the 21st Century*, Harper Business, New York.
4. This is not a new observation to the author. Working as a consultant for an international machine tool company in the early 1980s, the author could position the German machine tool makers to be clearly behind leading Japanese, American and Swedish companies as regards adaptation of CNC (Computerised Numerical Control) technologies at that point in time.
5. *A Survey of German Corporate Governance* by S. Prigge, Hamburg. Part of Chapter 12 of *Comparative Corporate Governance– The State of the Art and Emerging Research*, Klaus J. Hopt, et al. (Eds.). Clarendon Press, Oxford, 1998.
6. Sources: European Venture Capital Association (www.evca.com) and 3i (www.3i.com).

Chapter 6

1. See Charkham, ibid., pp. 130!
2. Le Figaro 25/02/1999 P32/Fabienne Boulineau and Sophie Beguerie. Information retrieved through REUTERS Business Briefing, 10-12-1999.
3. Source: Euromonitor, 990701.
4. OECD *Financial Market Trends*, No 73, June 1999. The definition of direct investments includes all investments of 10 percent or more of a company.
5. Claude Bébéar, CEO of AXA, the French insurance giant, is thus nicknamed in a Fortune article (December 20, 1999).
6. According to the Fortune article mentioned above.
7. Banque De France Bulletin Digest – No 71, November 1999.
8. The author took part in this forum as partner of Groupe Bossard, now part of the Cap Gemini group.
9. OECD *Financial Market Trends*, No 71, Nov. 1998.
10. Author's translation of Conseil National du Patronat Francais, CNPF, and Association Francaise des Entreprises Privée, AFEP, respectively.
11. Source: Straits Times (Singapore) 991203 refers to a study made by Davis Global Advisors.
12. *Europe Private Equity update*, no 13, June 1999 (www.evca.com).
13. The title of a book that attracted much attention when it was published in the late 1960s by

the leftist editor-in-chief, Jean-Jacques Servan-Schreiber, of L'Express, a French weekly magazine.

Chapter 7

1. Sources: PROMT, JEI Report 23/01/98 retrieved through REUTERS Business Briefing, 12-1-2000. A study carried out by the Commercial Law Center, a Japanese research body, is the original source of these findings.
2. Source: Tokyo Stock Exchange 'Fact Book'(1997) which is referred to by Kanda, Hideki in Comparative Corporate Governance – Country Report: Japan. Clarendon Press, Oxford, 1998.
3. Tokyo Stock Exchange: Shareholding at Market Value etc (www.tse.or.jp).
4. Quotation is taken from Karel van Wolferen's book The Enigma of Japanese Power (Vintage Books, New York, 1990). This seminal work by van Wolferen has been the main source as regards input concerning historical background and analysis of the power structure of the Japanese society for the review of the corporate governance situation in Japan in this book.
5. Edward Luttwak in his book Turbo Capitalism. Winners and losers in the global economy. Weidenfeld & Nicolson, London, 1998.
6. Source: Nikkei Weekly 15 November 1999, retrieved through Reuters Business Briefing.
7. JEI Report, Vol. 1999, No 22. Copyright 1999. Japan Economic Institute of America.
8. The New Economy. Special Report. Business Week January 31, 2000.

Chapter 8

1. In an interview by Lawrence Minard: Will Europe and Japan reform their corporate governance? Forbes Magazine, September 07, 1998.(Retrieved via http://forbes.com).
2. Sources: Market capitalisation figures (domestic shares only; US figures include NYSE and NASDAQ, German figures Deutsche Börse, respectively, only) refer to end of 1999 and have been retrieved at www.nyse.com (USA and Japan), and at www.fese.be (France, Germany, UK) respectively. GDP figures refer to 1998 (current prices) and have been retrieved at www.oecd.org.

Chapter 9

1. In his book The Post-Capitalist Society. Butterworth-Heinemann Ltd, Oxford, 1993.
2. Published in 1932 by Macmillan, New York.
3. Barnard, C.I., 1938. The Functions of the Executive. Harvard University Press, Cambridge, MA.
4. In his book Scale and Scope. The Dynamics of Industrial Capitalism. The Belknap Press of Harvard University Press. Cambridge, MA, 1990.
5. Lewis, Michael, 2000. The New New Thing. A Silicon Valley Story. Norton, New York.
6. There were different forms of companies and commercial co-operation projects with limited payment liability for partners long before this and these became more and more important during the eighteenth century, as reported by Fernand Braudel among others, the great French economic historian, in 'Civilisation and Capitalism 15th–18th Century, Volume II, The Wheels of Commerce', Paris, 1979.

Chapter 10

1. Up to 1972 referred to as 'Enskilda' in this chapter.
2. For further details, see reference list.
3. Companies and Finance: A Century of Investment Returns. Produced by the London Business School in association with ABN Amro. London, 2000.
4. In an interview with this author at the end of February, 2000.
5. S E-Banken is an abbreviation of Skandinaviska Enskilda Banken, the bank that was formed 1972 by the merger of Stockholms Enskilda Bank and Skandinaviska Banken. In 1997 this bank was renamed just SEB.
6. Glete, Jan 1994: Nätverk i Näringslivet. SNS Förlag.
7. Lindgren, Håkan: Summary. Active Ownership: Investor and the Wallenberg Group. English summary of 'Aktivt ägande. Investor under växlande konjunkturer.' Stockholm, 1994.
8. The companies by Investor classified as core holdings are briefly presented in the appendix.
9. Stora Kopparbergs Bergslags AB (translated: The Big Copper Mountain Company) is claimed to be the world's oldest corporation. It started copper mining in the 13th century.
10. Fagerfjäll.
11. The main sources for the Losec story here have been two books: (1) Holm, Erik 1992. Hässle 1904 – 1988. Astra Hässle, Mölndal; (2) Östholm, Ivan (co-writers: Gunnar Eliasson, Ulla Reinius, Nils-Eric Sandberg), 1996. Nya Skapelser. Losec-entreprenörens recept. Fischer & Co., Stockholm.
12. Free translation from the 1963 prospectus of Incentive.
13. Author's interpretation and translation of a Swedish word which corresponds to just 'acquisitiveness'. However, MW Sr. did not have the pejorative notion of that word in mind but more of a purposeful and constructive connotation. The biographer of MW Sr., professor Torsten Gårdlund uses the Swedish word within quotation marks.
14. Author's translation of a quotation from the autobiography of Olle Wijkström ('Och fort gick det'. Nynäshamn, 1994). Mr. Wijkström served as CEO of three companies (Lamco, a Liberian mining company, Papyrus, a Swedish pulp and paper company now part of Stora Enso, and the US subsidiary of Investor) during 17 years (1965–1982) under MW as chairman.
15. Ibid.
16. This was a favourite expression of this author's foremost mentor in meta-management and other demanding management issues for more than twenty years, the late Eric Rhenman, professor of business administration at the University of Lund and Harvard Business School, founder and chairman of SIAR and also a personal advisor to MW.
17. According to an estimate by Dagens Industri (week 18/96), a Swedish business daily.
18. Originally this motto was selected by MW Sr. in connection with when he was knighted of the Order of the Seraphim in 1931.
19. In an interview with the author in February 2000.
20. Marcus Wallenberg (MW) in this statement repeated what his father, MW Sr., had said earlier.
21. The statement was made in connection with the Wallenberg sphere's involvement in SILA (owner of SAS) and the selling off of their railway interests.

Chapter 11

1. The main sources of input for this part – in addition to publicly available information – have

been personal interviews with PB in the autumn of 1999 and internal memos PB handed over to the author at the interviews.

2. Interview by the author, August 1999.

3. The EU argument against the deal was that it would have damaged Nordic consumer interests by giving the merged company a too dominant market position. However, this was a rather static view since heavy trucks represent quite big investment decisions by transportation companies, and thus would lead to growth opportunities for other suppliers, e.g. Daimler Chrysler, Iveco and others already established on the Nordic markets. Furthermore, the Nordic market represented only a few percentage points of the intended merged company's total volume of trucks. The whole idea of the merger was to enhance the global market position of Volvo and Scania. If similar policies had been applied in the past, merged corporations such as ABB and Electrolux would not have existed today. The big merger steps, e.g. between ASEA and BBC were preceded by a restructuring of the Nordic electric equipment industry to make ASEA big enough to attract BBC. Thus, EU's ruling not only lacks historical perspective, it makes it more or less impossible for a company originating in a small home market to build a leading international position. Mr. Monti was the the EU Commissioner in charge. It seems that EU policy favours the big corporations home based in the large countries of Europe, e.g. a Mercedes–Benz of Germany or Fiat of Italy, at the expense of companies based in small home markets.

4. The stock market capitalisation of Investor is lower than its net asset value which is easily calculated since it mainly consists of listed companies. The difference between market capitalisation and net asset value is called the *investment company discount* since all Swedish investment companies are suffering from it.

5. Another name of the same phenomenon referring to the fact that there are owners behind – in the case of Investor the Wallenberg sphere – which are suspected of prioritising the owner control or power aspect before general shareholder value.

6. Quotations from Marcus Wallenberg's address to a business conference in Singapore, November 17, 1999.

7. Abstract from interview carried out by this author, February 2000.

Chapter 12

1. See Schumpeter, Joseph A., 1942. *Capitalism, Socialism, and Democracy.* First Harper Colophon edition, Harper & Row, New York, 1975, pp. 81–6.

2. See Appendix 2, Frame of reference, for a brief summary of *The SIAR School of Strategic Management*, the principal conceptual frame of reference of this author.

3. See his book, *The Economic Institutions of Capitalism*, The Free Press, New York 1985, Chapter 1: *Transaction Cost Economics*.

4. It should be recognised, though, that the early 1940s, when Schumpeter conceived his concept, was a rather gloomy period. The period between the two world wars had seen a lot of protective measures constraining world trade. The totalitarian powers of Nazi Germany, the USSR and Japan were still undefeated. It was still uncertain what parts of the world would enjoy the blessings of an open society after the war.

5. The theoretical foundation of this proposition is derived from cybernetics and general systems theory, specifically 'the law of requisite variety', formulated by W.R. Ashby (1956) Introduction to Cybernetics. Barnes and Noble University Paperbacks, New York, 1964.

6. *Business idea* is the most frequently used name of this concept that was developed by SIAR around 1970. Other terms, used by SIAR, included *ways of making money, system of superiority, system for dominance.* Peter F. Drucker has a somewhat similar concept, at least as

regards the concrete business system, called *The theory of the business* (outlined in an article in Harvard Business Review, Sept–Oct. 1994). Michael Porter also embarked on similar trains of thought in *What is Strategy?*, Harvard Business Review, Nov–Dec 1996.

7. The business-related risk category does not include risks normally being covered by insurance – accidents, fire, water damage etc.

8. The SIAR School of Strategic Management includes a set of concepts called the 'Differentiated Industry Analysis' which has provided the basis for the conceptualisation of different types of risk logic presented here. See also Dahlman, Carsten (2000).

9. This concept has been conceived by Professor Donald Schön: see his book *Beyond the Stable State!* Random House, New York, 1971.

10. Professor Rhenman founded SIAR and was the most important mentor of this author for a long time.

11. In her book, *The Drama of Leadership*. Wiley, New York, 1997.

12. This author's translation of a quotation from the preface of a book about IKEA and its founder, *IKEA– entreprenören, affärsidén, kulturen* (IKEA – the entrepreneur, the business idea, the culture) by Stellan Björk. Svenska Förlaget, Stockholm 1998.

13. At a board meeting of the SIAR Foundation, which has given the production of this book both moral and financial support. An author of several books on management and moral issues, Mr. von Hertzen was for many years the head of the Finnish group Cultor. He is a member of the boards of a number of Finnish, Swedish and Eastern European companies, and of the SIAR Foundation as well.

14. W.R. Ashby, 1964 (1956). *Introduction to Cybernetics*. Barnes and Noble, New York.

15. See among other things *The Fatal Conceit! The Errors of Socialism!*

16. The annual report of Skandia includes an account of the Navigator and Skandia's intellectual capital. See also www.skandia.com!

Chapter 13

1. Confucius. The whole quotation is: 'Learning without thinking is of no value. Thinking without learning is dangerous.'

2. Nobel laureate (1993) Douglass C. North is the most famous scholar on this topic. See his book *Institutions, Institutional Change and Economic Performance*. Cambridge University Press, 1990.

3. An expression used by Mr. Dale Hanson - former CEO of CalPERS and the driving force, together with Mr. Koppes, behind the development and implementation of CalPERS' pioneering corporate governance programme – when explaining some key success factors behind CalPERS' achievements.

Appendix 2

1. SIAR was founded in the mid 1960s. Its consulting operations were merged with Groupe Bossard in 1990, which was acquired by Gemini Consulting of the Cap Gemini Group in 1997. SIAR remains as an independent foundation and non-profit entity. The proceeds of its funds are used for the financing of research projects fulfilling certain criteria as outlined by the statutes and policies of the SIAR Foundation.

2. For an introduction in English to the SIAR School of Strategic Management, see Rhenman (1973), Normann (1977), and Lind, Rhenman (1989). In addition, several distinguished scholars, many of which have been visiting researchers to SIAR, have written about *The SIAR School*. See, for instance, Henry Mintzberg et al. (1998), pp. 272–274.

3. I am working on a forthcoming book (est. publication, autumn 2001), *The Fourth Knowledge Revolution* (prel. title) which will include a more comprehensive account of the *SIAR School* than what is possible and justified to have in the context of this book.
4. Normann, R. 1970/80 *A Personal Quest for Methodology*. SIAR-E-19, Stockholm and 1977 *Clinical Research and Clinical Theory– Some Epistemological Premises*. Appendix to Management for Growth, Wiley; Lind, J.-I. and Rhenman, E 1989 *The SIAR School of Strategic Management*, The Scandinavian Journal of Management; Carlsson, R 2000 Clinical Research – *The SIAR Way*, in IX *Conference on the Management of Business Organizations. Academic Research and Business Practice*. Tallinn Technical University, Tallinn.
5. This has also been a recurrent theme of earlier books I have written, see Carlsson, Hallberg (1994), Carlsson, Hallberg (1997), Carlsson (1998).

Appendix 3

1. The owner relations between these three elements can be found in Fig. 10.4.
2. Nilsson, Göran B.: *André Oscar Wallenberg. II. Gyllene Tider 1856–66*. Norstedt, Stockholm 1989.
3. *At the Centre of Development. Skandinaviska Enskilda Banken and its predecessors 1856–1996* by Ulf Olsson 1997.
4. Gasslander, Olle 1959: *Bank och Industriellt genombrott. Stockholms Enskilda Bank kring sekelskiftet 1900. II.*
5. This security which was issued by Kreuger's Match Corporation was something in between a bond and a preferential share. In addition to an interest of 5 percent, a premium of equal size to dividends larger than 5 percent was paid.
6. PB makes this distinction when he discusses corporate governance issues – where he emphasises the importance of being concerned with *substance* (value creation, board competence etc), rather than policies and procedures (formalities).
7. This is further explained in Chapter 10.
8. In addition to the important role he played in Asea and ABB (chairman until 1991, then honorary chairman) he had other important assignments in the Wallenberg sphere. He was also chairman of The Swedish Employers Confederation 1976–84 whose policy and practice he radicalised. He took a strong liberal stand against the socialist influence in Sweden's economic life and was a key driving force in fighting off an attempt by the socialist camp to introduce a massive programme, funded by company profits to have the labour unions take owner control of Swedish private industry.
9. Lindgren, Håkan, 1988: *Bank, Investmentbolag, Bankirfirma. Stockholms Enskilda Bank 1924–25*. Institutet för Ekonomisk Historisk Forskning, Stockholm.
10. See Hökerberg, Jan: *Spelet om Saab!*
11. See Lindgren, Håkan 1994: *Aktivt ägande. Investor under växlande konjunkturer*. Institutet för Ekonomisk Historisk Forskning, Stockholm.
12. Based on information and calculation supplied by Per Spångberg, Investor Relations Manager of Investor to the author in December 1999.

References

Ashby, W. R. (1956, 1964). *Introduction to Cybernetics*. New York: Barnes and Noble.

Barnard, C. I. (1938). *The Functions of the Executive*. Cambridge, MA: Harvard University Press.

Berle, A.A., and G.C. Means (1932). *The Modern Corporation and Private Property*. New York: Macmillan.

Berglöf, E., and E.-L. von Thadden (1999). *The Changing Corporate Governance Paradigm: Implications for Transition and Developing Countries*. The World Bank: Annual Bank Conference on Development Economics.

Björk, S. (1998). *IKEA – entreprenören, affärsidén, kulturen*. (IKEA – the Entrepreneur, the Business Idea, the Culture). Stockholm: Svenska Förlaget.

Bowen, W. G. (1994). *Inside the Boardroom. Governance by directors and trustees*. New York: Wiley.

Braudel, F. (1982). *The Wheels of Commerce, Vol. 2, Civilization and Capitalism, 15th–18th Century*. London: Collins.

Braunerhielm, P., and B. Carlsson (1998). *Varför växer företagen i Ohio – men inte i Sverige? Förutsättningar för tillväxten och sysselsättningen – en jämförelse av två industriella kluster i Sverige och Ohio*. (Why do companies grow in Ohio – but not in Sweden? Pre-requisites for growth and employment – a comparison of two industry clusters in Sweden and Ohio). Stockholm: Nutek and SAF.

Cadbury, A. (1992). *Report of the Committee on The Financial Aspects of Corporate Governance*.

Carlsson, R. H., and M. Hallberg (1994). *Sevicemonopolen och den nya tillväxten* (The Service Monopolies and New Growth). Stockholm: SAF.

Carlsson, R. H., and M. Hallberg (1997). *Ägarstyrning. Om corporate governance från Wallenberg sfär till offentlig sektor*. (Owner Control. On Corporate Governance from the Wallenberg Sphere to the Public Sector). Stockholm: Ekerlids Förlag.

Carlsson, R. H. (1998). *Riskkapital med mänskligt ansikte*. (Risk Capital with a Human Face). Stockholm: Timbro.

Carlsson, R. H. (2000). *Clinical Research – The SIAR Way in IX Conference on the Management of Business Organizations. Academic Research and Business Practice*. Tallinn: Tallinn Technical University.

Chandler Jr., A. D. (1990). *Scale and Scope. The Dynamics of Industrial Capitalism*. Cambridge, MA: The Belknap Press of Harvard University Press.

Charan, R. (1998). *Boards At Work. How Corporate Boards Create Competitive Advantage*. San Francisco, CA: Jossey-Bass Publishers.

Charkham, J. P. (1994) *Keeping Good Company. A study of Corporate Governance in Five Countries*. Oxford: Clarendon Press.

Cunningham, L. A. (1997). *The Essays of Warren Buffett: Lessons for Corporate America*. Yeshiva: Cunningham.

Dahlman, C. (2000). Industrilogikbaserad strategi- och organisationsutveckling (Industry Logic Based Strategy and Organisation Development). In *SIAR, Strategier för att tjäna pengar. Om 'affärsidén' och andra Siar-begrepp*, edited by R. H. Carlsson. Stockholm: Ekerlids Förlag.

Danielsson, C. (1974). *Studier i företags tillväxtförlopp*. (Studies in the Growth Process of Firms). Lund: SIAR.

Dimsdale, N., and M. Prevezer (1994). *Capital Markets and Corporate Governance*. Oxford: Clarendon Press.

Drucker, P. F. (1993). *Post-capitalist Society.* Oxford: Butterworth Heinemann.

Drucker, P. F. (1994). The Theory of the Business. *Harvard Business Review* (September–October).

Drucker, P. F., 1999. *Management Challenges for the 21st Century.* New York : Harper Collins.

Drucker, P. F. (1999). Beyond the Information Revolution. *Atlantic Monthly* (October 1999).

Fagerfjäll, R. (1998). *Företagsledarnas århundrade. Från Wallenbergs sidobolag till Wickmans statsföretag.* (The Century of Corporate executives. From Wallenberg's affiliated companies to the State Holding Company). Stockholm: Norstedts.

Fagerfjäll, R. (1999). *Företagsledarnas århundrade. Från Werthéns förvärvsstrategi till Barneviks globala nätverk.* (The Century of Corporate Executives. From Werthén's Acquisition Strategy to Barnevik's Global Networks). Stockholm: Norstedts.

Gårdlund, T. (1976). *Marcus Wallenberg 1864–1943. Hans liv och gärning.* (Marcus Wallenberg 1864–1943. His life and achievement). Stockholm: Norstedts & Söner Förlag.

Gasslander, O. (1956, 1959). *Bank och industriellt genombrott. Stockholms Enskilda Bank kring sekelskiftet 1900 I och II.* (Bank and industrial breakthrough. Stockholms Enskilda Bank around the turn of the century 1900). Stockholm: Generalstabens Litografiska Anstalts Förlag.

Glete, J. (1984). *ASEA under hundra år 1883–1983.* (ASEA during one hundred years 1883–1983). Stockholm: Stenströms Bokförlag/Interpublishing AB.

Glete, J. (1994). *Nätverk i näringslivet. Ägande och industriell omvandling i det mogna industrisamhället 1920–1990.* (Networks in industry. Ownership and industrial transformation in the mature industrialised society 1920–1990). Stockholm: SNS Förlag.

Greenbury, R. (1995). *Directors' Remuneration. Report of a Study Group.*

Gregory, H. J. (1999). *International Comparison of Board 'Best Practices' in Developed Markets.* New York: Weil, Gotshal & Manges, LLP.

Haag, M., and B. Pettersson (1998). *Percy Barnevik. Makten Myten Människan.* (Percy Barnevik, the power, the myth, the man). Stockholm: Ekerlids Förlag.

Hagstrom Jr., R. G. (1994). *The Warren Buffett Way. Investment Strategies of the World's Greatest Investor.* New York: Wiley.

Hagstrom Jr., R. G. (1999). *The Warren Buffett Portfolio. Mastering the Power of the Focus Investment Strategy.* New York: Wiley.

Hampel, R. (1998). *Committee on Corporate Governance. Final Report.* London: Gee Publishing Ltd.

Hayek, F.A. (1988). *The Fatal Conceit. The Errors of Socialism.* London: Routledge.

Hertzen, Gustav von (1993). *The Spirit of the Game. Navigational Aids for the Next Century,* Stockholm: Fritzes.

Holm, E. (1992). *Hässle 1904–1988.* Mölndal: Astra Hässle.

Hopt, K. J., H. Kanda, M. J. Roe, E. Wymeersch, and S. Prigge (1998).*Comparative Corporate Governance – The State of the Art and Emerging Research.* Oxford: Clarendon Press.

Hökerberg, J. (1992). *Spelet om SAAB. En biltillverkares uppgång, fall och väg tillbaka.*(The SAAB play. An automobile makers rise, fall, and come back). Stockholm: Bonnier Alba.

Jensen, M. C. (1988). Takeovers: Their Causes and Consequences. *Journal of Economic Perspectives:* 2.

Jensen, M. C. (1989). Eclipse of the Public Corporation. *Harvard Business Review* (September–October).

Jensen, M. C. (1993). The Modern Industrial Revolution, Exit, and the Failure of Internal Control Systems. *The Journal of Finance:* Vol. XLVIII, no. 3.

Jensen, M. C. (1994). Self-Interest, Altruism, Incentives, and Agency Theory. Bankamerica. *Journal of Applied Corporate Finance:* Vol. 7, no. 2.

Jensen, M. C., 1998. *Foundations of Organizational Strategy.* Cambridge, MA: Harvard University Press.

Jensen, M. C., G. Baker, C. Baldwin, and K.H. Wruck (1999). Organizations and Markets. In *The Intellectual Venture Capitalist,* edited by T. K. McCraw, and J. L. Cruickshank. Boston, MA: Harvard Business School Press.

Kelly, K. (1998). *New Rules for the New Economy.* Baltimore, MD: Viking Penguin.

Lewis, M. (2000). *The New New Thing. A Silicon Valley Story.* New York : W.W. Norton&Co.

Lind, J.-I., and E. Rhenman (1989). *The SIAR School of Strategic Management.* Oxford: Pergamon Press.

Lindgren, H. (1987). *Bank, Investmentbolag, Bankirfirma. Stockholms Enskilda Bank 1924–1945.* (Commercial Bank, Investment Company, Banking Firm: Stockholms Enskilda Bank 1924–45). Stockholm: EHF.

Lindgren, H. (1994). *Aktivt Ägande. Investor under växlande konjunkturer.* (Active Ownership: Investor and the Wallenberg Group). Uppsala: AFF.

London Stock Exchange, 1998. *Committee on Corporate Governance. The Combined Code.* London: Gee Publishing Ltd.

Lorsch, J. W., and E. MacIver (1989). *Pawns or Potentates: The Reality of America's Corporate Boards.* Cambridge, MA: Harvard Business School Press.

Lorsch, J. W. (1995). Empowering the Board. *Harvard Business Review* (January–February).

Luttwak, E. (1998). *Turbo-Capitalism. Winners and Losers in the Global Economy.* London: Weidenfeld & Nicolson.

Mintzberg, H., B. Ahlstrand, and J. Lampel (1998). *Strategy Safari. A Guided Tour Through the Wilds of Strategic Management.* New York: The Free Press.

Monks, R. A. G., and N. Minow (1996). *Corporate Governance for the 21st Century: Watching the Watchers.* Cambridge, MA: Blackwell Publishers.

Nilsson, G. B. (1989). *André Oscar Wallenberg. II. Gyllene Tider 1856–1866.* (André Oscar Wallenberg. II. Golden Times 1856–1866). Stockholm: Norstedts.

Nilsson, G. B. (1994). *André Oscar Wallenberg. III. Ett namn att försvara 1866–1886.* (AOW.III. A name to defend). Stockholm: Norstedts.

Normann, R. (1970/1980). *A Personal Quest for Methodology.* Stockholm: SIAR Dokumentation.

Normann, R. (1977). *Management for Growth.* New York: Wiley.

North, D. C. (1990). *Institutions, Institutional Change and Economic Performance.* Cambridge, UK: Cambridge University Press.

Nyberg, D. (1999). *Understanding Industrial Revolutions. Gerschenkron on Economic Backwardness – Banks as Promoters of Economic Growth and Political Origins of Banking Structures.* Stockholm: Department of Economics, Stockholm School of Economics.

Olsson, U. (1997). *At the Centre of Development. Skandinaviska Enskilda Banken and Its Predecessors 1856–1996.* Borås: Olsson and Skandinaviska Enskilda Banken.

Östholm, I., G. Eliasson, U. Reinius, N.-E. Sandberg (1996) *Nya Skapelser. Losec-entreprenörens recept.* (New Creations. The prescription of the Losec-entrepreneur). Stockholm: Fischer & Co.

Pitcher, P. (1997). *The Drama of Leadership.* New York: Wiley.

Porter, M. (1996). What is Strategy? *Harvard Business Review* (November–December).

Rhenman, E. (1973). *Organization Theory for Long-Range Planning.* Chichester: Wiley.

Roe, M. J. (1994). *Strong Managers, Weak Owners. The Political Roots of American Corporate Governance.* Princeton, NJ: Princeton University Press.

Schon, D. (1971). *Beyond the Stable State.* New York: Random House.

Schumpeter, J. A. (1942). *Capitalism, Socialism and Democracy.* New York: Harper & Row.

Sundin, A., and S.-V. Sundqvist (2000). *Ägarna och Makten i Sveriges Börsföretag 2000. Owners and Power in Sweden's Listed Companies.* Stockholm: Ägarservice.

Thunholm, L.-E. (1995). *Ivar KREUGER.* Stockholm: Bokförlaget T. Fischer & Co.

Thunholm, L.-E. (1996). *Den Stora Fusionen. Samgåendet mella Skandinaviska Banken och Stockholms Enskilda Bank.* (The Great Fusion. The Merger of Skandinaviska Banken and Stockholms Enskilda Bank). Stockholm: Fischer & Co.

Tichy, N. M., and S. Sherman (1993). *Control Your Destiny or Someone Else Will.* New York: Doubleday.

van Wolferen, K. (1989, 1990). *The Enigma of Japanese Power. People and Politics in a Stateless Nation.* New York; Vintage Books.

Veranen, J. (1987). The Ownership Function and the Performance of the Firm. *Acta Academiae Oeconomicae Helsingiensis*: Series A:54.

Wijkström, O. (1994). *Och fort gick det.* (And it happened fast). Lunds Offset AB.

Index